THE NASDAQ® HANDBOOK

THE STOCK MARKET FOR THE NEXT 100 YEARS

A Complete Reference for Investors,
Registered Representatives,
Company Executives, Researchers,
the Financial Press and
Students of Finance

PROBUS PUBLISHING COMPANY
Chicago, Illinois
Cambridge, England

This publication is designed to provide accurate and authoritative information in regard to the subject matter covered. It is sold with the understanding that the publisher is not engaged in rendering legal, accounting, or other professional service. If legal advice or other expert assistance is required, the services of a competent professional person should be sought.

FROM A DECLARATION OF PRINCIPLES JOINTLY ADOPTED BY A COMMITTEE OF THE AMERICAN BAR ASSOCIATION AND A COMMITTEE OF PUBLISHERS.

Editors:

Douglas F. Parrillo, Senior Vice President, NASD Communications Group
Enno R. Hobbing, Vice President, NASD News Bureau
Margo Vanover Porter, Director, NASD Communication Services
James H. Gutman, Assistant Director, NASD Communication Services

Contributing Editors:

Ilan Seidner, Peter S. Chandler, Michael Whitehouse, Richard DeLouise, Taisie Berkeley

Researchers:

D. Timothy McCormick, Robert W. Bannon, Peter Galbraith, Therese G. Cashmore, Peter Salmon, Christopher Spille

Production Editors:

Christine Hintz, Sharon Lippincott

Production Assistants:

Paige A. Jernigan, Lisa M. Jones

Contents

Preface

John M. Templeton, the chairman and founder of Templeton, Galbraith & Hansberger Ltd., is the author or coauthor of several books about investment. He has developed and sponsored a number of successful mutual funds, including Templeton Foreign and Templeton Growth. A chartered financial analyst, he has been a professional investment counselor for more than 50 years.

Preface

by John M. Templeton
Chairman and Founder
Templeton, Galbraith & Hansberger, Ltd.

Global investing is growing rapidly and will continue to do so. As current restraints and barriers become obsolete or transparent, the increased flow of information, more consistent accounting and reporting standards, improved security clearing and settlement methods, and continued deregulation and globalization of securities will result in greater acceptance of truly global investing. The Nasdaq Stock Market^{sm} will help expedite the trading of securities in a global marketplace. In fact, its role as a model market for the potential global trading of securities has been studied and copied by both the London Stock Exchange and the Singapore Stock Exchange.

For 50 years, I have believed in the superior profits of global investing. Although the world is moving inexorably to a global marketplace where you will be able to trade virtually all securities, regardless of origin, with an electronic command, the actual realization is still some time away. Frequently cited restraints are barriers to entry, difficulties in obtaining timely and necessary information, and different market trading systems. While Nasdaq cannot address the barriers to entry of some countries, Nasdaq — or at least a system like it — greatly lessens the problems of the other two restraints.

This book describes many aspects of Nasdaq, the stock market operated by the National Association of Securities Dealers, Inc. By merging advances in computer technology and telecommunications, Nasdaq has become a stock market unencumbered by physical or geographic boundaries. By implementing systems that help reduce costs, the market for equity investments is widened dramatically, particularly for those outside the U.S. who wish to make direct equity investments.

Nations Need Efficient Capital Markets

The conditions in the world today and in history show that many nations remain poor because of the neglect of wealth accumulation or the flight of wealth to safer places. There are many examples of poverty where the government alone owns all the wealth and neglects to stimulate entrepreneurship. Encouraging individuals to accumulate wealth brings prosperity to nations and happiness to workers.

It is clear that many nations will require efficient capital markets as a means to better allocate resources. The ability of a stock market to facilitate trading volumes at a low cost benefits not only brokerage houses but also the investing public. Therefore, the development of equity markets, and a means to efficiently trade securities in these markets, will be a natural consequence. The Nasdaq-type market represents one of the best models for accomplishing this goal.

A landmark for capitalism as well as for freedom was Adam Smith's 1776 publication of "An Inquiry Into the Nature and Causes of the Wealth of Nations." In the 200 years of relative freedom that followed, the yearly production of goods and services has increased more than a hundredfold. Before Adam Smith, there were fewer than 1,000 corporations on earth. Today, in 1991, corporations are being created, around the globe, at a rate of 4,000 every business day. Truly, we live in a world of spiraling progress.

Because business development continues around the globe, Nasdaq has extended its capabilities to global investors. It currently has more than 189,000 terminals in 52 countries from the United States to Australia to the United Arab Emirates. Notable foreign companies that have chosen Nasdaq for a listing of their shares include such leaders as Reuters, Akzo, and Volvo. There are in excess of 11 million investors in The Nasdaq Stock Market. Overall, the Nasdaq market consists of 415 market makers that hold more than 44,000 market-making positions covering companies worth in excess of $403 billion.

While the companies on Nasdaq possess many characteristics of the market itself, such as new technologies and exciting prospects, the average company has sales of $212 million and assets of $536 million. The age of Nasdaq-listed companies varies widely. While Nasdaq does attract many new, emerging companies, more than 100 of its companies have surpassed the 100-year mark, and more than 1,000 of its companies are more than 25 years old.

Nasdaq's Role in Free Market System

We live in a very exciting period. We have seen more progress in recent years than ever before in areas such as literature, music, agriculture, medicine, and business enterprise.

In terms of business enterprise, encouraging the efficient allocation of economic resources is vital for economic health. Nasdaq is playing a vital role in this area, both in the U.S. and increasingly with foreign companies. As the world moves toward greater freedom, economic prosperity, and a truly global marketplace, Nasdaq, and its system of trading securities, should continue to be an increasingly important part of the free market system for the benefit of all people.

PART I

America's Fastest Growing

Stock Market

Chapter
One

Joseph R. Hardiman is president and chief executive officer of the National Association of Securities Dealers, Inc., which operates The Nasdaq Stock Market. In this capacity, he guides and directs the organization's efforts to facilitate capital formation by developing, operating, and regulating quality electronic markets for the benefit of investors, issuers of securities, and member firms. Under Mr. Hardiman's leadership, the NASD has strengthened its regulatory capabilities to build and maintain the confidence of investors. Prior to assuming his current duties in 1987, Mr. Hardiman was the managing director and chief operating officer of the investment banking firm of Alex. Brown & Sons in Baltimore, Maryland.

The Nasdaq Stock Market: Two Decades of Growth

by Joseph R. Hardiman
President and Chief Executive Officer
National Association of Securities Dealers, Inc.

The rapid march of technology has forever changed our traditional ways of doing things. Whether at home or on the job, technology has become an integral part of our daily routine.

For the financial services industry, the impact of technological innovation is extraordinary. First and foremost, it provides instantaneous access to information worldwide. Second, it gives us the ability to execute transactions from remote locations as easily as if we were doing business from next door or in person. Third, it facilitates the creation of many new and sophisticated products to meet the needs of investors. Fourth, through a variety of applications, it is reducing the cost of processing business. Finally, technology is tearing down the traditional concept of having to do business from central locations and to have physical proximity to a customer.

No longer a trend but a constant, technology continues to revise and reshape the entire world of finance. Securities markets that have embraced technology have shown strong growth; those that have not run the risk of losing their franchise.

The means by which tomorrow's successful securities markets will incorporate technology is already clear to even the casual student of finance. They will be screen based, and their reach will be international. They will be highly automated, permitting pricing and transaction information to be simultaneously transmitted to a virtually unlimited number of investors across the nation and throughout the world.

Markets will not be dominated by a single dealer or specialist operating on a physical trading floor. Instead, prices will be driven by many competing dealers, disseminating buy and sell quotations over telecommunications networks to computer workstations or by investor orders received and matched against other investor orders. All this will take place electronically.

Securities markets will be equipped to offer a staggering array of innovative investment products and technology-based support services, ranging from immediate execution of orders and prompt clearance and settlement to round-the-clock accessibility.

The prototype for this market of the future is not under development in some university's financial research center. It is here, and it is operating today. It's The Nasdaq Stock Market — an indispensable information-age tool that is doing much to facilitate the capital-raising process for companies both at home and abroad.

The Nasdaq Stock Market Today

In view of its stature and importance in world financial markets, it is hard to believe that Nasdaq is only 20 years old. In its two short decades of existence, Nasdaq has become the second largest equity market in the United States and one of the largest in the world.

From a trading volume of 2.2 billion shares in its first full year of operation to an estimated 40 billion shares in 1991, Nasdaq has established itself as the fastest growing market in the U.S. (See Exhibit 1–1.) Already many times larger than the American Stock Exchange (Amex), Nasdaq is now challenging the New York Stock Exchange (NYSE) for share volume leadership. As recently as 1975, Nasdaq share volume was less than one third that of the NYSE. By 1980, it had climbed to nearly 60 percent. By 1991, Nasdaq share volume was nearly 90 percent of the NYSE. (See Exhibits 1–2 and 1–3.)

Exhibit 1–1   Change in Market Growth for Nasdaq, NYSE, and Amex 1981–1991*

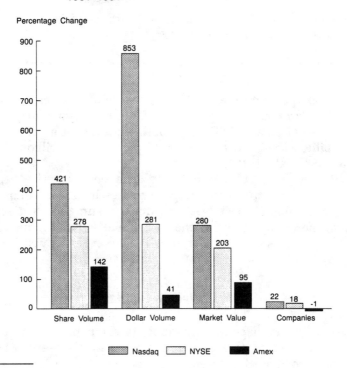

* Annualized based on data through October 31, 1991.

Exhibit 1–2   Share Volumes
             Nasdaq, NYSE, and Amex
             1981 vs. 1991*

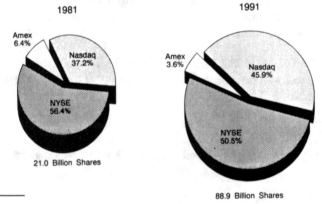

1981   1991

Amex
6.4%
Nasdaq
37.2%
Amex
3.6%
Nasdaq
45.9%
NYSE
56.4%
NYSE
50.5%

21.0 Billion Shares

88.9 Billion Shares

* Annualized based on data through October 31, 1991.

Nasdaq continues to gain a larger slice of a larger pie. Since 1981, Nasdaq's share of aggregate trading in the three major U.S. markets — Nasdaq, NYSE, and Amex — jumped from 37 percent of 21 billion shares to more than 45 percent of 93 billion shares traded. (See Exhibit 1–2.)

Rising share volume and long-term positive price performance have also produced huge increases in dollar volume of Nasdaq trading. In 1990, Nasdaq's dollar volume reached $452.4 billion, more than six times the 1981 dollar volume figure. And the 1991 figure is likely to exceed $670 billion. (See Exhibit 1–3.)

Enterprise on Display

Perhaps no community of companies sums up the diverse spirit of corporate enterprise better than those that listed on The Nasdaq Stock Market.

Today, investors can choose from among more than 4,000 Nasdaq companies. This mix reflects the fundamental shift taking

**Exhibit 1–3   Nasdaq Dollar Volume
1981–1991***

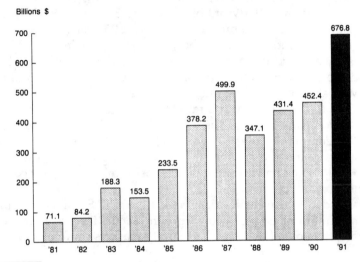

Billions $

'81	71.1
'82	84.2
'83	188.3
'84	153.5
'85	233.5
'86	378.2
'87	499.9
'88	347.1
'89	431.4
'90	452.4
'91	676.8

* Annualized based on data through October 31, 1991.

place in the nation's economy as it moves from a manufacturing base to one focused on services and technology.

Of the three principal U.S. stock markets, Nasdaq has the highest percentage of fast-growing, technology, and service companies, including:

- 84 percent of computer manufacturers.

- 86 percent of computer software and data processing firms.

- 74 percent of electronic-component makers and telecommunications companies.

- 81 percent of pharmaceutical and biotechnology companies.

Nasdaq companies come in all types and sizes, including many large internationally recognized companies such as Apple

Computer, Intel, MCI Communications, Microsoft, and Amgen. The Nasdaq market not only includes most of the young, innovative companies that are driving the U.S. economy, but also many that are more than 100 years old. Roughly 30 percent of Nasdaq companies have been in business for at least 25 years.

Nasdaq continues to be the primary market in the United States for new public companies. In the last 10 years, Nasdaq has listed more than 80 percent of all new issues. Dynamic and often growing at an exponential rate, these generally smaller firms add new jobs to the economy at a rate that far exceeds any other category of company. They are, as Bill McGowan, Chairman and CEO of MCI Communications Corporation, noted, "the innovators, the challengers, and the changers." Chances are good that a few of them will also go on to become the best-performing mega-companies of the next decade.

Nasdaq is also the leading market in the U.S. for the trading of international issues. More foreign securities are listed on Nasdaq than on all the other U.S. equity markets combined.

Technology Advances the Market

The first distinguishing characteristic of The Nasdaq Stock Market is technology. Nasdaq uses computers and telecommunications — the information-age technologies — to bring securities firms together electronically, enabling them to compete with one another over the computer rather than on a trading floor in a single location. All the information needed for trading is in the open, on the Nasdaq computer screen, available at the press of a button.

The central computer complex for the Nasdaq system is located in Trumbull, Connecticut. A second facility, located in Rockville, Maryland, provides backup computer systems and telecommunications circuits to continue service in the event of a major outage at the Trumbull location. Nasdaq is the world's first equity market to establish such a safety resource.

Trumbull and Rockville are connected by 80,000 miles of leased telephone lines to 3,400 trading terminals that are used by securities firms to display the prices at which they are offering to buy or sell securities, route orders, report trades, and send trade information to the clearing corporation for clearance and settlement.

Also connected to Trumbull and Rockville are the computers of market data vendors. They distribute best bid and ask prices and volume information on all Nasdaq securities to stockbrokers and others via 205,000 desktop terminals in nearly 50 countries.

Making Markets

The second distinguishing characteristic of The Nasdaq Stock Market is its competitive, multiple market-maker system. Market makers are dealers that buy and sell securities for their own accounts or inventories. They serve the market by selling stock when there is excess demand and buying stock when there is excess supply.

More than 400 securities firms are active Nasdaq market makers. The average Nasdaq security has nearly 11 market makers. The very active Nasdaq securities have in excess of 40.

Nasdaq market makers — which include large national full-service firms, regional firms, local firms, and wholesale market makers — are headquartered in 38 states and the District of Columbia.

Competing, multiple market makers offer five major advantages unavailable on traditional exchanges where trading is confined to a single specialist:

- Competition among market makers produces efficient pricing and provides the capacity to absorb large increases in volume without the trading halts that are common to the exchanges.

- The competitive, multiple market-maker system gives the Nasdaq market superior liquidity (i.e., the dollar volume of trading that can take place without affecting the price of a stock). Independent academic studies conclude that the principal reason for Nasdaq's superior liquidity is its market-making mechanism of competing dealers versus the single specialists of exchanges.

- Multiple market makers commit substantial capital to the support of a Nasdaq security.

- Unlike exchange specialists, market-making firms frequently prepare research reports on the companies in which they make markets. This activity greatly increases the visibility of a stock among investors.

- Most market-making firms have distribution units that merchandise securities in which they make a market. Exchange specialists, having exclusive franchises, have no retail distribution network because they are generally prohibited from handling customer accounts.

Most market-making firms, on the other hand, separate their distribution units from their research departments. These units merchandise securities in which their firms make markets, giving Nasdaq companies the benefit of sponsorship not found in other markets.

Automated Market Services

A number of automated trade execution, confirmation, and reporting systems serve the Nasdaq market. SOES^{sm}, SelectNet^{sm}, ACT^{sm}, and ACES^{sm} are acronyms for sophisticated systems that spell greater market efficiency.

The best known of these systems, SOES, the Small Order Execution System, permits automatic execution of a retail customer's order up to 1,000 shares, and it guarantees the customer the best price in Nasdaq at the time his or her order is entered.

A limit-order service, which operates as part of SOES, accepts and holds customer day orders and good-till-cancelled orders, executing these orders when the best bid or ask price in an issue is equal to or better than the limit-order price. The limit-order service also includes an order-match feature that enables public customers to receive automatic execution of matching limit orders priced within the best bid and ask when market makers do not participate.

Safeguards to Protect Investors

Nasdaq is a stock market built on integrity. Every quotation and transaction report that market makers enter into the Nasdaq computer is recorded and analyzed via statistical models that take into consideration security-specific price and volume parameters, breaking news, and general market trends. The system calculates the probability that an incident — for instance a market maker's quote change, volume report, or last-sale price report — reflects legitimate market forces or is subject to further analysis.

In addition, software and off-line market surveillance capabilities allow Nasdaq market surveillance specialists access to a wide spectrum of data, allowing them to reconstruct trading activity and trading patterns in each and every Nasdaq security.

Unusual trading patterns are automatically flagged and immediately reviewed by Nasdaq Market Surveillance analysts. The work of this department helps ensure that the Nasdaq market is fair, efficient, and effectively regulated.

The NASD, which operates and regulates Nasdaq, works to ensure market integrity in other ways as well . . . through a nationwide, on-site broker-dealer inspection program . . . through testing of all sales and supervisory personnel as a condition for registration . . . through a review of underwriting arrangements for companies going public . . . and through a review of members' sales literature and advertising.

In all, almost 5,400 member firms and their more than 400,000 registered employees are subject to NASD regulation.

Investors in the Nasdaq Market

About 11 million individual investors hold the bulk of Nasdaq securities by market value — some $121.8 billion. Individual investors account for nearly 40 percent of the shares held in Nasdaq National Market (Nasdaq/NMS)® securities; the average individual trade in these securities is about 1,300 shares.

Individual investors account for almost all of the share volume in the nearly 2,100 securities not in Nasdaq/NMS. As of the end of June 1991, these securities had an aggregate market value of more than $28 billion.

Institutions in 1991 held positions valued at $164.3 billion in virtually all Nasdaq/NMS common stocks, constituting approximately 43 percent of the aggregate market value of those securities. (See Exhibits 1–4 and 1–5.) Overall, the dollar value of Nasdaq stocks in institutional portfolios more than doubled between December 1985 and June 1991.

Exhibit 1–4   Distribution of Holdings of Nasdaq/NMS Stocks 1991*

Market Value
of Holdings

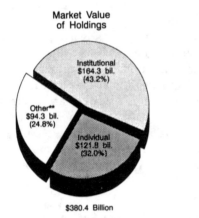

$380.4 Billion

Shares Held

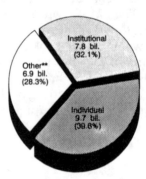

24.4 Billion Shares Outstanding

---

* Through June 30, 1991.

** Other includes holdings of officers, directors, or related persons, and beneficial owners of 10 percent or more.

Data Source: Vickers Stock Research Corporation.

Exhibit 1–5   **Nasdaq/NMS Companies and Their Profile Data**
October 1991

<u>Securities Data</u>

Number of Securities*	2,558
Average Share Price	$17.62
P/E Ratio	37.4
Average Number of Market Makers	11.7
Average Shares Outstanding Per Issue	9,800,000
Average Float (Shares)	7,100,000
Average Market Value	$173,300,000

<u>Company Data</u>

Number of Companies	2,529
Average Assets	$683,100,000
Average Equity	$110,700,000
Average Revenue	$264,700,000
Average Net Income	$7,700,000

---

* Domestic and foreign common stocks, ADRs, and shares of beneficial interest.

Nasdaq in the Global Perspective

As one of the largest stock markets in the world, Nasdaq is a major force in international equity trading. Nasdaq is not only the leading U.S. market for American Depositary Receipts and foreign stocks, it is the model for a growing number of overseas markets.

In 1986, London's International Stock Exchange patterned its new equities trading system after Nasdaq, complete with competing market makers and a computerized quotations system. In 1988, the Singapore Stock Exchange also launched a Nasdaq-like system. Soon, yet another market based on the Nasdaq model will be launched. Its name is JASDAQ, a screen-based market being developed by the Japan Securities Dealers Association.

In recognition of its world-class status, Nasdaq in 1988 became the first overseas stock market to be granted legal status as a "Recognized Investment Exchange" in the United Kingdom.

Nasdaq: The Evolution

Since its inception, the Nasdaq market has undergone a series of evolutionary changes, each designed to strengthen the market for investors and issuers alike. Nasdaq is continually changing, anticipating the future needs of market participants and improving its operations.

In commenting on Nasdaq's evolution, Paul Steiger, managing editor of *The Wall Street Journal*, recently commented: "It used to be that almost every major stock was listed on the Big Board, but that's not true nowadays. Nasdaq's National Market System is another vigorous, viable marketplace for trading stocks, including some very big ones, and both large institutional investors and individuals are active in it."

A Cable News Network commentator called Nasdaq one of the most powerful financial market stories of our time. *Fortune* hailed it as "The Stock Market of Tomorrow — Now." And as the NASD propels The Nasdaq Stock Market to new levels of achievement in the 1990s, *Business Week* has called it "A Computerized Mouse That's Roaring."

As it strives for ever-higher achievements in the interests of all its principal constituencies — investors, companies, and securities firms — Nasdaq remains committed to technological innovation and unsurpassed standards of market quality. Twenty years of growth are behind us, but Nasdaq is only just beginning to hit its stride.

Chapter Two

William G. McGowan is chairman and chief executive officer of MCI Communications Corporation. In his role as chairman since 1968, Mr. McGowan built MCI from a small firm to its current status as a worldwide communications giant with approximately $7.7 billion in annual revenues. Prior to founding MCI, Mr. McGowan was a management consultant concentrating in high technology industries.

Why Nasdaq?

by William G. McGowan
Chairman and Chief Executive Officer
MCI Communications Corporation

In 1972, MCI made its initial public offering in The Nasdaq Stock Market. Nasdaq had been operating for all of one year, and our choice of market caused many investors to ask, "Why Nasdaq?" My answer then was the same as it is today: Nasdaq is perfect for MCI, perfect for MCI's stockholders, perfect for today's information-based economy.

The reasons are not surprising.

Reason #1: The Competitive, Multiple Market-Maker System

The heart of The Nasdaq Stock Market is its competitive, multiple market-maker system, which is a vast improvement from monopoly systems, where a single specialist has control over trading in a given stock. However, some people still think that a stock listed on an exchange has greater market strength. This just is not true and has not been for years.

Three examples from MCI's experience concretely demonstrate the superiority of the multiple market-maker system.

At 12 noon, Friday, February 8, 1982, the Department of Justice announced American Telephone & Telegraph's (AT&T) divestiture of the Bell telephone operating companies. AT&T stock did not trade that day; the New York Stock Exchange (NYSE) called it a "regulatory halt."

Predictably, the media generated an outpouring of information about the divestiture over the weekend. Everybody had a chance to digest the news Friday, all day Saturday, and all day Sunday. On Monday morning, however, AT&T stock still did not open. Something was said about "an imbalance of orders." Finally, late on Monday afternoon, some NYSE trading in AT&T occurred.

Meanwhile, MCI stock traded all day Friday and Monday. If MCI had been listed on the NYSE and the exchange called a "regulatory halt," our shareholders might not have had the opportunity to buy or sell, which is, after all, what stock markets are all about.

A year and a half later, in August 1983, the Federal Communications Commission announced the charges that long-distance telecommunications companies would pay for access to local telephone companies' lines. Because these charges were exceptionally high, many in the securities industry believed they might have a negative effect on our earnings.

With the access-charge news on the wire, MCI traded 16.5 million shares in a day. The turnover represented 14 percent of our total capitalization. No halt was called; investors bought and sold MCI at will, without interruption, during the entire time. MCI and the Nasdaq National Market proved that they could handle such volume. On the NYSE, trading probably would have been halted, as was the case with the stocks of two companies at that time.

One was Warner Communications. On the Friday that Warner Communications first released bad news about its Atari unit, the Warner specialist on the New York Stock Exchange stopped trading. Trading did not resume until the following Monday afternoon. This was a protect-the-specialist halt, not a protect-the-public halt, because the news was already out. The specialist just needed to balance his books.

In another instance, during the tumultuous week of October 19–23, 1987, when volume and volatility hit highs in all markets, there were dozens of late openings and trading halts on the NYSE and the American Stock Exchange (Amex). In Nasdaq, the continuous market, MCI traded without interruption all week long.

These contrasting examples demonstrate that The Nasdaq Stock Market lets people buy and sell when they want to, providing access and liquidity. The sophisticated issuing company can decide where its stock will receive greater continuity of trading: in the market dominated by a "specialist" or in the market made up of multiple market makers.

Reason #2: Liquidity

The competitive, multiple market-maker system also contributes to superior liquidity. Liquidity, of course, is measured by the dollar volume of trading that it takes to move the price of a stock. With high liquidity, it takes a lot of money to bring about a small price change, a desirable effect.

Nasdaq's superior liquidity was first documented by an independent 1983 study,[1] conducted at Texas A&M University. The study found that ". . . OTC liquidity tends to dominate Amex liquidity for stocks of the same size . . . Moreover, for most size ranges short of very large companies, NYSE listing may well imply a lower liquidity than had the firm remained OTC."

A second study,[2] also conducted at Texas A&M in 1983, dealt more specifically with listing and the liquidity of bank stocks. It concluded that "listing [on the exchanges] does not appear to add to the liquidity of the stock of banking organizations . . . [and] . . . here is some surprising and reasonable evidence that listing actually significantly reduces the liquidity . . . for bank organizations."

Following these two studies, David A. Dubofsky and John C. Groth, of Texas A&M, published a paper,[3] which measured the liquidity of stocks, both before and after listing, of 112 companies that moved from Nasdaq to the Amex, and 128 that moved from Nasdaq to the NYSE, from 1975 to 1981.

Dubofsky and Groth summarized their findings as follows: "The results presented in this study indicate a marked decline in liquidity for securities moving from the [Nasdaq] market to either of the organized exchanges."

For securities moving from Nasdaq to the NYSE, the study reported a 24.4 percent decline in average liquidity 20 days after the listing and a further decline of 12.6 percent during the next 40 days. For stocks moving from Nasdaq to the Amex, liquidity increased slightly on Nasdaq — from 50 percent to 57.7 percent — as the moving day approached. Once a Nasdaq stock was listed on the Amex, however, liquidity declined by 26.4 percent.

Analyzing the cause, Dubofsky and Groth wrote: "The most logical reason for greater OTC liquidity is the different market-making mechanisms. Competing dealers in OTC securities may provide more continuous and liquid markets than the organized exchanges that employ monopolist specialists."

Eight years have elapsed since the first of the Texas A&M studies on Nasdaq's superior liquidity was published. During all that time, no independent study has seriously challenged their conclusions.

At MCI, our experience supports the findings of the Texas A&M studies. We measure the liquidity of our securities constantly, and we have found that our own securities are more liquid than are comparable securities on the NYSE.

Reason #3: Cost of Capital

Just as we measure our liquidity, we constantly measure our net cost of capital. MCI has more than $8 billion invested in its domestic and international communications network. Obviously, the cost of capital is very important to us. Our experience has shown that capital costs are no more expensive for us than they would be if MCI's stock were listed on an exchange.

Once again, broader academic studies bear out MCI's findings. A 1982 study, *The Impact of Exchange Listing on the Cost of Equity Capital*,[4] by H. Kent Baker, Professor of Finance, and James

Spitzfaden, Internal Auditor for Textron, concluded: "The cross-sectional and time-series analysis revealed that the cost of equity capital neither differed between matched pairs of Nasdaq/Amex and Nasdaq/NYSE firms nor changed significantly when a Nasdaq stock listed on either of these exchanges."

Another 1982 cost-of-capital study[5] was published by the Securities and Exchange Commission and prepared under NASD sponsorship at the University of Iowa by Susan M. Phillips and J. Richard Zecher, now chairman of Chase Investors Management Corporation. The study found that ". . . listing does not affect risk or the cost of capital for companies of similar asset size, industry group, and trading volume. Further, the decision to list does not appear to have any predictable effect on risk or the cost of capital for the listing company."

Reason #4: International Visibility

From a securities issuer's point of view, the Nasdaq market affords excellent visibility. MCI usually has more than 40 securities firms making a market in its stock. The trading, research, and sales departments of these firms all know MCI stock, follow it constantly, and discuss it with their customers. At the same time, quotations and last-sale data on MCI stock are displayed on more than 175,000 securities salespersons' terminals in the U.S. and 50 other countries. Some 225 newspapers carry MCI statistics in the U.S., Europe, and Asia. In fact, MCI has sold significant amounts of stock in Europe, mostly in England, Scotland, and Switzerland.

In addition, the largest concentration of non-U.S. securities on a U.S. stock market is found on Nasdaq. At year-end 1990, 87 American Depositary Receipts (ADRs) and 184 foreign securities from 20 countries traded in The Nasdaq Stock Market. This is substantially more than the foreign issues listed on either the New York or American stock exchanges.

There is no need to belabor the visibility issue. MCI stock traded in excess of 608 million shares in 1990. It continues to be the most actively traded security in any U.S. market.

Reason #5: It Doesn't Cost a Fortune

If MCI were to list on the NYSE, its listing costs would be many times higher than The Nasdaq Stock Market's annual cost of $8,000.

Another added cost of listing on the NYSE is for certificates. The reason for this difference in price is spelled out in the *New York Stock Exchange Handbook*, Section 502.01, "Certificates—Printing and Engraving Requirements."

"The face of a listed security in definitive form must be printed by the Intaglio plate process, to the extent prescribed below in this section for each particular type of security, from at least two engraved steel or nickel plates (unless the Split-Font Concept is utilized) which may be chromium plated, that is, one plate produced from original line engravings in steel from which a printing in color is made of the border and the tint underlying the face of the security; and a second plate produced from original hand cut engravings in steel from which a printing in black is made of the vignette, title and descriptive or promissory portion of the security."

All this for a piece of paper that is basically a receipt, which will languish for most of its existence in a fireproof vault and which contains information that is already stored electronically. Section 502.01 might be more appropriately called "a formula for the finest record-keeping system of the 19th century."

Reason #6: Advantages for Investors

The advantages of the Nasdaq market for MCI and its stock are advantages for investors, too. Continuity of trading, liquidity, reasonable cost of capital, and visibility all make for an efficient Nasdaq market. Investors benefit from this efficiency, just as issuers and the securities industry do.

I think the following statistics are a testimonial to what investors think of this 20-year-old market:

Nasdaq is by far the largest stock market in the U.S. in the number of companies represented and the second largest in terms of share and dollar volume.

Nasdaq's dollar volume of equity trading, $452 billion in 1990, secures its position as one of the world's five largest equity markets.

During the past 10 years, Nasdaq share volume has increased 100 percent more than has that of the Big Board. In 1990, Nasdaq share volume equalled 84 percent of that of the NYSE. On 27 days during the year, Nasdaq share volume exceeded that of the NYSE.

This immense growth says to me that the investing public sees Nasdaq as the future of global trading.

Reason #7: The Information Age

A final answer to "Why Nasdaq?" is simply this: Nasdaq is the prototype of future markets.

If we were just now starting a public market for trading securities in the United States, we would not even suggest, contemplate, or discuss trading stocks the way it is done on the New York and American stock exchanges.

When we visit foreign countries, we find that many still have markets for fruits and vegetables, where farmers and villagers meet each other. But why would we want to trade securities that way, in one building, in one place? Why would we want the melodramatic running about and paper waving of the exchanges? It's an exciting backdrop for stock market reports by television people but, for the rest of us, its inefficiency far outweighs any aesthetic benefit.

To trade years ago, it was necessary to bring people together. Today, we bring information together. Computers, linked by sophisticated networks, can do the job far better and more efficiently.

Technology has even eliminated the need for the human voice in trading. In December 1984, the first fully automated trade in a Nasdaq security took place. It took only three seconds, nearly 10 times quicker than a manual transaction. A computer in Trumbull, Connecticut bought 500 shares of Apple Computer common stock for an investor in California, with no voice communication between the investor's broker and the selling dealer in New York.

Today this automated system, known as SOES (for Small Order Execution System), handles individual investor orders for up to 1,000 shares in all Nasdaq National Market securities. It also allows individual investors to enter limit orders, at prices away from the prevailing market, and further allows the matching of limit orders against each other, automatically and without market-maker participation.

Other Nasdaq services allow market makers to negotiate orders of any size by computer, without voice contact; market makers to program their terminals automatically to accept and execute certain orders from established customers; and trades executed by telephone to be compared by the computer to be sure that buyers and sellers are in agreement on the terms.

In short, computers and telecommunications — the information technologies — are changing the way we trade stocks. Nasdaq itself is an innovation of the information technologies, and it is leading the rest of the world to screen-based trading, away from exchange floors.

The British have recognized this potential. With the "Big Bang" in 1986, the International Stock Exchange of London patterned its new equities trading system after Nasdaq, with competing market makers and a computerized quotations system. The Stock Exchange Council liked the efficiencies that computer technology brings to the dealing environment. It liked placing all members on an equal basis irrespective of geographical location. The Council absolutely and unequivocally refused to rely on the quality and state of mind of one individual specialist for the continuity of the market in any given stock. Finally, the Council liked Nasdaq's ability to lend itself readily to a 24-hour international market.

This capacity is another great strength of Nasdaq. As soon as the International Stock Exchange had its SEAQ (Stock Exchange Automated Quotations) system up and running, it began to exchange quotations and, later, transaction information with Nasdaq on some 700 United Kingdom (U.K.) and U.S. stocks via satellite. In May 1988, Nasdaq started an exchange of quotations with the SESDAQ system in Singapore. In 1991, Nasdaq went a big step further. Nasdaq installed its own computers in London so that firms there can make markets, as if they were located in the U.S., during the 12 hours of the day that either the U.K. or the U.S. markets are open. That is halfway to the 24-hour market.

As the London Council has, many American companies have recognized the potential of Nasdaq. Since 1980, the number of companies listed by Nasdaq has grown from 2,894 to in excess of 4,100, or more than 40 percent. More than 700 companies meeting the financial criteria for listing on the NYSE prefer Nasdaq. Meanwhile, listings on the NYSE are up only 12 percent or, in the case of Amex, are falling. And the public has recognized it — in 1990, Nasdaq traded 33.4 billion shares.

As usual, the redoubtable Peter Drucker has put his finger on it. He called the NYSE "a smoke stack part of the financial services industry," adding, "That is why Nasdaq is growing so quickly. The specialist system is a very poor substitute for communication. Such things hang on, but not forever."

The level of sophistication of computers and telecommunications, the speed of information, the diversity of this country, the desire of people to live where they want, and the sophistication of the investing public all demand a market exactly like the one in which MCI trades today — the Nasdaq market, a decentralized network of competing market makers, instantaneously and continuously linked by the automated Nasdaq system. I hope the New York and American stock exchanges will see the light and join the London exchange in following Nasdaq into the 21st century.

Endnotes

[1] K. Cooper, J.C. Groth, and W.E. Avera, *Liquidity, Exchange Listing, and Common Stock Performance*, Texas A&M University, College of Business Administration, Department of Finance, 1983.

[2] D.R. Fraser and J.C. Groth, *Listing and the Liquidity of Bank Stocks*, Texas A&M University, College of Business Administration, Department of Finance, 1983.

[3] D.A. Dubofsky and J.C. Groth, "Exchange Listing and Stock Liquidity," *The Journal of Financial Research*, Winter 1984, pp. 291–302.

[4] H.K. Baker and J. Spitzfaden, *The Impact of Exchange Listing on the Cost of Equity Capital*, The American University, Kogod College of Business Administration, Department of Finance and Business Institutions, 1982.

[5] S.M. Phillips and J.R. Zecher, *Capital Market Working Paper*, "Exchange Listing and the Cost of Equity Capital," Securities and Exchange Commission, Washington D.C., 1982.

Chapter Three

John G. McDonald is IBJ professor of finance at the Graduate School of Business, Stanford University, where he has taught investment management and corporate finance for 23 years. Since 1980, Mr. McDonald has concentrated on Asian equity markets and entrepreneurial companies in Japan, Korea, and Taiwan. He has served the NASD as vice chairman of its Board of Governors and as chairman of the international committee.

Competition and Technology: Driving Forces in Nasdaq's Emergence as an International Stock Market

by John G. McDonald
Professor of Finance
Stanford University

Financial markets around the world are rapidly changing. At the heart of this transformation are technology and competition. Equity markets provide dramatic testimony to the power that competition and technology hold to reshape financial arenas. Increasingly, stock markets around the world are turning from central trading floors to screen-based technology, which offers distinct competitive advantages in an increasingly global trading environment.

The international leader among screen-based equity markets is The Nasdaq Stock Market. Nasdaq's ground-breaking development of screen-based technology now allows it to compete with the New York Stock Exchange (NYSE) for listings and order flow. With a market capitalization of approximately $400 billion (equal to that of Australia, Hong Kong, Singapore and Malaysia, Denmark, Norway, Finland, and New Zealand combined) and trading volume currently running at 90 percent of that of the NYSE, Nasdaq has emerged as a formidable rival of the NYSE. With approximately 12 times the trading volume of the American Stock Exchange, Nasdaq has matured to become the second largest American stock market and a leading international equity market.

Since Nasdaq's inception in 1971, stock markets around the world have progressively adopted new computer technology, allowing screen-based technology to flourish — lowering costs and increasing efficiency and speed. A number of forces are driving this technological innovation and help explain why the U.S., in particular, offers a fertile environment for the growth and development of screen-based trading of securities.

Going Global

The trend toward globalization of securities markets is now widely appreciated. In recent years, foreign equity flows into the U.S. and flows of American equity to markets outside our borders have increased dramatically. The volume of cross-border equity trading is doubling about every three years. One equity trade in seven has a foreign investor on the other side. One trade in five involves a foreign share. In Europe, which in many respects foreshadows the financial environment of the future, one in three equity trades involves a foreign share.[1]

According to a Salomon Brothers study, cross-border equity trading has increased 16-fold since 1979. Investors around the world traded more than $1.5 trillion in stocks of foreign companies in 1990.

The flow of foreign equity into U.S. markets is likely to grow in the 1990s, as companies pursue more international capital-raising strategies and as international investors look to U.S. markets for investment opportunity. Similarly, American institutional investors will continue to seek investments abroad. I find that leading institutional investors generally agree on this potential for future growth.

International investment managers are playing an essential role in the globalization process. For example, American pension assets invested internationally have jumped from $3 billion in 1980 to in excess of $80 billion in 1991. International portfolio diversification strategies, long the norm in Europe, have grown in all major markets, leading to increased participation in markets outside one's country of domicile.

Given these trends, it is not surprising that we are seeing progress, in a variety of markets, toward round-the-clock activity. Leading the way have been markets that are intrinsically international — for example, the foreign exchange and the international bond markets. Futures and options markets are also making significant strides toward longer trading days, approaching the era of continuous trading.

In the 1980s, equity markets began to extend trading hours. Technological advances, many involving computer linkages and screen-based networks, have helped to facilitate cross-border transactions.

Rather than taking one universal form, globalization in equity markets is giving rise to a wide variety of market formats.[2] The predominant format continues to be the domestic market in which the stocks of companies based in that country are traded. A broad question for the future concerns the nature of equity markets: Will leading markets be centralized with all trades funneled through a single market maker (as on the NYSE specialist system) or will they include competitive market makers, linked through a screen-based system (as in the Nasdaq market)?

The number of stock markets has grown dramatically. Two decades ago, only 20 stock markets around the world drew the attention of investors and issuers outside the country in which the stock markets were located. Since then, many of these domestic markets have grown more than tenfold. In addition to these 20 equity markets, more than 20 "emerging markets," the largest of which are Taiwan, Korea, and Mexico, are in the process of increasing their access to foreign investors.[3]

A pioneering institutional investor in these newer markets is the Emerging Markets Growth Fund, which has monitored companies in all of these emerging stock markets since 1986. Latin American emerging markets, including Chile and Brazil as well as our neighbors in Mexico, have produced very competitive returns (in dollars) in recent years.

From Domestic to International

Brokerage firms with offices in Tokyo, London, New York, and other financial centers have developed systems to trade around the clock for their clients, either as agent or as dealer in common stocks. These firms span domestic markets and provide telephonic networks that link broker-dealers and institutional clients.

In a few instances, more formal "international markets" are taking shape where stocks from around the world are gathered into one central market for the trading convenience of investors in a given country or time zone.

Nasdaq has been a front-runner in designing a screen-based market expressly devoted to trading issues of leading companies around the world. Nasdaq International^{sm}, as this new service is called, will allow investors to choose the securities of several hundred companies with international investor interest, all of which can be traded in Nasdaq's central market.

An extension of the electronic, interdealer Nasdaq network in the United States, Nasdaq International operates from 3:30 a.m. to 9 a.m., Eastern Time (8:30 a.m. to 2 p.m. London Time) on each U.S. business day (excluding official U.S. holidays). These hours coincide with the opening hours of London financial markets.

The market comprises the top tier of Nasdaq companies and a select group of national and international stocks that trade on the New York and American stock exchanges. Members of the National Association of Securities Dealers located in the United Kingdom (U.K.) are among the market's participants, with the majority of investors/clients residing in the U.K. and continental Europe.

To handle the essential task of clearance and settlement, Nasdaq International offers automated trade comparison, the critical first step in settlement. The system compares trades either through one-sided input of trade details and confirmation by the contra party, or by two-sided input and matching by the system itself.

Private Placement Arena

In 1990, approximately 30 percent of all corporate equity and debt capital raised in the U.S. was raised through private placements. The private placement market is another intrinsically international financial arena, and it too is benefiting by automation. Under SEC Rule 144A (adopted April 1990), qualified institutional buyers may resell private placement securities without SEC registration, giving these securities an element of liquidity they had not previously possessed. Issuers can sell securities under this rule without reporting financial statements in the American format. With a primary market of almost $150 billion and a secondary market in the hundreds of billions, this is a marketplace that provided a prime opportunity for automation.

In 1990, in conjunction with Rule 144A, the NASD introduced screen-based technology to this market through a new automated system called The PORTAL^{sm} Market. Originally launched as a closed regulatory market, where privately placed securities could trade in a "safe harbor" setting within the 144A framework, PORTAL is now being expanded. The NASD has filed plans with the SEC to convert The PORTAL Market to an open information and trading system designed to attract more securities and more investors, brokers, and dealers. The NASD has determined that the automated PORTAL market will better serve participants when used primarily as a quotation and transaction service. Such a facility is needed and will do much to overcome the historic

fragmentation, obscurity, and inefficiency of the private placement market.

Elements of Change: Technology

How did we arrive at this level of cross-border activity, with increasingly automated trading and new markets to
handle this activity, in such a short time? It is primarily because
two ingredients for an international explosion in financial markets were in place: technology and competition. Let us focus first
on technology.

The internationalization of markets has been critically dependent on computer technology and global telecommunications. In
the early 1970s, technology afforded the securities industry an alternative to the idea that stocks needed to be traded in a central
location. Nasdaq was the first market to seize on automation and
make it the foundation of its market. In the process, Nasdaq revolutionized the American over-the-counter market in the 1970s,
with a nationwide system of on-line market makers in real-time
competition with one another.

Nasdaq's electronic, screen-based foundation demonstrated
that it was technologically feasible to remove equity trading from
the physical confines of the exchange floor and disperse information and market making around the country. This decentralized
market provided a conceptual and practical alternative to the centralized equity market "place," the principal stock market model
of the previous 350 years. It took nearly 40 man-years of development time to get Nasdaq up and running. Once operational, however, the technological barrier was broken; screen-based systems
have proliferated. Here are three examples in the 1980s:

- The London Stock Exchange switched to screen-based
  trading in 1986. Even before the so-called "Big Bang," the
  exchange designed an automated quotation system,
  called SEAQ, which emulated The Nasdaq Stock Market.

- The Stock Exchange of Singapore modeled an automated
  system, called SESDAQ, after Nasdaq.

- In Japan, Nasdaq has served as the prototype for a new automated information network, called JASDAQ, for Japan's over-the-counter market.

These markets are for the most part "dealer-quote driven," with competing market makers, rather than "order-driven" markets, with a central market maker.[4] A number of order-driven systems using electronic screens followed with the prototype of such systems being The Toronto Stock Exchange's CATS system.

The technology for CATS, which stands for Computer Assisted Trading System, has gained considerable acceptance in Europe. The exchanges in Paris, Brussels, Madrid, and elsewhere now use it. In fact, the question that many stock markets around the world now ask is "Can we afford *not* to use either a Nasdaq, CATS, or hybrid screen-based system?" This brings us to the other key ingredient responsible for the enormous change in equity markets in recent years — competition.

Elements of Change: Competition

Where change takes place most dramatically, you will find competition. European stock markets are now changing at a rapid pace as they prepare for the competitive challenges posed by a more unified market in Europe post-1992. More change has occurred since 1986 at the Paris Bourse, which recently redesigned along screen-based lines, than in the preceding century. This technological transformation accompanied the growth that allowed the Paris Bourse to surpass total equity capitalization in Germany in summer 1989.

In 1990, Germany once again took the lead in market capitalization in continental Europe. Not to be left behind, Germany's stock market has recently undergone a transformation of its own. The change began with the privatization of the Frankfurt Stock Exchange on January 1, 1991, and was accompanied shortly thereafter by the initiation, in April 1991, of electronic trading. Rudiger von Rosen, executive vice chairman of the Federation of German Stock Exchanges, acknowledged the competitive edge that screen-based trading provides. "We will be reaching Tokyo in the morning and connecting Europe with New York in the afternoon," he said. "We are sure in this respect the German market will pick up."[5]

Perhaps nowhere are competition and technological change more in evidence than in the United States, which has a number of competing stocks markets — the NYSE, The Nasdaq Stock Market, the considerably smaller American Stock Exchange, regional exchanges, and off-market networks. Unlike Japan, say, where the stock exchange in Osaka has substantial overlap with Tokyo (95 percent of Osaka issues also are listed on the Tokyo Stock Exchange), the three largest U.S. markets (NYSE, Nasdaq, and Amex) are separate and distinct, listing different companies. Overlap in the U.S. does occur in the so-called regional exchanges, where many securities listed on the NYSE, Amex, and Nasdaq (on the Midwest Stock Exchange only) are traded.

The existence of competition among U.S. equity markets encourages fast-paced change. The success of Nasdaq's electronic enhancements spurred the NYSE and Amex to invest in electronic systems of their own. No sooner did the NASD announce The PORTAL Market for private placements than the other stock markets began to enter this arena. Nasdaq's aggressive international agenda perhaps provided a background for NYSE Chairman William Donaldson's remark that, "[The NYSE] will be open and competitive 24 hours a day if there is a demand for it."[6]

U.S. stock markets realize they must change to stay competitive. As the old saying goes: *When you're finished changing, you're finished.*

Nasdaq: A Case Study of Change

Perhaps no stock market has come farther since the 1970s than The Nasdaq Stock Market. In many respects it illustrates the thesis that competition and technological innovation lead not only to change but also to growth. Today, Nasdaq is a major market in global trading of equities. Here is how it got there.

The groundwork for Nasdaq's international capacity was laid when building of the original system began in 1968. In 1971, central computers became operational in Trumbull, Connecticut, and a quantum advance in price transparency and competition occurred.

Nasdaq's progression from a national quotation system to a nationwide trading network began almost immediately. By the end of 1972, market makers traded 2.2 billion shares in nearly 3,500 securities. Trading activity and market-maker participation continued to grow. At the same time, quotation distribution quickly spanned continents. From the original 500 domestic Nasdaq quotation terminals back in 1971, the network has grown to almost 200,000 terminals in 1991, more than 30,000 of which are located outside the United States. It was the original screen-based technology that paved the way not only for Nasdaq's international capacity but for that of other markets as well.

As Nasdaq gained a reputation for technological sophistication and sound regulation, it achieved international recognition. In 1989, the Tokyo Stock Exchange began accepting applications for listing from Nasdaq National Market companies that meet its foreign listing requirements. Officials in Tokyo concluded that these securities traded in a highly organized market with a regulatory framework comparable to that of the NYSE.

In 1988, the U.K. designated Nasdaq as a "Recognized Investment Exchange." Canada followed with a similar designation for Nasdaq in early 1989.

Today, Nasdaq is the number one U.S. market for the trading of international issues, a large number of which trade in the form of American Depositary Receipts (ADRs). Today, more foreign securities and ADRs trade on Nasdaq than on all other U.S. equity markets combined. Examples include Cadbury Schweppes and Reuters in the U.K., Akzo in the Netherlands, LVMH in France, Volvo and Electrolux in Sweden, and many Japanese companies, including Nissan and Toyota.

In addition, the international community continues to call on Nasdaq's technological expertise. For instance, Nasdaq consultants are currently advising market officials in a number of countries on the development of their stock markets.

Future Progress

What does the international picture look like for screen-based markets?

The forces of competition and technology, which propelled screen-based systems into the forefront of equity and equity-derivative trading, show no signs of abating. We can expect continued head-to-head competition among U.S. markets, as they seek out international issuers and investors. This Darwinian competition should result in improved systems and services that in turn should lead to substantial international growth of all U.S. equity markets.

Technological advances have made it possible for Nasdaq to upgrade its systems to allow for the vast array of potential linkages and networking arrangements. Now, in the early 1990s, major changes in market systems' architecture are under way. They hold the potential for another quantum leap in technology, comparable to the development of Nasdaq in 1971. The systems change being installed and those considered by Nasdaq in the 1990s may result in breakthroughs that give new operational substance to the phrase "global stock market."

We can expect countries to continue to opt for screen-based markets. For example, Australia has closed regional trading floors around the country, and New Zealand is set to follow suit. Both have selected a screen-based market.

The continued evolution of global manufacturing and marketing is likely to encourage further issuance and trading of equities outside the community of domestic and corporate headquarters. The "multicultural corporation" continues to emerge in the 1990s. Signs included a marked increase in foreign research and development by U.S. companies, substantial increases in European investment in the U.S., the transformation of Eastern Europe, and the quest for new business beyond domestic borders among companies of all sizes. The "thirst for capital" is global in scope.

Given these trends, it is not surprising that more companies, of all sizes, are adopting a global approach to raising capital. The international financial arena, once the preserve of only large multinational companies, is now being used by smaller and mid-sized companies alike.[7] As American and non-U.S. companies of all sizes look to raise capital at the most attractive rate and gain exposure beyond their domestic borders, the number of companies traded "internationally" on The Nasdaq Stock Market and other major exchanges can be expected to increase well into the next century.

Endnotes

[1] For detailed source data on global equity markets and cross-border trading, see *Morgan Stanley Capital International Perspective*; and Salomon Brothers strategy paper, "The Forthcoming 1990s New Issue Boom: Will Smart Money Head to the U.S.," by Michael Howell, March 12, 1991.

[2] Allan W. Kleidon and Kenneth J. Singleton, "Liberalization in the Japanese Financial Markets," Research Paper No. 1069, Graduate School of Business, Stanford University, September 1989.

[3] *Emerging Stock Markets Factbook*, International Finance Corporation, World Bank, June 1991.

[4] Increasingly, markets such as Nasdaq and the Paris Bourse are incorporating aspects of both dealer and quote-driven systems. Nasdaq, for instance, has introduced a number of enhancements that allow for order-match capabilities, as part of its limit-order service for automatically executed small orders and in its SelectNet system for larger trades.

[5] *Investor's Daily*, March 8, 1991.

[6] William Donaldson, *New York Times* interview, December 30, 1990.

[7] Committee for the Study of the Causes and Consequences of the Internationalization of U.S. Manufacturing, *The Internationalization of U.S. Manufacturing: Causes and Consequences*, National Academy Press, 1991, p. 9.

Chapter Four

David S. Ruder is professor of law at Northwestern University School of Law, a member of the law firm of Baker & McKenzie, and a governor of the NASD. Mr. Ruder served as chairman of the Securities and Exchange Commission from August 1987 to September 1989. In that position, he was responsible for supervision of the securities markets, fostering international securities regulation, improving arbitration of broker-dealer customer disputes, implementation of corporate disclosure standards, enforcement of securities laws, and other areas.

How Securities Regulation Works

by David S. Ruder
Professor of Law
Northwestern University School of Law

Nowhere in the world are securities markets more thoroughly regulated or subjected to more intense oversight than in the United States. Multiple layers of regulation by federal and state regulators and by industry organizations provide a comprehensive system of investor protection.

The Securities and Exchange Commission (SEC) is the primary agency responsible for administering federal securities laws. These include the Securities Act of 1933 (the 1933 Act), the Securities Exchange Act of 1934 (the 1934 Act), the Public Utility Holding Act of 1935, the Trust Indenture Act of 1939, the Investment Company Act of 1940, the Investment Advisers Act of 1940, and the Securities Investor Protection Act of 1970.

Of all these pieces of legislation, the 1933 Act and 1934 Act are the most significant for issuers of securities and broker-dealers. The 1933 Act is a disclosure statute, which requires issuers to provide investors with facts about securities to be sold. The 1934 Act regulates securities markets and the business of securities brokers and dealers.

Securities Act of 1933

The 1933 Act compels companies going public to register their offerings with the SEC, unless an exception is obtained. The information required to be included in these registration statements is intended to give investors the facts they need to make informed investment decisions. It is prepared in two parts: a prospectus, which is widely distributed to underwriters, dealers, and investors; and additional information, which is filed with the SEC and available to the public. Failure to include or to state accurately material information in the registration statement or prospectus may result in civil or criminal penalties for those involved in its preparation.

The Act provides several exemptions from registration, including an exemption for private placements of securities directly with sophisticated investors who do not need the extensive protections afforded by registration because they can fend for themselves in the marketplace. Other exemptions include transactions that involve a limited number of investors, are limited to a certain dollar amount, or are to be offered on an intrastate basis only. For nonexempt offerings, the SEC provides a number of special registration forms for different issuers and types of offerings. The basic differences in these forms is the detail of information the issuer must disclose and the manner in which disclosure must be made.

The information required to be disclosed in a registration statement includes the following:

- Details regarding the issuer's assets and area of business.

- Information on the security being offered, how it fits in with the company's previously issued securities, and the method of offering contemplated (e.g., an underwritten offering, a rights offering, or a stock for stock offering).

■ Material information on how the issuer is managed.

■ Financial statements certified by independent public accountants.

In addition, the National Association of Securities Dealers, Inc. (NASD), which regulates most broker-dealers doing a public business in the United States, reviews the underwriting arrangements involved in most distributions to determine if the arrangements covering underwriter compensation are fair and reasonable.

Securities Exchange Act of 1934

To carry out its function under the 1934 Act, the SEC uses two approaches:

1. **Direct regulation.** The SEC provides direct regulation through statutory provisions or rules and regulations adopted under existing statutes. For example, the 1934 Act requires registration, or exemption, of broker-dealers, exchanges, and the securities traded on those exchanges. Other direct rules include:

   ■ Restrictions on borrowing by brokers and dealers.

   ■ Financial responsibility requirements, including net capital, recordkeeping, and segregation of fully paid customer securities.

   ■ Prohibition of security price manipulation or use of manipulative or deceptive devices in the sale or purchase of securities.

   ■ The authority to bar or suspend broker-dealers from the securities business.

   ■ The requirement that over-the-counter (OTC) public issuers and exchange-listed issuers file quarterly and annual reports with the SEC.

- Regulation of the proxy solicitation process.

- Provision for the recapture by issuers of "short swing" profits in transactions by insiders.

- The facilitation of a national market system for securities that removes burdens on competition, links markets, provides for price and quote reporting, and enhances opportunities for investors to ensure best execution of their orders.

2. **Delegation of regulatory authority.** The SEC delegates significant regulatory authority to private member owned and operated organizations charged with overseeing exchange and OTC trading, including the National Association of Securities Dealers Automated Quotation System (Nasdaq), an automated market for trading OTC securities. The SEC requires the self-regulatory organizations (SROs) — the NASD and the exchanges — to develop rules for trading in their markets and for the business conduct of their members.

As originally adopted, the 1934 Act provided SEC regulation of the exchange markets. In 1938, the Maloney Act Amendments to the 1934 Act authorized the registration of associations of brokers or dealers as national securities associations and entrusted the regulation of the business of their members to such associations, subject to the supervision and ultimate responsibility of the SEC.

Under the Maloney Act, OTC brokers or dealers became eligible for membership in the NASD (the only organization registered under the Maloney Amendments) unless they were guilty of certain violations of securities laws or NASD or exchange rules.

The SROs' Regulatory Role

The SROs — the NASD and the exchanges — play an important role in industry regulation. SRO responsibilities include establishing rules governing member firms' business conduct, setting qualifications standards for securities industry professionals, examining members for their financial operational condition and compliance with the rules, investigating alleged violations of securities laws, disciplining violators of SRO and SEC rules and regulations, and responding to inquiries and complaints from investors and members. The SROs also monitor and regulate the daily trading in their respective markets.

The SEC oversees SRO regulation by examining the SROs for compliance with their regulatory responsibilities, maintaining a surveillance capability of its own, reviewing and approving SRO rules and rule changes, and amending SRO rules where necessary and appropriate under the Act. The SEC also implements or changes existing regulations and conducts its own investigations, taking disciplinary or legal actions against those beyond SRO authority or against an SRO itself for not doing an adequate regulatory job.

Through their governing processes, SROs develop their own rules of conduct as required by the 1934 Act. The 1934 Act requires the SROs to design rules to protect both investors and the public interest, to promote a free and open market, to foster cooperation and competition in securities trading, and to prevent fraud and manipulation. New rules become effective after both the SRO governing bodies and the SEC have approved them.

Like other SROs, the NASD rules can change because of a new SEC regulation, a rule change by another SRO, a new product or service that the NASD wants to market, an SEC recommendation, or a conclusion that a rule is unenforceable, archaic, or not strict enough.

Generally, NASD rule changes are first considered by a committee representing the sector of the NASD most affected by the rule change or by a committee formed on an ad hoc basis. Following these deliberations, the NASD staff will prepare a draft of each new rule proposal and submit it to the committee where it originated for review. The committee will then accept, modify, or remand the staff draft.

The rule change is then presented to the NASD Board for approval and filed with the SEC. The SEC reviews the rule change, has it published in the *Federal Register* to solicit public comment, and then will either approve it, informally request that it be amended, or commence disapproval hearings. At any time during the process, the NASD may withdraw the rule change.

Registration With the SEC

The 1934 Act requires that securities broker-dealers register with the SEC. Firms dealing exclusively in commercial paper, bankers' acceptances, and commercial bills need not register. Firms that deal exclusively in either federal government or municipal securities register separately as government securities brokers or dealers or as municipal securities dealers. In addition, a broker or dealer whose business is exclusively intrastate and that does not use any facility of a national securities exchange is not required to register.

The registration process starts when the broker-dealer submits a completed application form and statement of financial condition to the SEC. The form requires the following information: a description of the firm's business, the applicant's disciplinary history, any felony or misdemeanor convictions, and a list of the firm's principals.

In addition to registering with the SEC, a broker-dealer must join at least one SRO. If a broker-dealer limits its business solely to securities listed on a national securities exchange, that exchange will be the appropriate SRO for that firm. If the broker-dealer transacts business in Nasdaq or the non-Nasdaq OTC market, it must become a member of the NASD. A broker-dealer that wishes to effect transactions directly on an exchange and also in the Nasdaq and OTC markets must become a member of both that exchange and the NASD.

Associated persons of a broker-dealer also must register with the appropriate SRO. These associated persons, which include any partner, officer, director, branch manager, controlling or controlled person, or employee of a broker-dealer, pass a general securities examination and have their employers file an application with the NASD. The registration form also requires information about the individual's prior employment and disciplinary history. The SRO has authority to exclude any person from associated person status where the person has, among other things, violated SEC requirements or committed a felony.

In addition, associated persons must provide fingerprints, which are then submitted to the Federal Bureau of Investigation for a criminal record check. Exempt from this requirement are those persons who do not sell securities, do not have access to securities, money, or original books and records, and do not supervise persons engaged in such activities.

Monitoring the Markets

As part of their self-regulatory functions, the NASD and exchanges maintain surveillance systems that monitor the trading of stocks and options in their markets. When the automated systems indicate unusual activity in a stock, SRO analysts look into the matter, to see whether it was the result of legitimate market forces or of law or SRO rule violations.

Some of the possible improprieties are:

- **Insider trading.** This occurs when corporate insiders effect securities transactions while in possession of material corporate information not publicly available. Other persons effecting securities transactions while in possession of material nonpublic information also may violate insider trading prohibitions if they misappropriate the information or otherwise have a duty not to trade on the information.

- **Manipulation.** Securities transactions that are effected to raise or depress prices artificially are illegal.

- **Excessive markups or commissions.** Firms are required to deal with customers at prices that are reasonably related to the current market. They are also prohibited from charging commissions that are excessive.

When unusual price or volume movements in a stock occur, SRO surveillance staff review current press releases; review historical trading activity in the stock; interview brokers, specialists, market makers, and issuer company officials; and send questionnaires to both the issuer and the brokerage firms involved in the stock. SRO staffs follow these procedures until the unusual movements are adequately explained.

If legitimate market forces were at work, the case is closed without action. If there appear to have been illegalities and if members of the SRO are involved, the SRO will usually initiate disciplinary action, but if members of the investing public are involved, the case will be referred to the SEC, whose jurisdiction is much broader than that of an SRO.

SEC Oversees SROs

Typically, the SEC does not conduct daily on-line surveillance of market activity. However, the SROs submit daily trade data to the SEC, which it stores in its own surveillance data base. The SEC also utilizes a computer system which, like that of the SROs, has pre-established parameters beyond which trades are noted as questionable.

When it detects questionable data for a stock, the SEC's Division of Market Regulation requests the appropriate SRO to supply its data for the same stock and the same time period. Market Regulation then compares its findings to those of the SRO to determine whether the SRO surveillance system overlooked anything. If the SEC determines that an SRO did not adequately capture certain data, it can direct the SRO to adjust its computer surveillance programming.

The inspection staff in SEC's Division of Market Regulation and investigators in its Enforcement Division also use the SEC surveillance system as a source of data. The data on this system provide information on broker-dealers and exchanges that can highlight areas for special attention during an examination and can be a source of evidence during investigations.

On-Site Member Examinations

If a firm belongs to more than one SRO, the SEC designates one such organization as the principal examining authority responsible for determining the firm's compliance with the financial responsibility requirements under federal securities laws. All SROs conduct on-site financial examinations and sales practice inspections of their member firms. Financial examinations seek to verify that securities firms are complying with SRO and SEC requirements and are maintaining a sound financial and operational condition. Sales practice inspections seek to ascertain whether firms and representatives have been fair in their dealings with their customers.

SRO financial exams include a review of the firm's books and records, verification of information submitted to the SRO in financial reports, and a review of compliance with SEC and SRO net capital and protection of customer securities rules. The net capital rule is a guide to measuring the liquidity of broker-dealer firms.

Sales practice examinations look for such activities as account "churning" (excessive transactions to create commission income), unauthorized trading, unsuitable recommendations to customers (suggesting transactions without regard to the customer's investment objectives and financial situation), conversion of customer funds for the firm's or employee's personal use, and misleading advertising, among other things. Compliance is analyzed by examining the way a firm opens customer accounts, files reports, confirms trades, handles monthly statements sent to customers, exercises supervision over accounts, responds to customer complaints, and uses advertising material, among other things.

On completion of an inspection, the SRO examiner staff holds an exit interview with the firm and advises it of any problems that have been found. If violations are noted, the staff classifies their seriousness. A minor violation might be a first-time, unintentional error in recordkeeping, which did not put customer funds in jeopardy. Major violations include intentional misuse of customer funds, repeated errors in bookkeeping, fraud, and any mistake that endangers customer funds.

When a firm is advised of a violation, it must assure the SRO that the problem will be corrected. A firm may be required to indicate, in writing, the steps it will take to avoid the problem in the future. This does not preclude the SRO from including the firm in an alert list, referring the matter to its enforcement section for a full-scale investigation, or taking disciplinary actions. In some cases, an SRO conducts special follow-up exams to be sure that the firm has rectified its procedures.

SROs submit to the SEC regular reports that detail ongoing and completed examinations and the problems identified.

SEC Oversight Extends to SRO Examination Procedures

The SEC's inspections of SROs consist of surveillance inspections and broker-dealer inspections:

- **Surveillance inspections of SROs.** These inspections focus on the SRO's ability to monitor trading in its market. The SEC tries to inspect each SRO every two years, with larger SROs inspected more frequently because of their high volume of activity. Inspections can also be initiated when a specific problem arises.

  On-site inspectors interview SRO staff, search files, and analyze surveillance activity with respect to possible violations. After an on-site inspection, the SEC team makes judgments as to whether initial inquiries about violations were thorough, follow-through efforts were adequate, and appropriate disciplinary actions were taken.

- **Broker-dealer inspections.** These inspections, which review financial operations, recordkeeping, and sales practices of securities firms, are conducted to ensure that SROs are effectively examining their broker-dealer members and taking prompt action on violations. SEC staff both reviews SRO-performed broker-dealer exams and also compares SRO exams with exams performed by the SEC itself.

The SEC performs two types of broker-dealer exams. The first are routine oversight exams. Results of the oversight exams are compared with findings from SRO audits to determine how well the SRO is performing its policing responsibilities.

As part of a routine oversight exam, SEC staff reviews a firm's compliance with the financial responsibility rules of the SRO and the commission. Two of these financial responsibility rules are the net capital rule and the customer-segregation rule. As already indicated, the net-capital rule sets standards regulating the liquidity of broker-dealer firms. The customer-segregation rule is designed to keep customers' funds and fully paid securities separate from the firm's operating funds or other assets.

The second type of broker-dealer inspection is an unannounced examination for cause. The cause may be a customer complaint, a report of a problem, recommendations by an SRO, or a potential violation that the SEC staff has discovered.

Disciplinary Actions

Where an SRO staff investigation indicates that a violation of the rules has occurred, the SRO initiates a disciplinary action. At the NASD, these actions are initiated by the NASD staff and heard first before one of the 11 District Business Conduct Committees located throughout the country.

In a disciplinary action, an SRO issues a formal complaint against a member firm or its associated persons. Hearings are held, at which the respondents are entitled to be represented by counsel, and appeals may be taken within the SRO structure. Ultimately, the complaint is dismissed or a penalty is imposed. Penalties include warnings, monetary fines, suspensions of individuals or firms, and the expulsion of a firm from an SRO or an individual from the SRO and therefore from the securities industry.

A final disciplinary action may be reviewed by the SEC on its own or on application by the penalized person. The SEC will affirm or modify the SRO's decision, or will remand the case to the SRO for further proceedings. A sanctioned firm or person may appeal the SEC decision directly to a U.S. Court of Appeals.

SRO rules permit the resolution of cases by negotiated settlement. In a settlement, the respondent agrees to the findings and the penalty but neither admits nor denies the allegations in the complaint.

International Regulation

The newest frontier for securities regulation is the international one. As cross-border trading has increased, the need has arisen to establish agreements between regulators of various countries and to seek establishment of compatible standards and procedures.

The securities regulators of 51 countries have banded together in the International Organization of Securities Commissions (IOSCO).

Particularly in the past five years, IOSCO has been active in addressing matters of concern to securities regulators throughout the world. Recently it has sought agreement regarding disclosure and accounting requirements that could apply across all markets, and agreement as to capital adequacy requirements for financial intermediaries in the various markets.

In the enforcement area, IOSCO has assisted in developing a series of bilateral cooperative agreements for the exchange of regulatory information and for cooperation in the investigation and the prosecution of wrongdoers. The SEC, for example, has bilateral agreements with Brazil, the United Kingdom, France, Italy, Japan, the Netherlands, and other countries.

The SROs have gone global also. The world's principal exchanges are joined in the Federation International des Bourses des Valeurs (FIBV), or International Federation of Stock Exchanges. The major dealers' associations have their own body, the International Councils of Securities Associations (ICSA), with representation from Australia, Canada, France, Japan, the United Kingdom, and the United States. Also significant is the Group of 30, an ad hoc group of leading financial firms, whose members have taken it upon themselves to devise worldwide standards for clearance and settlement of securities transactions.

Following domestic practice, the United States SROs cooperate with the government regulators in the global theater. The NASD, for example, is an associate member of IOSCO. The chief U.S. SROs, under the mantle of the SEC, have an agreement with the Securities Investments Board (SIB) in the U.K. to exchange information on the financial conditions of their member firms. The NASD has a separate agreement with the U.K. Stock and Futures Association (SFA) for the exchange of regulatory information on firms and individuals registered with them.

The search for effective international regulation should have the following objectives, among others:

1. Standards must exist to ensure adequate systems capacity and market integrity, including capital adequacy provisions.

2. Efficient trade comparisons and links to intermediated clearance and settlement systems must be in place.

3. There must be transparent prices through public dissemination of consolidated quotation and transaction information.

4. Rules providing fair treatment of customers must exist and be enforced.

5. There must be a capacity to provide surveillance of market activities, including effective audit trails.

6. Minimum standards for disclosure of information about companies should be established, worldwide accounting and audit standards should be agreed upon, and use of home country disclosure documents should be accepted.

7. Uniform standards for cross-border sales of professionally managed pools of capital should be promulgated.

8. Agreements must be reached between countries to cooperate in cross-border enforcement of securities law violations.

Extensive cooperation between the world's securities regulators is necessary for the development of international securities regulation. The standards of any one country cannot necessarily be applied to all others without change. There needs to be a gradual, pragmatic meeting of the minds regarding the regulatory practices from different countries that can be fitted together in a system that protects investors, issuers, and the public interest worldwide.

Chapter Five

John E. Pinto is executive vice president of compliance for the National Association of Securities Dealers, Inc. Mr. Pinto's division consists of 14 district offices that conduct on-site examinations of member firms to determine their compliance with NASD rules and federal securities laws. He is responsible for the surveillance of trading in Nasdaq issues and investigation of sales-practice abuses and fraudulent activities. His division also oversees the financial and operational viability of members.

Investor Protection Through NASD Regulation

by John E. Pinto
Executive Vice President, Compliance
National Association of Securities Dealers, Inc.

The integrity of a securities market depends on the quality and extent of regulation and surveillance applied to it. Markets need investors, and markets built on a foundation of trust and confidence attract investors.

In The Nasdaq Stock Market, trust and confidence are provided through regulatory programs administered by the National Association of Securities Dealers, Inc. (NASD). The NASD was established under the authority granted by the 1938 Maloney Act amendments to the Securities Exchange Act of 1934. Virtually every broker-dealer registered with the Securities and Exchange Commission (SEC) is required to become a member of the NASD.

The Principle of Self-Regulation

The principle guiding the NASD is that of true self-regulation, that is, volunteers from the securities industry elected or appointed to carry out policy making as well as enforcement and regulatory functions under the oversight of the SEC.

The NASD is the largest of all self-regulatory organizations for the securities industry in the United States.

The rationale for self-regulation is fourfold:

1. **Knowledge.** Securities industry professionals know their industry firsthand. They know, better than outsiders can, what is right with the industry, what is wrong, what needs most to be corrected, and how.

2. **Motivation.** The NASD's members have powerful incentives to craft sound rules for the markets, to prevent violations of the rules, and to detect infractions and punish those who commit them. Their enlightened views of self-regulation tell them that if the financial community does not manage its affairs properly, the investing public will lose confidence in the securities market, its reputation will be impaired, and its profitability will be negatively affected.

3. **Economy.** The NASD is privately financed and managed. U.S. taxpayers do not cover any of the NASD's operating expenses (nearly $175 million in 1990). The entire NASD budget is funded by its members and issuer companies.

4. **Public control.** The NASD's authority derives from federal legislation and can be withdrawn by legislation. The SEC reviews all of the NASD's rule and procedure changes as well as its disciplinary actions. As a result, the SEC may modify, reject, or approve these proposals or actions. The Justice Department, the Federal Bureau of Investigation, state securities commissions, and local law enforcement agencies all are involved in the policing of the securities industry. The NASD is active in working

on a cooperative basis with such agencies. The efficiency and integrity of The Nasdaq Stock Market is amply protected by public control at the federal, state, and local levels.

NASD and Nasdaq Regulatory History

In its more than 50 years, the NASD has compiled a strong record of regulatory achievement.

In its early years, the NASD established the program of on-site examinations of broker-dealer firms, qualifications testing of securities industry professionals, registration of sales and supervisory personnel, guidelines for markups, criteria for underwriting compensation, and standards for sales literature.

In 1963, the SEC declared that automation had the "potential for removing or alleviating some of the fundamental problems and limitations that have historically characterized both the operation and the regulation of the over-the-counter markets." The NASD agreed and built an automated quotations system. In February 1971, The Nasdaq Stock Market was born, and what had been a segment of the over-the-counter market became the over-the-computer market. The visibility and efficiency of the market increased enormously, and so did the capacity of the NASD to regulate it.

In 1975, Congress adopted the Securities Acts Amendments, which expanded the NASD's scope by giving it the sole responsibility among self-regulatory agencies for enforcing rules for the trading of municipal securities. Also, Congress called on the SEC to develop a "national market system" for equity trading. The Commission later determined that a number of Nasdaq securities — because of their high qualification standards and real-time transaction reporting — were of nationwide investor interest and should be incorporated into such a system. The NASD again responded effectively, and the Nasdaq National Market System (Nasdaq/NMS) began with 40 securities on April 1, 1982. Since that time, Nasdaq/NMS has grown to more than 2,500 issues.

Cooperation Produces Results

The NASD's involvement in cooperative regulation goes well beyond its relations with Congress and the SEC. For example, in the nationwide campaign against penny-stock fraud, the NASD has been engaged in joint investigations not only with the SEC but also with the Federal Bureau of Investigation (FBI), U.S. attorneys, the Internal Revenue Service, state securities commissioners, state attorneys general, and others. The NASD has participated in regional penny-stock sales-practice task forces in Florida, Denver, New York, New Jersey, and Los Angeles, assigning its senior enforcement staff on a full-time basis to prosecutors' offices.

In addition, the NASD participates in the U.S. Department of Justice's Securities and Commodities Fraud Working Group, which has produced many interagency referrals and cooperative actions. The NASD also conducts, on its own and in cooperation with the SEC, special training sessions on abusive practices for FBI agents, U.S. attorneys, and state securities examiners.

In order to ensure that its regulatory programs remain focused, the NASD frequently reviews its regulatory activities to make them more comprehensive and effective. For instance, in 1987, it appointed a Regulatory Review Task Force, headed by securities attorney and former SEC Commissioner A.A. Sommer, Jr. The task force recommended several improvements that were subsequently implemented. They included more precise computer systems to support the work of the Market Surveillance Department, sharper focus on the detection of questionable sales practices in member firms, and the crafting of sterner sanctions for violations.

Monitoring the Market

The NASD fulfills its self-regulatory responsibilities through an integrated plan involving both centralized, computerized surveillance of The Nasdaq Stock Market and nationwide on-site examinations of its member firms. The SEC defers the bulk of market surveillance and field examinations to the NASD and other self-regulatory organizations (SROs) and exercises its own responsibilities in these areas by oversight inspections of the SROs.

Market surveillance is the continuous monitoring of trading in The Nasdaq Stock Market that is conducted by the Market Surveillance Department in the NASD's Operations Center in Rockville, Maryland, 20 miles from NASD headquarters in downtown Washington, D.C. The Nasdaq Stock Market is a screen-based electronic market comprised of competing market makers located throughout the country and linked by the latest technology. Likewise, surveillance over trading in this market is facilitated by extensive state-of-the-art computerized systems.

Historical data on the price and volume trading patterns of each Nasdaq security are programmed into the market's central computers in Trumbull, Connecticut. As market makers in a given stock enter their quotations and transaction reports, the computer compares them with the historical parameters. It also factors in market-wide indicators and breaking news. If the market as a whole is rising and active and if good news comes out about the stock, the computer will be less ruffled by strong upward price and volume activity than under flat or falling market conditions.

If the computer finds the quotes or transaction reports on a stock to be unusual based on the trading characteristics of the particular security, Market Surveillance analysts begin looking for a reason for the unusual activity. The analyst's calls include the market makers that trade a significant volume in the stock under review. The analyst seeks to determine if there is any news or other unusual event affecting the company or the stock, what kind of investor interest there is in the stock, which firms are seeking to buy, which are seeking to sell — in short, what may be behind the unusual market activity that has caused a parameter break. The analyst also will call the Nasdaq company, asking one of its officers if any undisclosed corporate developments could account for the unusual activity or if the company knows or suspects some other reason for it.

In most cases, this rapid review turns up a logical explanation for the developments in the stock, and the matter can be closed. If doubt lingers, the Market Surveillance Department initiates more in-depth research.

Finding Insider Trading

When companies announce good or bad earnings, receipt or loss of a significant contract, or an attractive merger or acquisition proposal, the analysts seek to determine whether anyone has tried to profit from advance, insider information about the material development.

Let us take the hypothetical case of an announcement of a takeover. Prior to the news release disclosing the takeover to the public, the price of the stock surges upward, and trading volume is several times the historic average daily volume. An analyst now digs into past activity in the stock and finds several significant pockets of trading at various times in the period preceding the takeover news.

The NASD analyst contacts the acquiring and the acquired company and gets from both chronologies of meetings related to the acquisition. The chronologies may include the names and addresses of all participants in the meetings, including their outside advisors and their secretaries, and the duplicators and printers of documents developed from the meetings. Nasdaq companies must provide this information.

With the company chronologies in hand, the analyst queries Nasdaq market makers in the stock under investigation to see who did significant buying and selling in the stock at key times. Some insiders trade illegally shortly before company meetings if they feel sure about the meetings' outcome; others wait until the meetings are wrapped up. The accounts of investors with the market maker and other firms are scanned. If an investor has never shown interest in the stock of the acquired company and suddenly discovers it around the time of a meeting to discuss the acquisition, there is reason to look at that investor closely. If the investor is a corporate insider, or is related or associated with a corporate insider, and opens a brokerage account to trade the stock, that bears checking.

As the next step, the NASD analyst goes back to the company seeking to identify any of the major investors named by the market makers. Also, the Market Surveillance Department has a computerized file of all investors who have been involved in past investigations and reviews conducted by its analysts.

Disciplinary Actions

The Market Surveillance Committee, a group of 12 executives of securities firms across the country, reviews investigations that relate to market and trading practices conducted by the Market Surveillance Department. In a typical year, the committee takes some 35 formal disciplinary actions which lead to sanctions, including the barring of individuals from the securities industry, the suspension of firms or individuals, and the imposition of several million dollars in fines. In addition, the committee refers an average of more than 50 cases a year to the SEC for further action, many involving possible insider trading abuses.

Trading Halts

Daily, the Market Surveillance Department protects investors by imposing trading halts in securities. Nasdaq companies must promptly disclose to the press any material developments, positive or negative, that may affect investors' judgments about the value of their holdings. They must also inform the NASD about news before it is released to the press. When a company's news is material, Market Surveillance will institute a trading halt in the stock. During a halt, firms are prohibited from quoting or executing transactions in the stock.

A halt gives as many investors as possible access to the news and the opportunity to make judgments on the value of the stock. A halt normally lasts 30 minutes after the news appears on the press wire services; Market Surveillance institutes about 2,000 trading halts a year.

The NASD also monitors activity in OTC markets through its Anti-Fraud Department located in Washington, D.C. While focusing its attention primarily on non-Nasdaq OTC low-priced issues, the Anti-Fraud unit conducts extensive investigations involving fraud, manipulation, abusive sales practices, and other egregious conduct. Anti-Fraud has been particularly effective in spearheading the NASD's aggressive enforcement efforts in combating penny-stock fraud.

Broker-Dealer Surveillance

Broker-dealer surveillance focuses on the sales practices of NASD member firms and the financial and operational soundness of the firms. Market surveillance monitors trading activity, while broker-dealer surveillance looks critically at customer-protection and service-quality issues.

Some 750 full-time NASD professionals work on broker-dealer surveillance. Certain of these employees work out of the 14 district offices located in the Washington headquarters and 13 other major cities in the U.S.: San Francisco, Los Angeles, Denver, Seattle, Kansas City, New Orleans, Dallas, Atlanta, Chicago, Cleveland, Philadelphia, New York, and Boston. Each of these NASD offices investigates written complaints received from investors and utilizes a centralized computer data base as an additional regulatory tool to monitor and control these matters.

Investor complaints involving possible violations of federal securities laws or the NASD's Rules of Fair Practice may require special on-site examinations for cause.

NASD Rules of Fair Practice

In the regulation of firms, the centerpiece of the NASD's Rules of Fair Practice requires that "a member, in the conduct of his business, shall observe high standards of commercial honor and just and equitable principles of trade." The NASD enforces this rule to hold firms to strict standards of honesty, integrity, and fair dealing with customers, including prompt delivery of funds and securities, faithful adherence to customers' instructions, and much more.

Other significant NASD rules that govern a firm's conduct and relationship to its customers include:

- **Recommendations to customers.** When recommending to a customer the purchase, sale, or exchange of any security, a member must have reasonable grounds for believing that the recommendation is suitable based on the customer's other security holdings and his or her financial situation and needs. The Rules of Fair Practice list "practices that clearly violate this responsibility for fair dealing." Four of these include:

1. Recommending speculative low-priced securities to customers without adequate information on their financial situations. This practice results in a high probability that the recommendation will not be suitable for at least some customers.
2. Excessive activity, often referred to as "churning," in a customer's account designed to generate commissions for the representative and profits for the firm.
3. Fraudulent activity, such as the establishment of fictitious accounts, transactions in discretionary accounts in excess of, or without, actual authority from customers, unauthorized transactions, and misuse of customer funds or securities.
4. Recommending purchases beyond the customer's financial ability to meet such commitments.

- **Fair prices and commissions.** When determining what to charge customers for transactions, members must keep in mind the NASD's rule on fair prices and commissions, which says, in part, "It shall be deemed conduct inconsistent with just and equitable principles of trade for a member to enter into any transaction with a customer in any security at any price not reasonably related to the current market price of the security or to charge a commission which is not reasonable." This means, in effect, that a firm has to provide a customer with the best price available at the time of the trade.

- **Additional NASD rules.** Other rules require the publication of bona fide stock quotations, the adherence to bid and ask quotations represented to be firm, accurate disclosures on customer statements, and other essential elements of just and honorable dealing.

- **NASD Anti-Fraud rule**. This NASD rule prohibits the use of any manipulative, deceptive, or other fraudulent device in the purchase or sale of any security.

SEC Rules Enforced by the NASD

The NASD enforces federal securities laws and SEC rules, as well as its own Rules of Fair Practice. Certain of these SEC rules are detailed below:

- The net-capital rule, which governs the financial requirements that securities firms must meet to stay in business. This rule offers detailed instructions for determining a firm's financial condition.

- Requirements for firms to submit monthly and quarterly statements of financial condition, known as FOCUS (Financial and Operational Combined Uniform Single) reports.

- The customer-protection rule, which governs custody and segregation of customer funds and securities.

- The requirement for securities industry personnel to be fingerprinted.

- The SEC's anti-fraud rules, which prohibit the use of manipulative, deceptive, or other fraudulent devices in securities transactions.

- The SEC's cold-call rule designed to address high pressure and other abusive sales tactics involving penny stocks.

Supervision Within Firms

NASD strictly enforces its requirement that member firms closely supervise their personnel. A firm's supervisory system must cover all aspects of its business. Firm management must see to it that all supervisors are properly qualified, by being familiar with the regulations, familiar with the firm's product line, and capable of exercising authority.

A firm must regularly review the activities of each of its offices, particularly the handling of customer accounts, to prevent and detect irregularities. At a minimum, each registered representative of a firm must participate in an annual compliance review to discuss regulatory issues. The representatives must attend in person; telephone interviews or video conferences are not acceptable.

Violations of these NASD requirements have significant consequences. If registered representatives commit violations, the principals of the firms frequently are also penalized for failing to exercise proper supervision.

Registration Requirements

Supervisors, the people they supervise, and their employer firms are all subject to an assortment of registration requirements.

An individual seeking to be licensed must be sponsored by or be affiliated with an NASD member firm. He or she must fill out an application for registration, known as Form U-4, with all the details of his or her education, employment history, places of residence, and any regulatory problems or violations of the law that may have been committed. The forms are checked for accuracy and completeness by staff in the NASD's Central Registration Depository, where the records of hundreds of thousands of securities representatives and insurance agents are kept, and are updated as required. Fingerprints, which are checked by the FBI, must also be submitted.

If an individual's Form U-4 is acceptable, he or she may then take NASD-administered qualifications examinations. Insurance agents usually take an exam for a limited license, which allows them to sell only variable annuities and mutual funds. Anyone wishing to sell Nasdaq securities must be sponsored by an employer firm to take the General Securities Registered Representative examination, a six-hour test in which the average pass rate is about 65 percent.

The NASD requires sponsorship of the applicant to ensure that he or she, after passing the test, will be working under supervision. Passing other examinations can qualify individuals to be general securities principals and to become supervisors themselves. However, should they ever fall short of their responsibilities as supervisors, an NASD disciplinary decision could require them, among other things, to requalify as principals by retaking the exam.

Like individuals, firms entering the securities business must conform to the SEC's and the NASD's standards. Each firm trading Nasdaq securities must have a general securities principal to supervise dealings with investors and a financial and operational principal experienced in managing the books and records. It must comply with the SEC net-capital rule, which sets financial standards for the type of business that a firm wishes to do and specifies how liabilities and net liquid assets are to be computed.

Monitoring Operations

Once an individual and a firm become active in the industry, they are subject to NASD examination and monitoring. The SEC has designated the NASD as the examining authority for the vast majority of its 5,500 members. The New York Stock Exchange (NYSE) has the responsibility for the financial and operational condition of the 4,000 or so firms that belong to both the NASD and NYSE. During on-site examinations of those firms, when the NASD and NYSE jointly conduct the review, the NASD focuses on the member's sales practices that fall under the NASD's regulatory jurisdiction, such as Nasdaq and over-the-counter trading, municipal securities, mutual funds, and direct participation programs (tax shelters).

Every month, NASD members designated to the NASD must complete Part I of the SEC's FOCUS Report. This report sets forth financial and operational figures, including measures of a firm's volume, cash position, amount of customer exposure, inventory, monies, and securities due to or from other broker-dealers, profits, losses, and capital position. It is a key to the NASD's early-warning system for financial and operational problems. Quarterly, firms complete the more detailed Part II of the FOCUS Report, which is edited by computer for potential or actual difficulties.

The NASD recently adopted a requirement that members electronically transmit FOCUS data, which is fed directly into NASD computers for automated review and analysis. This process gets important financial and operations data to the NASD on a more timely and efficient basis, and gives the NASD greater resources to protect investors by enhancing its ability to detect potential financial problems.

Firms whose net capital falls below the required level are not permitted to continue doing a securities business. They must then report what steps they are taking to return to compliance with the requirements and must have the resumption of business approved.

Annual financial reports of member firms, certified by independent auditors, are also required by SEC rule and are reviewed by the NASD.

On-Site Examinations

The firms that are designated to the NASD and trade in Nasdaq and other equities, municipal securities, and options are subject to on-site routine examinations annually or every two years. Specialty firms that are engaged exclusively in either tax shelters, insurance, or mutual funds are examined on-site every three years. Under agreements with the Boston, Cincinnati, Midwest, and Pacific stock exchanges, the NASD has regulatory responsibility for on-site examinations of joint NASD/exchange members.

During a routine examination, an NASD examiner typically reviews a firm's books and records for currency and accuracy, its sales practices, its activities in Nasdaq market-making activities, the fairness of its dealings with customers, the rules of the Municipal Securities Rulemaking Board, other OTC securities activities, and its compliance with the anti-fraud provisions of the Securities Exchange Act of 1934, the registration requirements of the Securities Act of 1933, disclosure-of-capacity requirements, advertising rules, and the Federal Reserve System's regulations regarding the

extension of credit (i.e., margin requirements) on securities transactions.

Financial and Operational Examinations

A financial and operational examination is part of
the routine examination. This determines whether a firm's condition is sufficiently sound for it to continue transacting business.
The examination includes tests for compliance with all financial
responsibility rules, a verification of FOCUS Reports Part I and
Part II, and a net-capital computation that is prepared in accordance with the SEC's net-capital rule. A reserve-requirement computation is made, pursuant to the SEC's Customer Protection
Rule, to verify that the firm has properly reserved for sufficient
liquid assets to cover indebtedness related to customer accounts.
The examination also covers bank and omnibus account reconcili-
ations and cash-flow analysis.

Action on Examination Reports

The 11 District Business Conduct Committees
(DBCCs), which are composed of volunteers from member firms
who are elected by their peers to three-year terms, review examination reports prepared by the NASD staff. While most examination reports reflect general compliance with relevant securities
laws and regulations, those that indicate apparent violations of
rules and regulations are reviewed by the DBCC for possible disciplinary action. If a district committee orders formal disciplinary
action, the firms and individuals involved are entitled to hearings, at which they may be represented by counsel. If a district
committee finds that violations were indeed committed, it may
impose penalties ranging from a censure to the expulsion of a
firm from the NASD and the barring of an individual from association with any NASD member firm. Fines may also be imposed.
In 1990, the NASD collected the largest fine (over $2 million) ever
imposed in a disciplinary action.

The National Business Conduct Committee, one of the principal committees of the NASD Board of Governors, reviews all disciplinary actions by the DBCCs and Market Surveillance Committee. This review ensures that sanctions imposed in disciplinary proceedings are consistent, uniform, and fair, and serves as an avenue of appeal from district decisions. The Board of Governors may also intervene on request or of its own volition. Penalties handed down by the NASD may be appealed to the SEC and, ultimately, to a United States Court of Appeals.

In 1990, the NASD filed a total of 1,080 disciplinary actions against its member firms and registered persons. Of these, 135 stemmed from customer complaints. The 945 others resulted from broker-dealer surveillance, which included 3,856 on-site examinations. The actions led to the expulsion of 25 firms from the NASD, the barring of 344 individuals from association with any member firm, the temporary suspensions of 17 firms and 233 individuals, and the imposition of more than $30 million in fines.

In a word, NASD regulation works.

PART II

Nasdaq Companies:
Who Are They?

Chapter Six

Mary C. Farrell, a first vice president and member of the investment strategy team at PaineWebber Incorporated, has more than 18 years of experience as an investment research analyst. Ms. Farrell is a member of the New York Society of Security Analysts and is a regular panelist on *Wall $treet Week*.

The Panorama
of Companies

by Mary C. Farrell
Research Analyst and First Vice President
PaineWebber Incorporated

Since its inception in 1971, The Nasdaq Stock Market has played an increasingly important role in the U.S. securities industry and more recently in the world markets. No longer the province of smaller issues awaiting the opportunity to list on an exchange, Nasdaq has proven to be the market of choice for numerous publicly held companies, both small and large. It is this panorama of companies, some of the fastest growing in America, that has contributed to the growth of The Nasdaq Stock Market. By providing them with liquidity and access to capital, Nasdaq has contributed to the growth of these companies and the growth of America.

Nasdaq Growth Outpaces Exchanges

In 1991, the securities of 4,077 companies were traded on the Nasdaq market, compared with 1,851 on the New York Stock Exchange (NYSE) and 864 on the American Stock Exchange (Amex). The number of issues (many companies have more than one type of security trading) was 4,657 for Nasdaq, 2,387 for the NYSE, and 1,058 for the Amex. (See Exhibit 6–1.)

More impressive than these numbers is the growth of the Nasdaq market, as measured by the number of issues. While the number of issues on the NYSE has expanded slowly and that on the Amex has declined, the Nasdaq market has grown significantly — from 2,827 issues at its inception in 1971 to 4,657 in 1991, a 65 percent increase. During the same period, NYSE issues increased only to 2,387 from 1,927 and Amex issues declined 19 percent, from 1,308 to 1,058.

The advantage of being part of a computerized market with an ample number of market makers has for many companies out-

---

Exhibit 6–1   10-Year Comparisons of Nasdaq, NYSE, and Amex

| | | | | | | | (In Millions) | | |
| | Companies | | | Issues | | | Share Volume | | |
Year	Nasdaq	NYSE	Amex	Nasdaq	NYSE	Amex	Nasdaq	NYSE	Amex
1991*	4,077	1,851	864	4,657	2,387	1,058	33,970	37,384	2,713
1990	4,132	1,769	859	4,706	2,284	1,063	33,380	39,665	3,329
1989	4,293	1,719	859	4,963	2,241	1,069	33,530	41,699	3,125
1988	4,451	1,681	896	5,144	2,234	1,101	31,070	40,850	2,515
1987	4,706	1,647	869	5,537	2,244	1,077	37,890	47,801	3,506
1986	4,417	1,573	796	5,189	2,257	957	28,737	35,680	2,979
1985	4,136	1,540	783	4,784	2,298	940	20,699	27,511	2,101
1984	4,097	1,543	792	4,728	2,319	930	15,159	23,071	1,545
1983	3,901	1,550	822	4,467	2,307	948	15,909	21,590	2,081
1982	3,264	1,562	834	3,664	2,225	945	8,432	16,458	1,338
1981	3,353	1,565	867	3,687	2,220	959	7,823	11,854	1,343

---

* As of October 31, 1991.

weighed any advantage of listing on an exchange, keeping some of the bluest of America's "blue chips" on Nasdaq. Increasing globalization and computerization of the marketplace can only enhance these advantages.

A Large Volume Market

In 1972, the year after it was established, Nasdaq accounted for 42 percent of the combined share volume of the NYSE and Amex. In 1990, Nasdaq volume of 33.38 billion shares was nearly 78 percent of the combined exchange volume, (see Exhibit 6–2) and the percentage continued to grow in 1991, reaching 84 percent by the end of October. In fact, Nasdaq volume occasionally exceeds NYSE volume, a possible harbinger of the future. As larger companies increasingly opt to maintain their Nasdaq status and new issues are continually added to the market, volume will continue to grow.

Volume has declined somewhat since the record year of 1987 but, as the number of terminals expands and the number of companies and issues grows, Nasdaq should more than hold its share of worldwide trading, aided by increasing exposure of its companies abroad. In the first quarter of 1991, Nasdaq share volume ran at a record pace.

Exhibit 6–2   U.S. Equity Markets: 1990 Share and Dollar Volumes

	Share Volume		Dollar Volume	
	(In Millions)	Percent	(In Millions)	Percent
Nasdaq	33,380	39.2%	$ 452,430	21.8
Nasdaq/OTC Trading in Listed Securities	2,589	3.0	86,494	4.2
Amex	3,329	3.9	37,715	1.8
Regionals (BSE, CSE, MSE, PSE, and Phlx)	6,208	7.3	178,139	8.5
NYSE	39,665	46.6	1,325,332	63.7
Totals	**85,171**	**100.0**	**2,080,110**	**100.0**

A Broad Array of Companies

Nasdaq is host to a broad array of companies. A Nasdaq company can range from Microsoft's $15.5 billion to a company with less than $10 million in market valuation.

The typical Nasdaq company has total assets of $555.7 million, shareholders' equity of $99.5 million, total revenues of $234.1 million, and net income of $8.0 million. The typical security sells for $11.44 a share, has 10.2 million shares outstanding with a public float of 6.8 million, and has a market value of $116.2 million. (See Exhibit 6–3.) In the aggregate, Nasdaq companies represent $2.24 trillion in total assets, $400.2 billion in shareholders' equity, total revenues of $942.6 billion, and net income of $32.2 billion. The typical price-to-earnings ratio is 42.5.

What Makes Nasdaq Companies Special?

Nasdaq companies are notable for the large concentration of ownership by insiders (officers, directors, or related

---

Exhibit 6–3   Profile of Typical Nasdaq Company and Issue*: October 31, 1991

Nasdaq Company		Nasdaq Security	
Total Assets	$555.7 million	Share Price	$11.44
Shareholders' Equity	$99.5 million	Number of Market Makers	10.5
Total Revenues	$234.1 million	Total Shares Outstanding	10.2 million
Net Income	$8.0 million	Public Float (Shares)	6.8 million
P/E Ratio**	42.5	Market Value of Shares Outstanding	$116.2 million

---

* Includes domestic and foreign common stocks, ADRs, and shares of beneficial interest.
** Domestic common stocks and shares of beneficial interest only. Total market value divided by earnings.

persons, or owners of 10 percent or more of stock). As of year-end 1990, insiders held 28 percent of the outstanding shares of Nasdaq/NMS stocks. This inside ownership is a major strength of Nasdaq companies, suggesting that management, in many cases, retains an entrepreneurial interest. More importantly, a high level of inside ownership assures that management's interest is closely aligned with shareholders' interests.

Nasdaq remains the province of the individual investor, who held 42.1 percent of the shares in 1990. (See Exhibit 6–4.) While institutions may dominate trading on the exchanges, the individual investor remains a mainstay of the Nasdaq market. Despite reports that individuals are abandoning the stock market, Nasdaq numbers tell a different story, a tribute to the quality companies comprising it.

Exhibit 6–4   Distribution of Holdings of Nasdaq/NMS Stocks: 1990

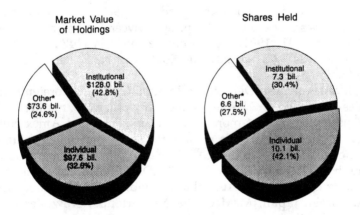

Market Value
of Holdings

Shares Held

---

* Other includes holdings of officers, directors, or related persons, and beneficial owners of 10 percent or more.

Data Source: Vickers Stock Research Corporation.

Individuals and insiders dominate as holders of Nasdaq shares, but ownership has evolved toward more institutional holdings, reflecting the attractive opportunities offered by Nasdaq companies, increased liquidity associated with the Nasdaq market over the years, the historical outperformance of smaller issues, and, more recently, the better values available among smaller companies, particularly growth stocks. Institutions now hold 42.8 percent of the market value of Nasdaq National Market securities.

Geographic and Company Diversity

Nasdaq companies are headquartered in all 50 states, as well as the District of Columbia and Puerto Rico, ranging from 576 in California and 358 in New York to two in North Dakota and one in South Dakota. (See Exhibit 6–5.)

They also represent virtually every major industry group, a total of 35 industries. Commercial banks comprise by far the greatest number (572), followed by foreign securities (255) and computer and data processing products (196). Not surprisingly, the categories that grew most rapidly between December 31, 1990, and October 31, 1991, were pharmaceuticals (147.7 percent), health services (93.8 percent), and Southwest banks (83.0 percent). (See Exhibit 6–6.)

More American Depositary Receipts (ADRs) of foreign companies are traded on Nasdaq than on any other U.S. market — in fact, nearly 60 percent more than on the NYSE and Amex combined. In 1990, Nasdaq set records for share and dollar volume, trading more than 2 billion ADR shares with a dollar value of more than $21 billion. Currently, 87 ADRs trade on Nasdaq, representing companies in Australia, Finland, France, Germany, Ireland, Israel, Japan, Mexico, the Netherlands, New Zealand, Norway, South Africa, Sweden, and the United Kingdom. In addition, 170 foreign companies trade on Nasdaq, representing additional countries as well, with 132 Canadian, 78 percent of the total.

Like the financial markets in general, Nasdaq companies have seen the shift away from heavy industry toward more service-related industries such as technology and health

Exhibit 6–5   Nationwide Distribution of Nasdaq Company Headquarters
(Number of Nasdaq Companies Alphabetically by State)

State	Number of Cos.	State	Number of Cos.
Alabama	34	Montana	9
Alaska	5	Nebraska	18
Arizona	46	Nevada	33
Arkansas	10	New Hampshire	25
California	576	New Jersey	237
Colorado	134	New Mexico	14
Connecticut	108	New York	358
Delaware	6	North Carolina	69
District of Columbia	12	North Dakota	2
Florida	206	Ohio	133
Georgia	77	Oklahoma	36
Hawaii	8	Oregon	33
Idaho	4	Pennsylvania	193
Illinois	118	Puerto Rico	7
Indiana	58	Rhode Island	13
Iowa	22	South Carolina	34
Kansas	24	South Dakota	1
Kentucky	26	Tennessee	44
Louisiana	20	Texas	245
Maine	8	Utah	61
Maryland	71	Vermont	11
Massachusetts	194	Virginia	86
Michigan	92	Washington	60
Minnesota	132	West Virginia	18
Mississippi	15	Wisconsin	63
Missouri	51	Wyoming	9
		Total	**3,869**

Exhibit 6–6   Nasdaq Major Industry Groups Ranked by Growth

Major Industry Groups	Percent Change 12/31/90- 10/31/91	(In Billions) Market Value	Number of Companies
Pharmaceuticals	147.66%	$30.0	139
Health Services	93.78	12.0	95
Commercial Banks & Bank Holding Companies Southwest	82.97	2.3	18
Computer & Data Processing Services	81.33	48.1	196
Apparel	74.00	6.9	51
Medical Instruments & Supplies	68.32	15.8	132
Commercial Banks & Bank Holding Companies Great Lakes	68.16	21.9	98
Business Services	64.22	8.6	117
Electrical Equipment	61.16	4.6	72
Commercial Banks & Bank Holding Companies Midwest	58.83	6.0	36
Wholesale Trade	55.78	15.6	165
Retail Trade	53.33	21.7·	128
Commercial Banks & Bank Holding Companies South	50.91	13.2	122
Restaurants	50.76	6.1	65
Instrumentation	48.79	3.8	109
Savings & Loans	46.20	2.7	81
Communications Equipment	46.05	5.8	112
Commercial Banks & Bank Holding Companies Northeast	37.98	18.1	231
Trucking & Transportation	35.98	12.3	90
Primary Manufacturing	34.38	11.6	123
Commercial Banks & Bank Holding Companies West	32.38	7.9	67
Life Insurance	30.59	4.4	45
Computer Manufacturers	29.17	20.4	136
Machinery	29.11	6.4	99
Electronic Components	27.27	15.1	108
Foreign Securities	27.02	21.1	255
Electric, Gas, & Sanitary Services	24.31	8.7	83

(Exhibit continues)

Exhibit 6–6   Nasdaq Major Industry Groups Ranked by Growth (Continued)

Major Industry Groups	Percent Change 12/31/90- 10/31/91	(In Billions) Market Value	Number of Companies
Property/Casualty Insurance	23.30	11.9	41
Telecommunications	20.37	29.7	84
Food Products	16.51	9.6	60
Construction	14.57	1.3	32
Printing & Publishing	11.68	5.6	46
Travel & Entertainment	10.34	1.7	86
Oil & Gas	2.49	3.7	137
Gold & Silver	0.67	0.5	31
Totals		**$415.0**	**3,490**

care. Because so many initial public offerings of smaller growth companies are on Nasdaq, the shift is more apparent than on other securities markets. Currently, about 40 percent of the market value of Nasdaq is represented by service-related companies.

Some specific stock categories have their own indexes. Aside from the Nasdaq Composite, they are the Industrial, Other Finance, Bank, Insurance, Utility, Transportation, Nasdaq/NMS Composite, Nasdaq/NMS Industrial, Nasdaq-100®, and Nasdaq-Financial®. (See Exhibit 6–7.) In an increasingly complex marketplace, these indexes provide market watchers more tools to track market movements within sectors and to monitor relative performance in particular industries.

The Nasdaq market boasts many companies with billionaire status; 73 companies as of September 30, 1991, with market capitalizations of more than $1 billion. It is worth noting that the 50 market-value leaders of Nasdaq range from $16.3 billion to $1.4 billion. The top four include Microsoft, Intel, MCI Communications, and Amgen, all with market valuations above $7 billion. (See Exhibit 6–8.)

Exhibit 6–7   Nasdaq Index Performance Through October 31, 1991

Indexes	Record High	Date Established	10/31/91	10/31/81	10-Year % Change
Composite	542.98	10/31/91	542.98	195.24	+178%
Industrial	612.01	10/31/91	612.01	233.02	+163
Other Finance	567.23	10/09/89	536.37	169.80	+216
Bank	526.64	3/20/87	333.45	136.23	+145
Insurance	585.08	4/17/91	549.79	189.04	+191
Utility	788.51	10/09/89	602.29	174.82	+245
Transportation	546.57	10/31/91	546.57	173.10	+216
Nasdaq/NMS Composite	239.72	10/31/91	239.72	*	*
Nasdaq/NMS Industrial	243.94	10/31/91	243.94	*	*
Nasdaq-100®	595.31	10/16/91	585.01	**	**
Nasdaq-Financial®	479.87	10/30/91	479.66	**	**

* The Nasdaq/NMS indexes began on July 10, 1984, valued at 100.
** The Nasdaq-100® and Nasdaq Financial® indexes began on February 1, 1985, valued at 250.

On the other hand, as of September 1991, 2,144 companies had less than $25 million in market capitalization; they averaged $8.0 million. Only 16 percent, or 553, had market valuations above $100 million, (see Exhibit 6–9) but these companies accounted for about 90 percent of the total market value.

The Companies of Nasdaq

What companies are listed on Nasdaq? In the technology area, well-known names such as Intel, AST Research, Apple Computer, Lotus Development, Sun Microsystems, and Microsoft are leaders of the technology revolution in America. In fact, the top eight volume leaders on Nasdaq are also technology companies, representing not only computer firms but also

Exhibit 6–8   50 Nasdaq/NMS Market-Value Leaders as of September 30, 1991

Symbol	Company Name	Total Shares Outstanding (000's)	Market Value (000's)
1. MSFT	Microsoft Corp.	174,094	$15,494,366
2. INTC	Intel Corp.	202,649	8,561,920
3. MCIC	MCI Comm. Corp.	255,993	7,263,801
4. AMGN	Amgen Inc.	130,223	7,194,821
5. AAPL	Apple Computer, Inc.	117,490	5,815,755
6. NOVL	Novell, Inc.	143,846	5,340,283
7. TCOMA	Tele-Comm., Inc. Cl A	305,159	4,691,820
8. LINB	LIN Broadcasting Corp.	51,400	3,790,750
9. NOBE	Nordstrom, Inc.	81,740	3,678,300
10. COST	Costco Wholesale Corp.	76,732	3,663,953
11. MCCS	Medco Containment Srvs., Inc.	54,345	3,607,149
12. MCAWA	McCaw Cellular Comm., Inc. Cl A	117,335	3,402,715
13. SUNW	Sun Microsystems, Inc.	100,904	3,052,346
14. FDLNA	Food Lion, Inc. Cl A	162,647	3,049,631
15. FDLNB	Food Lion, Inc. Cl B	159,715	2,974,692
16. PCLB	Price Co. (The)	48,385	2,915,196
17. STPL	St. Paul Companies, Inc. (The)	42,370	2,595,162
18. RTRSY	Reuters Holdings PLC	51,710	2,579,036
19. STJM	St. Jude Med., Inc.	47,075	2,447,900
20. SAFC	SAFECO Corp.	62,746	2,368,662
21. CSFN	CoreStates Fin. Corp.	54,400	2,359,600
22. FITB	Fifth Third Bancorp	39,325	2,221,862
23. ROAD	Roadway Srvs., Inc.	38,742	2,111,439
24. BMET	Biomet, Inc.	56,189	2,107,088
25. SIAL	Sigma-Aldrich Corp.	49,710	2,075,392
26. USBC	U.S. Bancorp	97,992	2,057,832
27. STBK	State Street Boston Corp.	36,543	2,032,704
28. UNIT	Unitrin, Inc.	53,207	1,968,659
29. CINF	Cincinnati Fin. Corp.	16,477	1,894,855
30. ORCL	Oracle Sys. Corp.	136,297	1,822,972
31. USHC	U.S. Healthcare, Inc.	63,962	1,774,946

(Exhibit continues)

**Exhibit 6–8   50 Nasdaq/NMS Market-Value Leaders as of
September 30, 1991   (Continued)**

Symbol	Company Name	Total Shares Outstanding (000's)	Market Value (000's)
32. CNTO	Centocor, Inc.	35,504	1,730,820
33. CPER	Consolidated Papers, Inc.	43,657	1,713,537
34. BOAT	Boatmen's Bcshs., Inc.	37,809	1,696,679
35. UNIH	United HealthCare Corp.	31,204	1,685,016
36. NTRS	Northern Trust Corp.	34,209	1,684,793
37. MMBLF	MacMillan Bloedel Ltd.	110,441	1,684,225
38. PHYB	Pioneer Hi-Bred Int'l, Inc.	30,222	1,647,099
39. PCAR	PACCAR Inc.	33,814	1,631,526
40. BETZ	Betz Labs., Inc.	28,631	1,553,232
41. SOCI	Society Corp.	32,844	1,535,457
42. SONO	Sonoco Products Co.	43,172	1,467,848
43. WMTT	Willamette Inds., Inc	25,477	1,449,004
44. LOTS	Lotus Development Corp.	43,296	1,439,592
45. SCIXF	Scitex Corporation Ltd.	37,347	1,391,176
46. MEDC	Medical Care International	20,545	1,381,651
47. BMCS	BMC Software, Inc.	25,064	1,359,722
48. TYSNA	Tyson Foods, Inc.	68,955	1,344,622
49. CHIR	Chiron Corporation	19,042	1,337,700
50. STRY	Stryker Corporation	47,517	1,330,476

Note: Only domestic common and foreign Nasdaq/NMS securities appear on this list.

telecommunications companies such as MCI Communications. Nasdaq has historically provided the means for technology companies such as these to access the marketplace for capital.

Other Nasdaq companies pioneered new industries years ago. They include Herman Miller and HON Industries, still benefiting from growth in the open office systems market, as well as Price Company and Costco Wholesale Club, bringing wholesaling directly to the public.

Some of the most exciting Nasdaq companies are among the leaders in fledgling industries with explosive growth potential,

Exhibit 6–9   Performance of Nasdaq Stocks by Market Value: January-September 1991

(In Millions) Market Value Range	(In Millions) Market Value Average January 1991	Number of Companies	Price Weighted*	Market-Value Weighted**	Equal (Percent) Weighted***
$ 0-24.9	$ 8.0	2,144	+39.0%	+60.6%	+93.0%
25-49.9	35.6	422	+35.9	+54.2	+55.6
50-74.9	61.9	199	+38.5	+48.5	+48.5
75-99.9	88.0	128	+31.3	+41.3	+41.2
100-199.9	143.6	274	+34.6	+44.5	+43.7
200-499.9	301.8	174	+35.9	+42.3	+41.8
Over 500	1,238.4	105	+34.0	+42.6	+39.2
Overall	$ 79.6	3,446	+36.1%	+44.8%	+75.8%

* Percent change in average price.
** Percent change in average market value.
*** Average percent price change.

Note: Consists of all common stocks trading on Nasdaq since the beginning of 1991. Performance does not include dividends.

such as Amgen and Cetus in the biotechnology group. Enormous startup costs have been funded through Nasdaq's public markets, and the benefits have begun to multiply.

In the health care area, St. Jude Medical, Medco Containment Services, National Health Laboratories, and U.S. Healthcare have accrued aggressive earnings growth while providing products or services for dealing with the nation's burgeoning health care problems.

The environmental area, expected to be one of enormous growth in the future, is also well represented on Nasdaq by companies such as BHA Group, Sevenson Environmental, and Clean Harbors.

Companies representing less exciting industries, in true Nasdaq fashion, have been able to achieve exciting growth rates through innovation and excellent management. They include the

Bruno's and Food Lion supermarket chains, as well as spice and flavoring manufacturer McCormick. Smaller A&W Brands competes successfully with the global giants of the beverage industry both domestically and internationally. Basic industry as well is more than adequately represented on Nasdaq — Cross & Trecker, PACCAR, and Masco Industries are prominent examples.

Many of the top-performing issues are relatively new companies, either incorporated or going public within the most recent 10-year period, and the vast majority of these are traded on the Nasdaq market. Many of the market leaders over extended periods of time have been those involved in new technologies that have taken the risks of innovation long associated with companies in the Nasdaq market. Initial public offerings have resulted in a constant flow of new companies on Nasdaq, offset in some years by the fact that Nasdaq companies have provided fertile ground for mergers and acquisitions. (See Exhibit 6–10.)

Although their generally smaller sizes have meant less attention than was given to some of the mega-deals garnered during the last decade, Nasdaq companies, through their inherent values, have attracted a share of the takeover activity. Until 1984, the number of mergers and acquisitions of Nasdaq companies was negligible. But it accelerated rapidly, reaching 125 deals worth $25 billion in market capitalization in 1989. In 1984, the market value of Nasdaq mergers and acquisitions was less than 7 percent of the value of the NYSE deals, but by 1989 that figure reached 20 percent.

A recent event confirmed that Nasdaq is home to companies ranging from small and emerging to large and seasoned. Nasdaq's Roadway Services was included in The Dow Jones Transportation Index, the first non-NYSE company to be part of a Dow Jones average but undoubtedly not the last.

The Nasdaq National Market

In 1982, the Nasdaq National Market System (Nasdaq/NMS) was created so that qualified companies could enjoy facilitated and up-to-the-minute reporting of transactions. Even though companies must meet stringent quantitative and

Exhibit 6-10   Nasdaq Initial Public Offerings: 1981-1991*

Year	Number of Offerings	(In Billions) Dollar Value Offerings**
1981	333	$ 3.01
1982	110	1.15
1983	637	11.21
1984	304	2.77
1985	294	4.00
1986	570	9.65
1987	402	6.11
1988	159	2.13
1989	**148**	**2.16**
1Q	23	0.17
2Q	37	0.44
3Q	35	0.64
4Q	53	0.91
1990	**135**	**2.38**
1Q	34	0.57
2Q	48	1.01
3Q	38	0.69
4Q	15	0.11
1991	**200**	**4.93**
1Q	23	0.51
2Q	94	2.33
3Q	83	2.09

*   Through September 30, 1991.
**   Includes overallotment shares.

Data Source: IDD Information Services, Inc. Excludes closed-end mutual funds. Firm-commitment underwritings only.

qualitative standards to be included on it, 2,494 of the 4,706 Nasdaq issues were listed on Nasdaq/NMS at the end of 1990.

**Exhibit 6–11   Profile of Typical Nasdaq/NMS
Company and Issue*: October 31, 1991**

Nasdaq/NMS Company		Nasdaq/NMS Issue	
Total Assets	$683.1 million	Share Price	$17.62
Shareholders' Equity	$110.7 million	Number of Market Makers	11.7
Total Revenues	$264.7 million	Total Shares	
Net Income	$7.7 million	Outstanding	9.8 million
P/E Ratio**	37.4	Public Float (Shares)	7.1 million
		Market Value of Shares Outstanding	$173.3 million

---

* Includes domestic and foreign common stocks, ADRs, and shares of beneficial interest.
** Domestic common stocks and shares of beneficial interest only. Total market value divided by earnings.

Being on Nasdaq/NMS provides important benefits. Qualified Nasdaq/NMS companies may be purchased on margin, and most states exempt them from blue-sky registration. Although only 53 percent of Nasdaq issues are part of Nasdaq/NMS, they account for 96 percent of the total market capitalization of Nasdaq. Moreover, they have an average of 11.7 market makers per security, compared with 9.9 for all Nasdaq securities. (See Exhibit 6–11.) Of the top 50 Nasdaq/NMS companies in market value at the end of 1990, 48 had more than $1 billion in market capitalization.

Smaller companies that do not yet meet the Nasdaq/NMS standards are still an integral part of Nasdaq, which provides liquidity, marketability, and visibility to many of America's smaller publicly held companies. It will continue to offer new companies their first trading arena, nurture them through their emerging growth, and then as the market of the future provide a global arena as they mature into "blue chips." Some of America's finest companies have chosen to be part of the most technologically advanced market in the world, a partnership with significant benefits today and for the future.

Chapter Seven

Gordon S. Macklin joined Hambrecht & Quist, Inc., as chairman and co-chief executive officer in July 1987. Before joining Hambrecht & Quist, Mr. Macklin was president of the National Association of Securities Dealers, Inc., for 17 years. From 1950 to 1970, Mr. Macklin was with McDonald & Company where he was a partner and member of the firm's executive committee.

Abby M. Adlerman is an investment banker who specializes in emerging growth and high technology companies. In 1988, she joined Hambrecht & Quist and is a principal of the firm. Previously, she spent two years with L. F. Rothschild in New York.

Kenneth Y. Hao is a financial analyst in Hambrecht & Quist's corporate finance department, where he participates in public financings as well as merger and acquisition assignments for high technology and life science companies.

Going Public and the Nasdaq Market

by Gordon S. Macklin
Chairman and Co-Chief Executive Officer
Hambrecht & Quist Incorporated

Abby M. Adlerman
Principal
Hambrecht & Quist Incorporated

Kenneth Y. Hao
Financial Analyst
Hambrecht & Quist Incorporated

Going public can be one of the most significant events in the life of a company. The initial public offering (IPO) process is comparable to a rite of passage, after which the company joins the ranks of some of the country's largest and most well-known companies.

The rewards of going public are great. Through an IPO, a company can raise a significant amount of capital and also have substantial latitude in deciding where to channel the funds. The stock market enables a public company and its shareholders to sell and buy equity at third-party-established valuations. The added liquidity and up-to-the-minute market valuations enhance the ability of the company to use stock options to attract and retain employees and to acquire businesses with its stock. In addition, since new developments in publicly traded companies will affect the public's investment decisions, public companies enjoy greater visibility through both the research of investment firms as well as articles in the financial press.

Like all rites of passage, the IPO process is challenging. It spans many months, during which all details about the company, including its past and projected financial performance, are subject to analysis by various "experts." The company will assemble an "IPO team" of investment bankers, lawyers, and auditors who will be actively involved in the complex underwriting and legal procedures of a public offering. The greatest challenge, however, lies on the shoulders of the company's management, whose ability to convey the company's story to investors significantly influences both the success of the IPO and the perception of the company in the following public market.

Basic Offering Issues

The first issues facing a company considering an IPO usually involve four basic questions: (1) When should the IPO occur? (2) How large should the offering be? (3) What will be the approximate valuation? (4) Which trading market should the company choose? Answering such questions typically is more of an art than a science, and enlisting the advice of an experienced investment banking firm can be extremely helpful. While timing and trading market issues should be determined in advance of the IPO process, the offering size and price will not be finalized until the end of the IPO process and directly before the actual offering to investors.

Timing the Offering

The company first should consider whether it is indeed ready to go public. The more predictable a company's profitability, the more "ready" it is for an IPO. Examining the operating margins and growth rates of comparable companies that have recently gone public and their subsequent performance in the stock market provides essential guidance in determining whether a particular company is ready to go public. An earnings disappointment or volatile operating performance by a public company can cause a dramatic reaction in its stock market valuation, particularly if it is a new issue. For companies that do not have a long or consistent operating history, meeting performance expectations for one or two additional quarters before going public often can add immeasurably to their credibility with investors during the IPO.

The level and consistency of profitability of companies that have successfully gone public vary greatly with the company's industry. For example, while sustainable revenues and consistent operating margins are almost mandatory for most IPOs, companies in particular industries can successfully go public with radically different financial models.

When Centocor, Inc., a developer and marketer of biological substances for immunotherapy and immunodiagnostics, went public in 1982, it had an extremely short operating history, having been founded in the fall of 1979. At the time of the IPO, Centocor had accumulated large losses and had not yet received significant revenues from product sales. Furthermore, most analysts believed that operating losses would continue for at least two more years.

However, Centocor attracted strong demand from investors during the IPO and in several subsequent public offerings because of the size of its potential market, its proprietary technology, its strong management, and its relationships with major corporate partners. Because of the successful performances of both the company and its stock, Centocor helped set a precedent for the numerous biotechnology companies that have gone public in recent years.

Once a company has decided on a public offering, its financial condition can affect the timing of the IPO. This is particularly true for companies that designate the IPO proceeds for use in re-paying debt, pursuing large research and development projects, or building sales and marketing channels. Other companies that are using the IPO primarily to provide liquidity for current share-holders and will use the net proceeds to fund operations and for general corporate purposes may have more flexibility on the tim-ing.

The state of the stock market is always an important deter-minant in the timing of an IPO. It is only natural for companies in industries that are currently in favor with equity investors to seek to catch the "open window" and obtain attractive valuations. Cer-tainly, the stock market's demand for new issues does vary greatly over time, and ongoing market conditions can dramati-cally influence the IPO valuation.

However, embarking on and then rushing through an IPO process primarily to catch an "open window" is inadvisable. The minimum time from choosing investment bankers to the close of the offering is approximately two months, and there can be little assurance that stock market conditions at the time of the offering will not be radically different than are the conditions at the start of the IPO process. The expenses and disappointments associated with an offering that is delayed or abandoned are considerable. At the same time, it may be unwise to disregard the ramifications of a strong bull market or an extremely volatile market. In any case, though, stock market conditions should be only one of sev-eral factors to consider in timing the IPO.

Offering Size

The company's capital requirements should be a primary determinant of the dollar amount of the offering. While it is not imperative for the company to have designated specific uses for the proceeds of the IPO, it is important to carefully con-sider how much capital the company can effectively assimilate. It is advisable for the company to settle on a tentative offering size, as measured in both shares offered and dollars raised, early in the IPO process.

The size of the offering also affects the stock's liquidity and potential price volatility in the aftermarket (the period following the IPO). The number of shares that are available for free trade in the public markets is called the public "float." Generally, to provide liquidity levels that are attractive to large institutional investors, a stock should have a float of at least 1 1/2 million shares. Smaller floats tend to be more narrowly distributed, which causes decreased liquidity, as buyers cannot as easily find sellers and vice versa. Stocks with small float sizes tend to be more susceptible to volatility in the aftermarket because sizable trades may involve a large percentage of the total shares available and can cause substantial price movement in the stock. On the other hand, an excessively large offering of shares may result in too much dilution in ownership and earnings per share.

Many companies have successfully pursued a "seasoning strategy," which involves a small IPO and, sometime afterward, a larger follow-on offering. This strategy can be particularly effective when the company's IPO valuation is under pressure because of difficult market conditions or because the company is not well known and is perceived as higher risk. The company can structure a small IPO at a conservative valuation and allow the stock to become better known in the investment community. As the stock prices appreciate due to improving market conditions or as the company builds credibility with investors, the company can structure a larger follow-on offering at a higher valuation.

In this scenario, the company incurs a high cost of capital for only a portion of the total funds raised. Furthermore, the upward momentum of its stock price appeals to existing and new investors and generates positive visibility for the company. Most importantly, this strategy can provide a company with access to funding through the equity markets under almost any conditions.

The public offerings on Nasdaq of Octel Communications Corporation provide a good example of the seasoning strategy. Octel completed the first technology IPO following the market crash of October 1987, raising $16.9 million at an offering price of $7 per share. A year later, Octel's stock price had appreciated substantially due to the company's growth and improving stock market conditions. At this time, Octel completed a $40.3 million follow-on offering at $23.375 per share. Through the seasoning strategy, Octel obtained access to the capital needed to fund its

growth, gained credibility with investors, and benefited from upward momentum in its stock price.

The proposed offering size influences the company's choice
of investment bankers for "lead manager" or "co-managers."
Most major-bracket investment banks will not manage IPOs of
less than $15 million. Very small IPOs are considered more specu-
lative and usually are managed by certain regional or "boutique"
investment banks that specialize in such higher-risk underwriting.

Offering sizes sometimes change during the IPO process in
response to company developments and changes in the expected
offering price. In addition, in a typical IPO, the company gives
the underwriters the option to sell up to an additional 15 percent
of the entire offering to investors during the 30 days following the
IPO. This is called the "overallotment" or "green shoe" and allows the underwriters to stabilize the market by using additional
shares to manage their trading positions.

Valuation

For the company and selling shareholders, the cost
of capital is lower with a higher IPO valuation because fewer
shares, and hence a smaller percentage of equity, can be sold for a
given amount of proceeds. However, pushing a company's valuation to the limit may result in a trade-off between the cost of capital and the aftermarket price performance of the stock. An
aggressive IPO valuation will cause investors to put more pressure on the company's financial results in the aftermarket. Furthermore, a higher valuation, given the higher starting price of
the stock, is likely to reduce the stock price's rate of appreciation.

As discussed earlier, a strong aftermarket performance
makes a follow-on offering more attractive and creates credibility
with investors. The company should seek the highest sustainable
valuation rather than the highest attainable valuation. Typically,
investment bankers will advise a company to offer its stock at 10
to 15 percent below where they expect the stock to trade shortly
after the IPO.

An investment bank usually completes its first valuation before being retained by the company since the numbers on the

table are important criteria in selecting investment bankers. During the IPO process, the investment bankers will frequently refine their valuation analysis to incorporate the constantly changing business conditions and stock market environment. While investment banks conduct the most comprehensive valuations, it is critical for the company's management to understand the logic behind the valuation. Therefore, management should be an active participant in the valuation of the company rather than merely a judge of the outcome.

The list of specific factors that can affect valuation varies for each company as well as over time. Factors such as earnings history, company size, market share, industry, competitive profile, growth potential, economic conditions, and state of the stock market all can play roles in the valuation of a company's stock. The investment bankers consider these factors in relation to the investment outlook to determine an appropriate valuation range for the company. During the IPO process, the investment banks must justify their valuation by communicating the important characteristics of the company and its strategies to potential new investors. This is termed "positioning" the company. The more unique a company's business, the more impact positioning has on the company's IPO valuation.

An analysis of the stock market's current valuation of "comparable" companies is the most basic and effective valuation tool for investment bankers. The analysis involves composing a list of publicly traded companies that best match the business, size, profitability, risk structure, and growth potential of the company going public. The company's management provides the most valuable input in helping to identify these companies. An ideal comparables list is not necessarily one that contains exclusively companies trading at high market-value ratios. Rather, it should contain a set of companies that investors will feel is most representative of the IPO candidate. After the comparables list is assembled, the investment bankers will compile a set of data for each comparable company and calculate various financial and market-value ratios. Ultimately, the investment bankers will use such comparables to determine and substantiate the proposed IPO valuation.

Trading Market Issues

Selecting the market in which a company's stock will trade represents an important decision. The overwhelming majority of companies go public on The Nasdaq Stock Market, partly because of its significant benefits in obtaining sponsorship in the investment community. The multiple market makers in Nasdaq, unlike the single specialists on the exchanges, play a key role in helping a newly public company enhance its reputation among investors and promote liquidity in the stock. And since its daily quotes are available on desktop terminals all over the world, Nasdaq enables emerging companies to enjoy a broad-based trading market.

Nasdaq in 1990 accounted for 134 of the 158 IPOs on major U.S. markets, and the dollar value of Nasdaq IPOs exceeded that on the New York Stock Exchange (NYSE) and American Stock Exchange (Amex) combined, as it has in 7 of the last 10 years. Of the more than 1,700 IPOs that were eligible to list on the NYSE or Amex from the beginning of 1984 through the end of March 1991, almost 1,300 of them listed on Nasdaq. Over the past 10 years, between 64 percent and 98 percent of the IPOs eligible for exchange listing have listed on Nasdaq.

Investment Banks

Because of the many challenges and potential pitfalls of the IPO process, early advice from experienced investment bankers is valuable. Companies raising more than $20 million usually retain two or more investment banks to manage and underwrite the IPO. Because of these two roles, an IPO's investment bankers are referred to both as "managers" and as "managing underwriters." When chosen to manage a Nasdaq IPO, investment banks usually commit to providing aftermarket support in the form of investment research and market-making functions.

As the main advisors and managers of the IPO process, the investment bankers draw on their experience in public offerings to guide the company through all aspects of the IPO process. The investment bankers provide particularly important input on the timing and size of the offering, valuation, preparation of the prospectus, and investor meetings. In examining these issues, the managing underwriters analyze the company in the context of their financial expertise and broad knowledge of the investing public and the financial markets.

The investment bankers, particularly the managing underwriter designated the "lead manager," must lead the IPO team through the complex steps of the IPO process as well as create and coordinate a group of other investment firms that will participate in the underwriting. The IPO process is time-sensitive and requires a consensus every step of the way among the numerous groups and individuals who are involved, including company executives, managing underwriters, company counsel, underwriters' counsel, and auditors. The leadership and experience of the investment bankers in coordinating the process contribute greatly to the effectiveness of the IPO.

The second role of the investment banks involves their underwriting function. After the distribution of the preliminary prospectuses, the lead manager usually organizes a group of underwriters into a "syndicate" to participate in the offering. Dealers and brokers, many of whom are also members of the underwriting syndicate, take "indications of interest" for purchase of the stock from institutional and retail investors. Based on the receipt of these indications of interest, the lead underwriter recommends a final offering size and offering price to the company. When these two parameters are finalized, the lead underwriter can determine the final allocation of stock to the investors.

Following pricing and allocation, the underwriters purchase the entire offering directly from the company (in the case of a "firm commitment" underwriting) and fulfill the orders. The underwriters earn their fees in this case by arranging to purchase the stock from the company at a discount, called the "gross spread," from the final offering price.

In the aftermarket, the managing underwriters of the IPO usually provide services for the company through their research, sales, and trading departments. The research department of each managing underwriter writes and distributes periodic reports that provide an evaluation of the company's stock as an investment through an analysis of the company's past performance and detailed projections for the company's near-term financial results.

Such reports target an audience of institutional investors, brokers, and the financial press. Active and effective research coverage can influence the stock price of a company by stimulating buying demand or selling interest.

The sales and trading departments of the managing underwriters devote resources to making a market in Nasdaq stocks. For a substantial period after the offering, the managing underwriters of an IPO on the Nasdaq market will be the most active participants in the trading of the stock. The managing underwriters' familiarity and relationship with the major buyers and sellers of the stock and their active market making provide increased support for the stock. Because investors typically are more inclined to hold stock that can easily be bought and sold, trading support has a positive effect on the stock price.

Selecting Investment Banks

Investment banks compete intensely for IPOs and can be aggressive in promoting their qualifications and preparing valuation analyses. To build the most effective IPO team, the company should evaluate investment banks on their ability to manage the IPO process, perform the underwriting function and, most importantly, provide aftermarket support. The company's management can and should call on an investment bank's past IPO clients in their evaluation processes. However, an investment bank that performed well for one IPO client may not be an appropriate managing underwriter for a different company. The following criteria are the key considerations in determining the best choices:

- **Experience and Focus.** The complexities of going public and the potential liability involved make managing underwriters with experience in the IPO arena absolutely necessary. It is important to examine the set of companies taken public by the investment bank and also by the individual bankers who would be assigned to the transaction. Experience in the company's particular industry or niche, especially in the research and sales disciplines, is instrumental to an investment bank's ability to understand the business of the company and its ability to convey the company's story to investors. The focus and depth of the research department also may prove extremely valuable in ensuring that consistent, accurate, and insightful research coverage will follow in the aftermarket. Investment banks that concentrate their activity on particular industries will tend to have the greatest access to investors who are most likely to invest in such sectors.

- **Aftermarket Performance.** Calculate the stock price appreciation of the companies taken public by the investment bank in recent years. This measure of aftermarket price performance gives a clear indication of the investment bank's credibility with investors. Investors will be more interested in purchasing stock in an IPO managed by an investment bank that has a history of taking quality companies public. A solid track record of aftermarket performance gives the investment bank's sales force an advantage in selling subsequent IPOs.

- **Pricing.** Examine the past IPOs of the investment bank and determine the offering prices' deviations from the initial filing ranges. Because the filing range stems from the investment bankers' expectations for valuation, the proximity of the offering price to the range indicates how accurate these expectations were. The deviation of the final number of shares offered from the number of shares filed also can indicate whether the underwriters were able to sell the full number of shares at an offering price satisfactory to the company. These analyses also reflect the credibility of the investment bank with investors. If the final offering prices consistently fall beneath the filing range for a particular investment bank, investors will tend to expect more downward flexibility on price in future IPOs managed by that firm.

- **Research.** The investment bank usually will assign coverage of the company to a particular research analyst. The company should examine the quantity and quality of this analyst's research coverage. The knowledge, focus, and reputation of this individual plays a great role in the effectiveness of the research coverage.

- **Sales and Trading**. Look for an investment bank with an experienced group of sales people who have long-term relationships with individual and institutional investors. To evaluate trading commitment, obtain statistics on the percentage of trades an investment bank has participated in for companies it took public and its ongoing trading position relative to other investment banks. These data are readily available for Nasdaq market stocks.

- **Long-Term Relationship**. Companies that receive quality investment banking services during an IPO and in the aftermarket will tend to use the same bankers for future financings and other transactions. Information concerning the investment bank's participation in subsequent financings or mergers and acquisitions services for IPO clients will provide a valuable perspective.

The Process

The other key advisors to the company in the IPO process are its legal counsel and accountants. Often before selecting investment bankers, the company will have enlisted these professionals to assist in its periodic management decisions. Gaining in-depth knowledge about the company will be extremely important for the legal counsel, who will play a major role in determining legal disclosure issues for the company. It will also be important for the accountants, who will need to conduct audits, guide management on certain accounting principles, and approve the accounting practices of the company. Experience in IPOs and an established reputation are important criteria for choosing both company counsel and accountants. The regulations and the review process of the Securities and Exchange Commission (SEC) are complex and will require much attention during the offering. Lawyers and accountants who are knowledgeable and experienced in such matters can expedite the process and minimize the risk of subsequent delays and additional expenses.

The most time-consuming part of the IPO process involves the preparation of the prospectus. This is a document of descriptive and financial information that the members of the IPO team create under the guidelines of SEC regulations. The prospectus functions both as a disclosure document from a regulatory perspective and a selling document from a marketing perspective. This sometimes "schizophrenic" character of the document is the main reason why it is so difficult to write. Ideally, the document should stimulate investor interest in the company and also protect the company from litigation by disclosing all pertinent facts and risks. The prospectus serves as the definitive source of information about the company for potential investors.

The SEC requires that the company use the prospectus to disclose all information about the company and its businesses that could be relevant to an investor. The cover of the preliminary prospectus contains the basic offering data, including the proposed size of the IPO as well as the filing range, which gives investors their first indication on valuation. The body of the prospectus includes information about the company's products and services, manufacturing facilities, competition, and the possible risks of investing in the company.

The prospectus also must contain the audited historical financial results of the company and various exhibits that show the effects of the planned offering on its financial position. The legal counsels of the company and the underwriters play the most important roles in ensuring compliance with SEC regulations and determining appropriate disclosure. The contention that a company's prospectus either omitted pertinent information or included misleading information could serve as the main vehicle for a class-action, securities-fraud lawsuit.

The selling nature of the prospectus must stem from factual statements about the company or its historical financial performance. Statements about the company that cannot be substantiated or verified must be qualified to indicate that they are the company's beliefs or intentions. Particularly speculative remarks about topics such as the company's growth prospects or reputation should not be included in the prospectus. The investment bankers' expertise in addressing the concerns of investors and emphasizing the company's strengths while working within the stringent disclosure regulations of the SEC is a key factor in the effectiveness of the prospectus and the IPO.

The Filing

The final form of the document that emerges from numerous drafting sessions is called the "preliminary prospectus." At this point, the company files a registration statement, which includes both that prospectus and several other IPO documents with the SEC for review. The SEC forbids companies from engaging in unusual public promotional activity during the public offering process. Before filing, the company must keep careful watch over its contact with the press, since any company action that could be construed as a selling effort is against SEC regulations. Such actions are termed "gun jumping" and could delay or preclude the offering.

Once the registration is filed, however, the company may release a statement to the press within the SEC's guidelines. The investment banks then will distribute thousands of copies of the preliminary prospectus to the other underwriters, dealers, and investors across the country. The covers of all preliminary prospectuses contain warning language stating that the registration statement has not yet become effective and that the prospectus is subject to amendment. Because the SEC requires that this warning be printed in a bright red color, preliminary prospectuses are often called "red herrings."

After it is filed, the registration statement will be thoroughly reviewed by the SEC. After approximately one month, an SEC staff member will respond with comments and suggestions for revisions. In most cases, the company may file with the SEC a response letter drafted by the company counsel that addresses the SEC's comments and outlines proposed revisions for an amended prospectus. If the response letter and the amended prospectus adequately address the issues raised by the SEC, the registration statement will be declared effective on request.

If the SEC determines that a serious omission or misstatement exists in the preliminary prospectus, the Commission may require the company to recirculate an amended version of the preliminary prospectus. Although recirculation is atypical, when it occurs, the company must undergo costly time delays and printing expenses in moving forward with the IPO.

During the period between the filing and when the registration statement is declared effective, the company's management team and the managing underwriters of the IPO begin a series of presentations to investors in major cities across the U.S. and sometimes overseas. This tour is called the "road show" and gives major investors the opportunity to meet the company's management team and directly ask questions. Because investors place significant emphasis on these presentations, the management team and managing underwriters undergo substantial preparation for the road show.

Also during the waiting period, the syndicate of underwriters and a "selling group" composed of other broker-dealers begin marketing the stock to investors. Consequently, orders known as "indications of interest" for the stock begin to arrive from investors, although no money changes hands and no actual sales are made. Investors in no way are obligated to purchase stock on the basis of indications of interest. The lead manager is responsible for organizing and compiling these indications of interest, an action known as "building the book." Through building the book, the lead manager can recommend a final offering size and offering price to the company for acceptance once the registration statement becomes effective. The size and composition of the book can have a major impact on the final offering size and offering price. For example, exceptionally high demand for an IPO often can lead to a final offering price well above the filing range and an increase in the number of shares offered.

Other Regulatory Review

Concurrent with the SEC review, the National Association of Securities Dealers (NASD) must review the registration statement and ancillary documents. The NASD typically focuses on issues related to underwriting arrangements and compensation to ensure that transactions stay at "arm's length." As does the SEC, the NASD assigns to the transaction a reviewer who will return comments to the company. While the SEC and NASD are distinct regulatory authorities, their reviewers typically coordinate clearance on documentation to ensure that all authorizations have been received before the registration statement is granted effectiveness.

In addition, all states have established securities commissions, some of which conduct a review process before allowing the initial public sale of securities within that state. The rules pertaining to state securities registrations are referred to as "blue sky" laws, and typically the underwriters' counsel assumes responsibility for obtaining those approvals. The blue-sky laws focus on the fairness of internal corporate transactions to new shareholders by maintaining fair shareholder voting rights, monitoring insider option terms, limiting corporate loans to officers, and similar actions.

By qualifying to have its securities traded on the Nasdaq National Market System (Nasdaq/NMS), a company is exempt from the blue-sky laws of most states and will obtain automatic approval to sell stock in those states when the SEC and NASD declare the registration effective. Because a Nasdaq/NMS listing also has numerous advantages beyond the initial blue-sky exemptions, the vast majority of eligible companies seek a Nasdaq/NMS listing for their IPOs.

The Final Steps

When the SEC declares the registration statement effective, the managing underwriters recommend the appropriate offering price and offering size which, on acceptance by the company, is called the "pricing" of the IPO. The lead manager also finalizes the allocation of the stock, and the syndicate and selling group return to the investors who indicated interest and confirm the price and quantity of the individual sales. Shortly afterward, the stock begins to trade on the open market. The final offering size and price are reflected on the cover of the amended version of the prospectus to compose the final prospectus.

Typically five business days after the effective date, when all the paperwork is finalized by the company, underwriters, lawyers, and accountants, the official closing of the offering occurs. At this time, the company exchanges stock certificates for a check from the underwriters for the proceeds from the IPO. Although the company's stock has been publicly traded for one week, the IPO process only now is complete.

The Responsibilities of Public Ownership

It is important to note that the IPO process is only the beginning of a company's existence as a public company. Public ownership provides tremendous opportunity, but the many new responsibilities that arrive with it require a strong commitment by the company. For a public company, communication and continuous interaction with the investment community are key elements in establishing effective shareholder relationships. While the SEC and other regulatory authorities require public companies to file periodic financial statements and to disseminate certain material information to shareholders on a timely basis, a company should go beyond these minimum requirements.

Within the limits of nonselective disclosure, a company should encourage securities analysts to obtain guidance on the company's financial outlook through regular contact. To ensure active research coverage and trading support, a company should maintain its relationships with its investment bankers while seeking to develop new ties to other securities analysts and market makers. Through these actions, the company helps provide the market with the full and fair disclosure necessary to determine efficient prices for its stock.

Life in the public market can be rewarding albeit challenging, and the IPO process is merely the launching point. Nonetheless, it serves as an excellent learning experience for the company which, having experienced its complexities, will be far more prepared to meet the responsibilities of public ownership.

Chapter Eight

Irving M. Pollack is a lawyer and consultant specializing in securities and capital markets matters. He served for 33 years at the Securities and Exchange Commission, where he held the positions of commissioner, director of the division of enforcement, director of the division of trading and markets, and assistant general counsel.

Listing Requirements and Obligations of a Nasdaq National Market Company

by Irving M. Pollack
Lawyer and Consultant

In recent years, The Nasdaq Stock Market has become the market of choice for the companies that list on it. It is becoming less and less common for companies to move to an exchange as they grow and mature. The principal reason for this is that Nasdaq has established itself as a major national and international market. Indeed, Nasdaq is ahead of the exchanges in moving toward the global trading system of the future.

Today, this competitive alternative to the exchanges is a very visible, highly organized, and well-regulated market with which a growing number of companies identify — a market that marries competition among dealers with new-age, screen-based technology.

As a precondition to listing on The Nasdaq Stock Market, securities must be registered with the Securities and Exchange Commission (SEC) under Section 12(g) of the Securities Exchange Act of 1934 (the "1934 Act"). This section requires a company selling securities to the public to disclose information about its business, results of operations, financial condition, principal shareholders, and management. As a practical matter, companies listed on Nasdaq are subject to the same requirements as exchange-listed companies that are covered under Section 12b-1 of this Act.

In addition to SEC registration, the company must meet various qualitative and quantitative standards prescribed by the NASD. (See Exhibit 8–1.) The minimum qualifications for a company to be admitted to listing on the Nasdaq National Market System (Nasdaq/NMS) have been raised from time to time and today are equal to or exceed those of the American Stock Exchange in every area.

What the Quantitative Standards Mean to Investors

Quantitative standards inherently convey a great deal of information to investors.

The requirement for SEC registration means that Nasdaq/NMS companies are required to make the same extensive, quarterly, interim, and annual disclosures of their financial and operational condition as are companies listed in other major markets. In making disclosures, those enterprises follow uniform standards prescribed by the SEC, the most exacting by any government securities regulator in the world. The financial requirements for operating companies — those that have a product or a service in the market — immediately tell investors that, at the time of listing, they were basically profitable, having appreciable pretax and net income in the last fiscal year or in two of the last three. The requirements also show that these companies have substantial tangible assets (which do not include goodwill) and a sizeable shareholder base.

The financial requirements for development companies — those that are not yet marketing a product or a service — are

Exhibit 8–1   Nasdaq National Market Quantitative Standards

Standard	Initial Nasdaq/NMS Inclusion		Continued Nasdaq/NMS Inclusion
	Alternative 1	Alternative 2	
Registration under Section 12(g) of the Securities Exchange Act of 1934 or equivalent	Yes	Yes	Yes
Net Tangible Assets[1]	$4 million	$12 million	$2 million or $4 million[2]
Net Income (in last fiscal year or two of last three fiscal years)	$400,000	—	—
Pretax Income (in last fiscal year or two of last three fiscal years)	$750,000	—	—
Public Float (Shares)[3]	500,000	1 million	200,000
Operating History	—	3 years	—
Market Value of Float	$3 million	$15 million	$1 million
Minimum Bid	$5	—	—
Shareholders		400	400[4]
—if between 0.5 and 1 million shares publicly held	800	—	—
—if more than 1 million shares publicly held	400	—	—
—if more than 0.5 million shares publicly held and average daily volume in excess of 2,000 shares	400	—	—
Number of Market Makers	2	2	2

[1] "Net tangible assets" means total assets (excluding goodwill) minus total liabilities.

[2] Continued Nasdaq/NMS inclusion requires net tangible assets of at least $2 million if the issuer has sustained losses from continuing operations and/or net losses in two of its three most recent fiscal years or $4 million if the issuer has sustained losses from the continuing operations and/or net losses in three of its four most recent fiscal years.

[3] Public float is defined as shares that are not "held directly or indirectly by any officer or director of the issuer and by any person who is the beneficial owner of more than 10 percent of the total shares outstanding. . ."

[4] Or 300 shareholders of round lots.

much higher than those for operating companies. There is also a requirement for a three-year operating history. These standards indicate that the company, although it is still without earnings, is of appreciable size and has a minimum of three years' experience and effort invested in building its future.

The Corporate Governance Requirements

To qualify for admission to Nasdaq/NMS, a company must also adhere to a wide array of corporate governance standards. These standards give shareholders a level of participation in corporate affairs fully comparable to that afforded to shareholders in exchange-listed companies. The standards require each Nasdaq/NMS company to:

- Have a minimum of two independent directors on its board. "Independent director" is defined to exclude officers or employees of the company or other individuals having a relationship that would interfere with the exercise of independent judgment in carrying out the responsibilities of a director.

- Maintain an audit committee composed of a majority of independent directors. This requirement supports detached review of a company's financial and other operations.

- Provide shareholders with annual reports and make quarterly as well as other reports available. Annual reports must be distributed a reasonable period of time prior to the company's annual meeting.

- Solicit proxies and provide proxy statements for all meetings of shareholders, as well as file such proxy solicitations with the NASD.

- Hold an annual meeting of shareholders and provide notice of such meeting to the NASD. This gives shareholders the opportunity to meet with management face to face.

- Specify in its bylaws a quorum of not less than 33 1/3 percent of the outstanding shares of the company's common stock.

- Examine all related-party transactions for potential conflicts of interest. The audit committee or a comparable body performs such reviews.

- Secure shareholder approval for certain transactions and increases in the amount of stock outstanding. Such transactions will generally include stock options or purchase plans pursuant to which stock may be acquired by officers or directors. In cases of stock issuance, an amount equivalent to 20 percent or more of the stock outstanding before the issuance will usually require shareholder approval. If approval is required, at least a majority of the total votes cast in person or by proxy is necessary to grant the approval.

- Finally, each Nasdaq/NMS company must execute a listing agreement with the NASD.

Shareholder Voting Rights Rule

By virtue of its listing agreement, a Nasdaq/NMS company is obligated to comply with the shareholder voting rights rule that the NASD adopted and the SEC approved in 1990. The NASD shareholder voting rights rule specifies the following conditions:

- Nasdaq/NMS companies are prohibited from issuing any class of securities or taking any other corporate action that would restrict, nullify, or disparately reduce the voting rights of holders of an outstanding class or classes of publicly traded securities of the issuer.

- Transactions presumed *not* to restrict, nullify, or disparately reduce voting rights include: (1) issuance of securities in an initial public offering; (2) issuance of securities in a public offering with voting rights not greater than those of any outstanding class of the issuer's common stock; (3) issuance of securities approved by shareholder vote pursuant to a proxy statement in a merger, acquisition, or a stock dividend transaction in which the voting rights of the securities would not be greater than those of any outstanding class of the issuer's common stock; and (4) corporate action taken pursuant to state law requiring a state's domestic corporation to condition the voting rights of a beneficial or record holder of a specified threshold percentage of the corporation's voting stock on the approval of the corporation's independent shareholders.

- Transactions that *are* presumed to restrict, nullify, or disparately reduce voting rights include: (1) restrictions on voting power based on the number of shares held; (2) restrictions on voting power based on the length of time shares have been held; (3) issuance of securities pursuant to an exchange offer where the securities being issued result in a restriction, nullification, or disparate reduction of voting rights of outstanding common stock; and (4) any issuance of securities pursuant to a stock dividend, or any other type of distribution of stock, in which the securities issued have voting rights greater than the per-share voting rights of any outstanding class of the common stock of the issuer.

The cumulative effect of the corporate governance and shareholder voting rights rules is to establish the Nasdaq/NMS companies that are bound by them as good corporate citizens with an abiding respect for the rights of investors.

What the Listing Standards Mean to Companies

To Nasdaq/NMS companies, listing standards mean that their securities are traded in a market that is recognized as being on a par with other major markets by those who have responsibilities for regulating and overseeing their operation. For example, in 1987 the SEC, in commenting on a Memorandum of Understanding entered into between the NASD and the North American Securities Administrators Association, said, "The Commission believes that Nasdaq/NMS and exchange-listed securities trade in an environment subject to substantially equivalent disclosure, regulatory, and surveillance protections, and deserve to be treated comparably."

Much earlier, in 1984, the Federal Reserve Board ruled that Nasdaq/NMS securities were automatically eligible for purchase in margin accounts, just as exchange-listed securities are. Similar determinations have been made by the states which, one after the other, have granted Nasdaq/NMS securities the same exemptions from state registration that exchange-listed securities have enjoyed for many years. Overseas, the United Kingdom's Department of Trade and Industry has certified Nasdaq as a Recognized Investment Exchange, and the Tokyo Stock Exchange has declared Nasdaq/NMS securities to be eligible for listing on it, precisely because the regulatory system for them is as strong as that of the exchanges.

The many Nasdaq/NMS companies that are eligible to list on a stock exchange no longer take that step to gain marginability of their securities, an exemption from state registration, or acceptance overseas. Parity has been achieved in each of these areas.

Requirements for Continued Inclusion

In addition to the requirements for initial listing, Nasdaq/NMS has a set of standards, which are lower, for continued inclusion. (See Exhibit 8–1.) The rationale is that companies can run into temporary difficulties and that neither they nor their investors are served by a delisting while the company is working to repair its fortunes.

Under the continued inclusion requirements for Nasdaq/NMS, the company must maintain its SEC registration. Its net tangible assets may drop from $4 million to $2 million if it has sustained losses from continuing operations and/or experiences net losses in two of its most recent three fiscal years. However, it must continue to have $4 million in net tangible assets if it has sustained such losses in three of its four most recent fiscal years. The public float of the stock may decline from the 500,000 shares to 200,000, and the market value of the float may drop to $1 million. There must be at least 400 shareholders, or 300 holders of round lots.

Deviation from the corporate governance and shareholder voting rights requirements is not permitted. If it occurs, the company is dropped from Nasdaq/NMS, and it loses the benefits of trade-by-trade transaction reporting and the widespread visibility associated with securities traded in this market.

When a company and its security fall below any of the financial minimums, Nasdaq advises the company that it is subject to delisting. The company is then entitled to a hearing before a Nasdaq panel. If it can demonstrate that it has prospects of being able to get back up to the maintenance standards in a reasonable period of time, the stock will continue to be listed on Nasdaq, with the letter "C" appended to its symbol. This advises investors and brokers that the stock is not fully in compliance. If the company comes back into compliance, the "C" is removed. If it does not, the security is delisted from Nasdaq/NMS.

Quality Information on Companies

After listing standards, the second requirement of a quality market is quality information on the companies. In Nasdaq/NMS, this is assured by the requirements of SEC registration or the comparable requirements of such other regulatory bodies as state insurance commissions, the Comptroller of the Currency, the Federal Reserve Board, the Federal Deposit Insurance Corporation, or the Office of Thrift Supervision in the Treasury Department.

Included in this information is a variety of required reports that together serve to give shareholders the best available data on their company's business operations and financial condition. The SEC Form 10-Q for a company's quarterly report and the Form 10-K for its annual report call for the following:

- A precise description of the nature of the business.

- Summary financial information.

- Management Discussion & Analysis, which provides management's explanation of its financial results and assessment of future trends that will affect the company.

- A description of properties owned by the company.

- Security ownership of certain beneficial owners and managers.

- Names and titles of directors and executive officers.

- Executive compensation details.

- An account of certain relationships and related transactions.

- Reports on legal proceedings.

- Analysis of market price and dividends on common equity and related stockholder matters.

- A report on recent sales of unregistered securities.

- Description of indemnification of directors and officers.

- Full financial statements and supplementary data.

- A report on changes in and disagreements with accountants on accounting and financial disclosure.

- Further financial statements and exhibits.

- Such further material information necessary to assure that a misleading picture is not created by the statements contained in the report.

Nasdaq/NMS companies must provide their shareholders with their annual reports and proxy statements and furnish quarterly reports and SEC Form 10-Ks on request. Investors studying these disclosure documents can get a very good picture of a company's past, present, and future. In addition, a company must make interim reports on Form 8-K about material events that affect it and investors.

All these SEC-required documents are filed with Nasdaq as well as with the SEC. Nasdaq reviews them primarily to make sure that a company qualifies for continued listing. It and the SEC also look for possible errors and omissions. If errors or omissions are detected, the SEC may raise questions about the financial statements and halt trading in the stock until the questions are satisfactorily answered. The SEC by law can halt trading for only 10 days, although it can extend that period in increments of 10 days. Similarly, Nasdaq can implement a "qualifications halt" in the stock if the financial statements are not clarified.

Nasdaq also requires companies to provide it with duplicate copies of filings with the SEC. These are turned over to Disclosure, Inc., a private organization that duplicates them, for a fee, for all interested parties. This makes it possible for investors, attorneys, the media, and others to learn all about a company and makes the company's affairs truly public.

Required SEC Notifications

Under other SEC rules, a Nasdaq company must report certain information on its securities to the NASD in a timely manner.

SEC Rule 10b-17 requires that notice be sent to the NASD 10 days prior to the record date for the following:

- A dividend or other distribution in cash or in kind, including a dividend or distribution of any security.

- A stock split or reverse split.

- A rights or other subscription offering.

When issuing rights and warrants, advance notice 10 days prior to the record date may not be practicable. In this instance, companies must provide distribution information to the NASD on or before the record date and no later than the date the registration statement becomes effective with the SEC or another regulatory agency.

Under SEC Rules 13a-17 and 15d-17, Nasdaq companies must notify the SEC and the NASD no later than 10 days after the effective date of a corporate name change and changes of 5 percent or greater than last reported in the number of shares outstanding for Nasdaq issues.

Again, these requirements generate information about companies that is important to investors.

Quality Trading Information

An essential of a quality market, namely quality trading information, is the responsibility of the NASD as the operator and regulator of The Nasdaq Stock Market. However, Nasdaq/NMS companies are required to contribute to such trading information in one important way — notifying Nasdaq Market Surveillance and the public, through the press, of any material news that may affect the value of their securities or influence investors' decisions.

Material news can include the following events:

- A merger, acquisition, or joint venture.

- A stock split or stock dividend.

- Earnings or dividends of an unusual nature.

- The acquisition or loss of a significant contract.

- A significant new product or discovery.

- A change in control or a significant change in management.

- A call for redemption of securities.

- The purchase or sale of a significant asset.

- The public or private sale of a significant amount of additional securities.

- The planned issuance of a significant amount of additional securities.

- A substantial change in capital investment plans.

- A significant labor dispute.

- Establishment of a program to purchase a company's own shares.

- A tender offer for another company's securities.

- An event requiring the filing of a current report, such as an 8-K report, under the 1934 Act.

A Nasdaq/NMS company must report material news to the public through the press so that actual or potential investors have current information on which to base their judgments. A company is further obligated to report the news to Nasdaq Market Surveillance before releasing it to the press wire services, so that Market Surveillance can decide whether it is sufficiently important to merit a trading halt in the company's stock.

During a halt, NASD member firms are prohibited from executing any transactions in the halted stock, and no quotation or other information on the stock is displayed on Nasdaq terminals. The purpose of the halt is to provide time for the dissemination of the material news, so that investors have equal opportunities to become aware of it. A halt generally lasts 30 minutes after the news has appeared on the wires, but it may last longer if it appears that the news has not been adequately disseminated.

In a given year, Nasdaq Market Surveillance implements about 2,000 trading halts, or eight per trading day.

Being Public

The requirements and obligations of Nasdaq/NMS companies are consistent with their being public. When a company issues stock, it takes on investors as partners, and it owes them good management, good corporate citizenship, and full, frank, and timely disclosure of its affairs. Listing on Nasdaq/NMS helps make certain that companies discharge these responsibilities.

Chapter Nine

J. Lynton Jones, managing director of Nasdaq International, Ltd., represents the NASD with European exchanges and securities regulatory bodies. He also provides services to European issuers of Nasdaq securities and those interested in The Nasdaq Stock Market. Prior to joining Nasdaq, Mr. Jones was head of public affairs for the London Stock Exchange.

Nasdaq: The Preferred U.S. Market for Overseas Companies

by J. Lynton Jones
Managing Director
Nasdaq International, Ltd.

On July 28, 1987, English China Clays (ECC) issued new shares (in American Depositary Receipt form) and listed on The Nasdaq Stock Market. Its purpose: to raise new capital to acquire an American company. By the time the acquisition was completed, in November 1987, the October stock market crash had taken place, and ECC found that its acquisition was going to cost considerably less than it had anticipated. Not everyone has the good fortune to raise capital while the market is at its peak and then to make an acquisition when the market is near its bottom. But then, ECC has a knack for getting its timing right.

ECC is one of Britain's more successful companies, and its shares are actively traded on the London Stock Exchange. Why did ECC choose to list on The Nasdaq Stock Market rather than on the New York Stock Exchange (NYSE)?

The answer that ECC gives is not dissimilar from the answer given by the other 86 foreign companies that list their ADRs on Nasdaq or the 184 companies that list their underlying shares on Nasdaq. (See Exhibits 9–1 and 9–2.) These companies are, generally speaking, well-known in their domestic markets and, more often than not, are listed on the main domestic stock exchanges. In addition, they are followed by the major domestic research houses and have a substantial level of domestic institutional investor interest in their stocks.

Exhibit 9–1   ADR Share Volume and Issues
Nasdaq/NMS, NYSE, and Amex: 1990

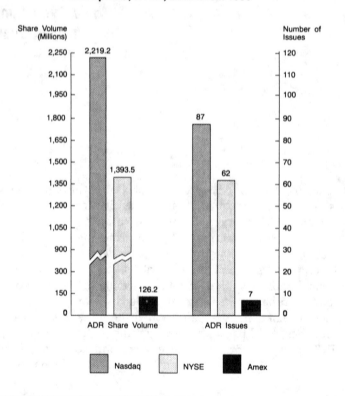

Exhibit 9–2   Trading of ADRs and Foreign Securities on Nasdaq, 1986–1990

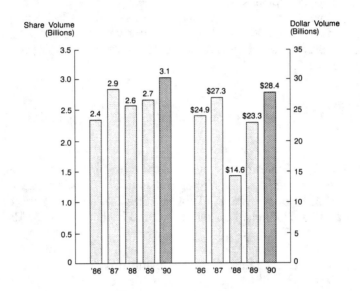

A Stranger Away From Home

But in the United States, they are relative un-knowns, the equivalent of startup companies in terms of investor knowledge of their activities. Apart from some very well-known foreign companies that are followed closely by U.S. investors, the majority of foreign companies seeking to sell their shares in the U.S. have to make a major effort to gain the sort of recognition that they can take for granted in their home markets.

Given that situation, one question that they must answer to ensure a successful launch for their shares in the U.S. is, "Which stock market will be the most effective in helping us achieve the investor interest we seek?"

To answer this question, the majority of foreign companies begin by examining the relative merits of each U.S. market that trades foreign stocks. Most limit their examination to The Nasdaq Stock Market and the NYSE. Each of these markets has a respectable story to tell. When these comparative tests are done, The Nasdaq Stock Market consistently gets high marks for the reasons described below.

Companies Want to Raise Their Profiles

The majority of foreign companies seeking to enter the U.S. capital markets for purposes of a listing have as a specific objective the need to raise their profiles in the United States. This is not simply because they want to raise awareness of the company and its products. It is also because a higher profile holds out the prospect of investor interest in the company's stock. And this in turn leads to a greater flow of orders, which generates the liquidity that the stock needs to survive and prosper.

The Nasdaq Stock Market scores high on this test. Whatever the level of efficiency that the NYSE specialist system has at transacting existing order flow, the one thing it does not have is the ability to *generate* order flow. For companies such as General Motors and American Telephone & Telegraph, in which there is nearly always a healthy flow of both buy and sell orders, the specialist market provides a satisfactory means of matching orders. But consider the case of a typical foreign company that is not a household name in the U.S.

The British consumer electronics retailer, Dixons, well known in its domestic market but virtually a complete unknown in the U.S., decided some time ago to apply for a listing in the U.S. It considered the competing claims of both The Nasdaq Stock Market and the NYSE. It chose the New York. After two years on the NYSE, Dixons had less than 20 shareholders. It had been a victim of the "small fish/big pond" syndrome. The NYSE listing did not generate investor interest, and Dixons simply failed to get noticed. Finally, the company cut its losses, delisted, withdrew its

SEC registration, and returned to the United Kingdom, chastened but wiser.

Comparisons Provide the Evidence

Compare that with the case of ECC. Confronted with the same choice as Dixons, it opted for Nasdaq, citing a variety of reasons:

- It would more likely be noticed on Nasdaq than on the NYSE.

- Nasdaq had a better understanding of the needs of foreign issuers.

- ECC would rank well among its peer group on The Nasdaq Stock Market.

- It was comfortable and pleased with Nasdaq's market-making system, which is the same as the trading system that operates in the U.K.

- The cost of a Nasdaq listing is less onerous than that of the NYSE.

- It was more likely to achieve its objectives on The Nasdaq Stock Market.

It was right. In its first year on Nasdaq, ECC's share price consistently outperformed the FTSE 100 index (the prime British index), and the number of its U.S. ADRs rose from 2.5 million at the time of issue to well above 3 million one year later.

In many respects, ECC and Dixons are comparable companies. Although ECC's market capitalization of £872M exceeds Dixons' £684M, Dixons is possibly more well known in the U.K. So why didn't Dixons enjoy the same success in the United States capital markets as did ECC?

To answer that question, let's look at the experience of other European companies using The Nasdaq Stock Market for the listing of their ADRs. Some of the better known examples have included Reuters, Jaguar, and Glaxo. Where are they now?

Reuters has for some time been a very popular stock on The Nasdaq Stock Market. After its launch in 1985, initial trading volumes were not high because Reuters was not well known in the United States. But with a well-planned investor relations program, making full use of Nasdaq's market-maker system with its ability to generate order flow to build up liquidity in the stock, trading in Reuters has grown dramatically over the years. By 1990, Reuters was one of the most heavily traded stocks on The Nasdaq Stock Market. It was the number one foreign stock in the Nasdaq National Market, and number one in dollar volume among ADRs. (See Exhibits 9–3 and 9–4.) Reuters succeeded by taking full advantage of the ability of Nasdaq to generate order flow.

Jaguar plc was one of Nasdaq's all-time favorite stocks. In four years on Nasdaq, more than 800 million Jaguar ADRs traded with a total dollar volume of $5.7 billion. By 1989, it was without doubt the most popular foreign stock traded on the Nasdaq market. Combining the support of its ADR program with an effective advertising campaign, Jaguar discovered that the people who bought the stock were more likely to buy the car, and those who bought the car were more likely to buy the stock. But it got to this enviable situation primarily because Nasdaq's market-maker system succeeded in generating the order flow necessary for the liquid trading of the stock.

The Example of Glaxo

The most heavily traded of all Nasdaq ADRs was Glaxo, the British pharmaceutical company. Throughout 1985 and 1986, Glaxo was not only the most heavily traded ADR, but in 1986 it became the most heavily traded of all the stocks on the Nasdaq market. But then Glaxo decided to move to the NYSE.

It is perhaps worth taking a minute to consider the ramifications of this move. In talking to potential ADR issuers, Nasdaq staff members always say that one of the market's significant advantages is the fact that, unlike the situation with the NYSE, the process of delisting from Nasdaq is painless. The company simply writes to the NASD explaining its intention to move.

Exhibit 9-3   Top 20 Foreign and ADR Share-Volume Leaders on Nasdaq

Symbol	Company Name	Closing Price 12/31/90	1990 Share Volume
1. RTRSY	Reuters Holdings PLC	$40.500	190,206,000
2. ADTLY	ADT Ltd.	21.625	66,903,000
3. DBRSY	De Beers Consolidated Mines	19.375	44,672,000
4. NNCXF	Newbridge Networks Corp.	3.250	32,758,000
5. SCIXF	Scitex Corp. Ltd.	15.125	31,802,000
6. CLCDF	Clearly Canadian Beverage Corp.	4.625	29,301,000
7. VAALY	Vaal Reefs Explor. & Mining Co. Ltd.	6.438	22,870,000
8. ERICY	LM Ericsson Telephone Co.	32.250	22,601,000
9. CCTVY	Carlton Comm. Plc	15.125	18,763,000
10. QSNDF	Archer Comm., Inc.	10.125	17,398,000
11. SHKIF	SHL Systemhouse Inc.	3.250	16,607,000
12. MNRCY	Minorco	13.750	16,005,000
13. DRFNY	Driefontein Consolidated	10.750	14,624,000
14. KLOFY	Kloof Gold Mining Co., Ltd.	8.875	14,270,000
15. IITCF	INTERA Info. Technologies Corp.	11.500	14,179,000
16. AKZOY	Akzo N.V.	22.000	14,058,000
17. STLTF	Stolt Tankers & Terminals (Holdings) S.A.	14.625	13,035,000
18. FSCNY	Free State Consol. Gold Mining Co. LTD.	8.500	12,245,000
19. AEAGF	Agnico-Eagle Mines Ltd.	6.125	10,321,000
20. BTBTY	BT Shipping Ltd.	5.250	10,033,000

Note: This list includes only securities with a 1990 closing price of $3 or more.

It can hardly be any surprise, therefore, when some companies like Glaxo move to the NYSE. That is not to say that we do not regret such a move — especially because we know that the NYSE cannot provide a tangible market benefit to Nasdaq companies. However, we are content to keep companies on Nasdaq by the quality of our market rather than by using restrictive delisting rules as the NYSE does.

In the case of Glaxo, officials decided that the order flow for its stock was sufficient to be able to move to the NYSE without significant damage. When you consider the volume of its stock

Exhibit 9–4   Top 20 Foreign and ADR Dollar-Volume Leaders on Nasdaq

Symbol	Company Name	Closing Price 12/31/90	1990 Dollar Volume
1. RTRSY	Reuters Holdings PLC	$40.500	$8,929,080,000
2. ERICY	LM Ericsson Telephone Co.	32.250	1,880,522,000
3. ADTLY	ADT Ltd.	21.625	1,793,786,000
4. DBRSY	De Beers Consolidated Mines	19.375	914,131,000
5. SCIXF	Scitex Corp. Ltd.	15.125	753,999,000
6. ASEAY	ASEA AB	85.000	499,804,000
7. AKZOY	Akzo N.V.	22.000	395,829,000
8. CADBY	Cadbury Schweppes PLC	61.250	326,745,000
9. CCTVY	Carlton Comm. PLC	15.125	317,708,000
10. QSNDF	Archer Comm., Inc.	10.125	266,729,000
11. MNRCY	Minorco	13.750	257,372,000
12. STLTF	Stolt Tankers & Terminals (Holdings) S.A.	14.625	257,361,000
13. NNCXF	Newbridge Networks Corp.	3.250	243,472,000
14. DRSDY	Dresdner Bank AG	230.000	242,523,000
15. VAALY	Vaal Reefs Explor. & Mining Co. Ltd.	6.438	215,826,000
16. ECILF	ECI Telecom Ltd.	25.000	209,328,000
17. DRFNY	Driefontein Consolidated	10.750	191,461,000
18. IITCF	INTERA Info. Technologies Corp.	11.500	188,357,000
19. FISNY	Fisons PLC	28.000	184,162,000
20. WDEPY	Western Deep Levels Ltd.	30.750	157,603,000

Note: This list includes only securities with a 1990 closing price of $3 or more.

that was being traded on Nasdaq, this was hardly a surprising conclusion. And yet what happened? When it moved to the NYSE, the volume of trading in its stock dropped by more than 40 percent. This took Glaxo by surprise. It took the company more than two years before trading volume of its stock on the NYSE returned to near the levels it had enjoyed on Nasdaq.

Glaxo is not an isolated example. The same story has proved to be the case for Saatchi and Saatchi (trading volume down 70 percent), Philips (down 40 percent), and many other companies. Why is this?

For one very simple reason: the market-making trading system on Nasdaq generates a level of "sponsorship" that the NYSE specialists (effectively monopoly market makers) are neither equipped nor allowed to perform. The specialists, unlike the market makers on Nasdaq, are allowed to deal with only broker member firms on the NYSE. This means that they are precluded from dealing directly with potential investors, they produce no research on the stocks in which they are making markets, and their monopoly provides no direct incentive for them (as the competing market-maker system on Nasdaq encourages) to trade more stock in any particular company.

Registration Considerations

Before a foreign company can list its ADRs on The Nasdaq Stock Market or the NYSE, it must register its stocks with the SEC. This is a major disincentive. Among other things, SEC registration requires a company to ensure that its accounts are reconciled with U.S. Generally Accepted Accounting Principles (GAAP). For a company registered in the U.K., this is possible even though it may be time consuming and expensive. For a German or Swiss company, it is impossible because it would require them to provide a level of disclosure of their company's affairs that they would not want to reach their competitors.

For example, it is a common practice in Germany for companies to maintain hidden reserves. Were these companies to reconcile their accounts with U.S. GAAP, they would need to disclose these reserves. This disclosure would enable a U.S. investor to make a meaningful comparison between the German company and a similar U.S. company. But it would also mean that the German company was disclosing to its German competitors the sort of information that it would dearly love to keep to itself.

A few years ago, it was rumored that a particular German company suffered some losses because of rather incautious use of the foreign-exchange markets. However, when its annual report and accounts were issued, the company used hidden reserves to provide a bottom-line figure in line with previous expectations. The company would argue that this enabled it to protect the interests of its investors by stabilizing the share price and protecting them from violent fluctuations. An American regulator might argue that this tactic had the effect of hiding the true situation from the investor.

Similar problems arise concerning the question of segmented accounting. Under U.S. GAAP, it is necessary to provide separate profit and loss accounts for any subsidiary responsible for contributing in excess of 10 percent of the total revenues of the company. Germany has no such provision. If they operate in a multinational environment and raise only a small proportion of their funds in the United States, German companies ask why they should be forced to change their entire accounting procedures to bring them into line with U.S. practices? The counter argument to this is that if U.S. investment dollars are sought, then U.S. disclosures should be provided.

It is a difficult problem, but a solution will be found in the years to come. Possibly by means of providing major foreign companies with an exemption, possibly by the adoption of international accounting standards (presently the holy grail of the accounting profession), or possibly by some means not yet addressed. But change will most certainly occur.

PORTAL Can Help Raise Capital

To help bridge the gap until that time, the NASD has introduced two markets that offer alternatives to filing a full-scale SEC registration. The first is The PORTAL Market, and the second the OTC Bulletin Board^{sm}. PORTAL is an electronic market devised by the NASD for trading securities distributed in the United States under the terms of SEC Rule 144A. This 1990 rule stipulates that an issuer does not have to register a distribution with the SEC if the issue is distributed to so-called "Qualified Institutional Buyers" or QIBs. A QIB is defined as an institution having more than $100 million invested in securities. The advantages that this market has for the foreign issuer not wanting to access the retail market in the U.S. but nevertheless eager to tap the institutional market are clear. It can raise capital efficiently and flexibly without the need for complex and expensive SEC-registration procedures.

In its initial version, PORTAL was designed as a market within the 144A closed market to give investors and other participants the guarantee that all were qualified and that, as the SEC was demanding, there was no seepage of these stocks into the regular public markets. It quickly became apparent that the private-placement market did not need the level of protection on which the SEC was insisting. The NASD then introduced measures to liberalize The PORTAL Market and turn it into a more open system specifically designed for the secondary trading of 144A stock rather than for its initial placement. These steps will result in the consolidation of The PORTAL Market as the premier price-discovery mechanism for the 144A market. Already, a number of foreign companies, including CGE from France and the British privatized electricity companies, have used The PORTAL Market for the secondary trading of their ADRs.

Bulletin Board Can Raise Visibility

Unlike PORTAL and The Nasdaq Stock Market, the OTC Bulletin Board cannot be used to raise new capital in the United States. Foreign companies can, however, use the OTC Bulletin Board as a low-effort means of "dipping their toes" into the U.S. market. Companies can have their ADRs (or underlying shares) quoted on the Bulletin Board, the pages of which are accessible on Nasdaq Workstation[sm] screens. In this way, a company can, to a small degree, raise its visibility in the U.S. and provide a level of marketability for its shares without devoting considerable resources to that. The OTC Bulletin Board, in effect, is a highly regulated, automatic version of the so-called "Pink Sheet" market for companies not listed on Nasdaq or one of the national exchanges.

The NASD today is capable of providing foreign companies with the broadest range of markets of any stock market in the United States. Whether the issuer's objective is to raise capital via the public or private markets, heighten the visibility and investor support of an existing ADR program, or simply take the first step in testing and understanding the U.S. capital markets, the NASD has the means by which these objectives can be accomplished. Likewise, it offers the most effective alternative irrespective of company size or industry. This flexibility and efficiency make the markets of the NASD — The Nasdaq Stock Market, The PORTAL Market, and the OTC Bulletin Board — the preferred choice of international companies.

PART III

Investing in Nasdaq

Chapter
Ten

Gene L. Finn, as vice president and chief economist of the National Association of Securities Dealers, Inc., advises senior management on the effect of proposed rules and external economic events on NASD activities. He also directs economic and statistical programs involving the securities industry and its markets. Before joining the NASD in 1983, Mr. Finn was chief economist for the Securities and Exchange Commission.

Nasdaq Investors: Individual and Institutional, Domestic and Foreign

by Gene L. Finn
Vice President and Chief Economist
National Association of Securities Dealers, Inc.

Most stock is held either directly by or indirectly for the benefit of individuals. Individual investor surveys reveal that in 1990 approximately 42.1 million individuals held stock directly and an additional 9.3 million exclusively through equity mutual funds.[1] A much broader universe of individuals and households is affected by equity market investments through pension fund coverage. In 1985, 42.8 percent of wage and salary workers were covered by a pension plan.[2] Finally, though the focus here is equity investment in Nasdaq securities, individual and institutional investment in fixed-income (debt) securities expands the number of persons and households affected by securities markets as direct and/or indirect participants to a still broader percentage of the public.

When we talk about individual and institutional investor participation in Nasdaq, we are really talking about the medium (direct or indirect) through which the funds of individuals find their way into equity investments. The long-term trend in the institutionalization of equity savings flows (see Exhibit 10–1) is up, reflecting the changing underlying demand on the part of individuals for pensions and money-management services. During the whole post-World War II period, spanning the past 45 years, there has been a generally gradual but continuous trend toward the institutionalization of equity savings. In 1946, 93.1 percent of corporate equities was held directly by households; in 1990, that share had declined to 54.4 percent.

The ability to shield savings from income taxes has found individuals wisely seeking to shelter retirement savings through pensions and other tax-sheltered methods, reducing the share of direct investment by individuals. Perhaps most important, mutual funds have been able to substantially enhance the value of equity market investing to individuals by providing them with an efficient means to obtain cost-effective diversification and professional management of their savings funds. These factors are reflected in the accelerated shift that occurred in the 1980s in the proportion of stock held directly by households and indirectly through institutional money managers.

This most recent decline in the share of individual direct investment appears to reflect further basic shifts in income-tax regulations, including individual retirement accounts (IRAs), 401(k) plans, and similar opportunities to shelter savings from taxes through processes that make saving through institutions more attractive relative to direct investment. It also undoubtedly reflects a tremendous expansion in money-management services, particularly mutual funds, being made available to investors on a cost-effective basis. Individual investment through equity mutual funds grew from $39.7 billion in 1970 to $225.8 billion in 1990, or from 1 percent to 12.2 percent of individual direct holdings. (See Exhibit 10–2.)

Nevertheless, the individual as a direct investor should not be written off. Households at the end of 1990 still held 54.4 percent of the aggregate value of corporate equity securities, com-

Exhibit 10–1   Household Holdings of Corporate Equities — 1946–1990

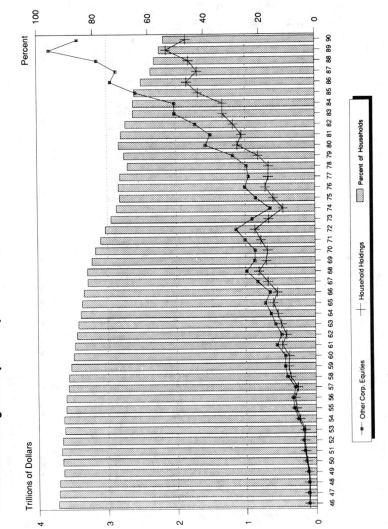

Data Source: Federal Reserve Board Flow of Fund data.

Exhibit 10–2   Corporate Stockholdings of Households, Direct and Through Mutual Funds — 1946–1990

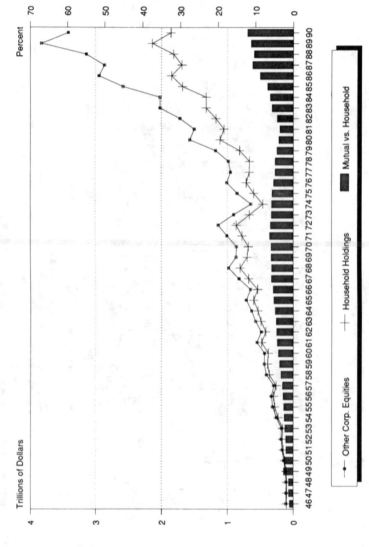

Data Source: Federal Reserve Board Flow of Fund data.

pared with 45.6 percent held by institutions. Moreover, the long-term trend in the number of shareowners is up, rising from approximately 6.5 million in the early 1950s to more than 51.4 million in mid-1990. (See Exhibit 10–3.)[3] The absolute number of individuals holding equities fluctuates, as it grows, rising sharply in economic expansions and declining, sometimes sharply, following bear markets. But over the long term, growth continues to expand the size of the individual investor market even though its proportionate share of holdings declines.

Characteristics of Individual Investors in Nasdaq Stocks

Approximately 26 percent of all individuals holding stock directly hold shares in a Nasdaq/NMS-listed company. About two-thirds of these individuals hold only Nasdaq/NMS issues. The others also hold equity mutual funds, exchange-listed stock, or over-the-counter shares. The Nasdaq/NMS shareholder population has a greater proportion of men than women (63 percent vs. 37 percent), with approximately 82 percent of Nasdaq/NMS shareowners owning their home.[4] About 70 percent are married, and 54 percent have a college education or beyond. The typical Nasdaq/NMS shareholder is 43 years old, holds two stocks, has a household income of about $40,000 to $50,000 per year, and owns assets approximating $75,000.

Growing Institutional Presence in Nasdaq/NMS Companies

The NASD, by bringing organization, visibility, and regulation to over-the-counter (OTC) securities, has enabled mutual funds and other institutions to expand the coverage of their portfolios to include thousands of companies whose market under pre-Nasdaq trading arrangements did not possess the pricing and liquidity characteristics required by most institutions. By substantially increasing the efficiency of the market for Nasdaq stocks, the NASD has vastly improved the investment process for both individual and institutional participants.

Exhibit 10–3   U.S. Shareowner Population

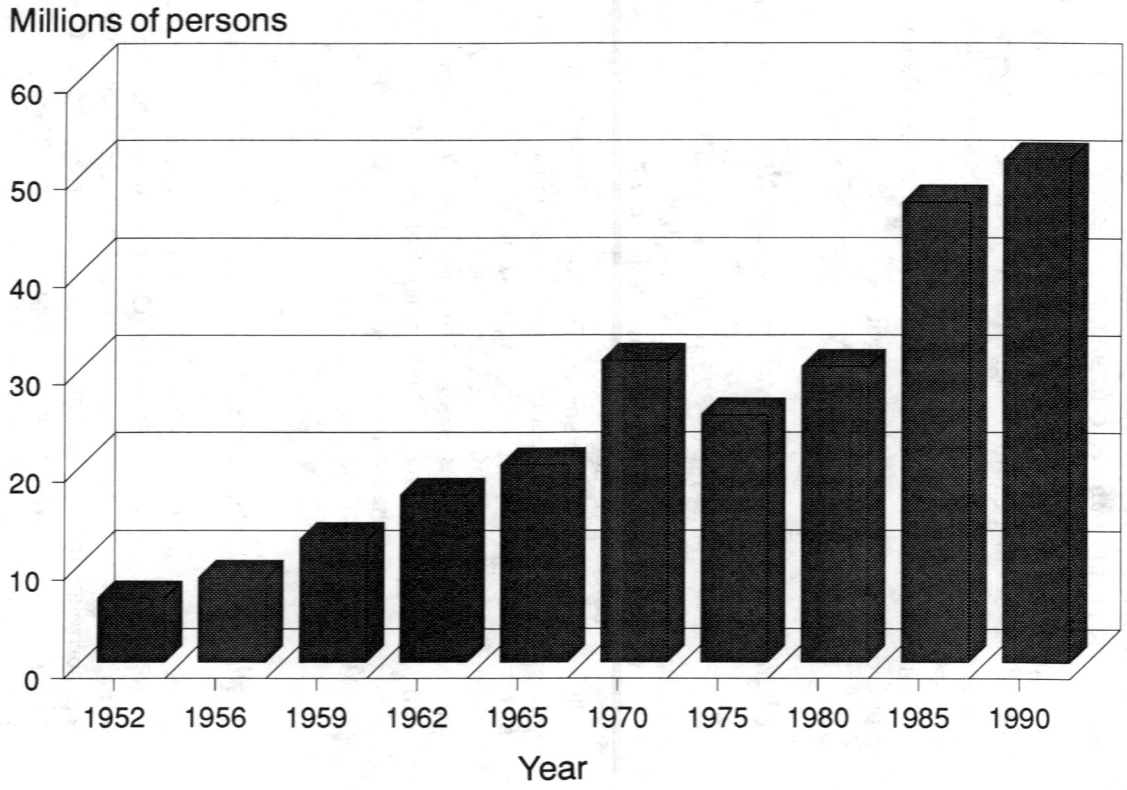

Millions of persons

Year

The mix of individual and institutional shareholdings in Nasdaq/NMS stocks has changed dramatically as Nasdaq gained recognition as a highly organized, highly regulated, efficient electronic market. As recently as 1979, the first year for which such data have been assembled, institutions held approximately 14 percent of the market value of Nasdaq stock.[5] The proportion of institutional holdings increased at a rapid rate throughout the 1980s, reaching 42.8 percent at year-end 1990. (See Exhibit 10–4.) This growth in the share of institutional holdings reflects both decisions on the part of companies, attractive to institutional investors, to remain in Nasdaq and decisions on the part of institutional managers that companies in Nasdaq possess the corporate and market characteristics that make them attractive for institutional portfolios.

Among the 2,576 Nasdaq/NMS-listed issues at the end of 1990, there were 2,419 issues with at least one institutional shareholder. Indeed, Nasdaq/NMS stocks in the market-value range between $50 million and $1 billion have a larger proportion of the dollar value of their shares held by institutions than do NYSE companies of comparable size. (See Exhibit 10–5.) Institutional holdings probably reflect differences in the industry and growth characteristics of the companies themselves, but they also reflect the liquidity provided by the market.

Since its startup in 1971, Nasdaq market facilities have been characterized by state-of-the-art technology and regulation equivalent to that imposed on the traditional stock exchanges. Quality companies, recognizing the quality of the Nasdaq market, have decided to keep their shares in that market in increasing numbers. For example, in 1980 there were four companies with in excess of $1 billion of market value. In 1990, there were 48 such companies. Also by 1990, there were 611 companies with market value exceeding $100 million.

Number of Institutional Positions Expands

Nasdaq stocks have attracted an expanded institutional following. During the last five years, institutions have increased their presence in Nasdaq stocks by nearly 60 percent from

Exhibit 10—4 Foreign Institution Holdings of Nasdaq Securities — 1985–1990

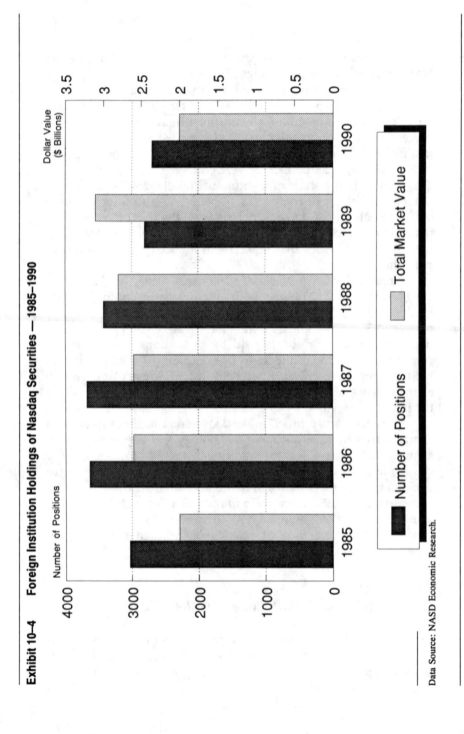

Data Source: NASD Economic Research.

Exhibit 10–5   Distribution of Nasdaq/NMS & NYSE Securities With Institutional Holdings (December 31, 1990)

| | Nasdaq/NMS | | NYSE | |
Market Value ($ Millions)	Number of Stocks	Market Value Held by Institutions	Number of Stocks	Market Value Held by Institutions
$25.0 or less	1,080	28.0%	130	34.3%
$25.1 to 50.0	411	24.1%	115	20.8%
$50.1 to 100.0	336	29.9%	203	21.7%
$100.1 to 250.0	344	35.9%	315	28.4%
$250.1 to 500.0	126	45.2%	212	36.7%
$500.1 to 1,000.0	70	47.3%	223	40.2%
$1,000.1 or more	52	43.5%	469	47.5%

Data Source: Vickers Stock Research Corporation.

48,646 positions in 1985 to 74,768 positions in 1990. (See Exhibit 10–6.) During the same time period, the value of institutional holdings in Nasdaq stocks rose 58 percent from $81.4 to $129.0 billion while total Nasdaq market value rose only 8 percent from $287.3 billion to $310.9 billion. Thus, institutions became increasingly important shareowners of Nasdaq stocks.

Domestic institutions accounted for the bulk of the expansion in institutional shareownership. The value of domestic institutional holdings rose from $79.4 billion in 1985 to $146.2 billion in 1989, only to decline to $127.0 billion in 1990, due to the bear market. At the same time, domestic institutions continued to add positions in Nasdaq stocks from 45,614 in 1985 to 72,075 in 1990. Institutional money managers have recognized the growth potential of many Nasdaq companies and have current investments in more than 3,000 Nasdaq issues. Domestic money managers now account for 31,488 positions, followed by domestic banking companies with 18,175 positions, domestic investment companies with 16,806 positions, and domestic insurance companies with 5,200 positions at the end of 1990.

Exhibit 10–6   Historical Nasdaq Institutional Participation: 1985–1990

	Domestic Institutions		Foreign Institutions		Total	
	Number of Positions	Total Market Value ($ Billions)	Number of Positions	Total Market Value ($ Billions)	Number of Positions	Total Market Value ($ Billions)
1985	45,614	$ 79.4	3,032	$2.0	48,646	$ 81.4
1986	57,409	102.1	3,636	2.6	61,045	104.7
1987	66,337	103.9	3,677	2.6	70,014	106.5
1988	71,820	115.7	3,428	2.8	75,248	118.5
1989	73,412	146.2	2,802	3.1	76,214	149.3
1990	72,075	127.0	2,693	2.0	74,768	129.0

Note: Includes only securities in an index.

Foreign institutions, responding to the favorable conditions for investing equity portfolio funds in quality companies listed on Nasdaq, increased their participation in the Nasdaq market in much of the 1980s. Foreign holdings data are incomplete because, unlike the mandatory reporting requirements that generate complete holdings data for domestic institutions, foreign holdings reports in the data bases are voluntary and presumably incomplete.

Nevertheless, known foreign institutional holdings rose from $2.0 billion in value of Nasdaq stock in 1985 to $3.1 billion in 1989, before declining in the 1990 bear market to $2.0 billion. (See Exhibit 10–7.) Foreign institutional ownership of Nasdaq companies, though much smaller than domestic institutional ownership, is essentially reflective of foreign holdings of U.S. stocks generally.[6] For the most part, investors domestic and foreign are attracted to quality companies by the same forces and in comparable degrees as long as a quality market is also available.

Companies With Large Institutional Shareholdings

The mix of a company's shareholder population is determined not only by the relative attractiveness of the company to individual and institutional investors but, in the case of institu-

Exhibit 10-7   Market Value of Institutional/Individual Nasdaq/NMS Shareholdings — 1985–1990

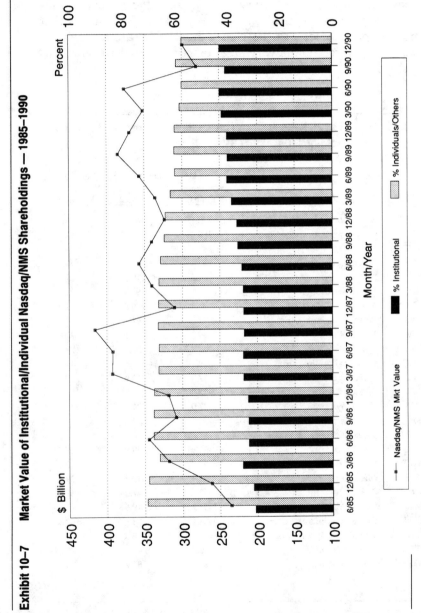

Data Source: NASD Economic Research.

tions, by the size and liquidity of the market for the company's stock. The market merely reflects in a highly efficient manner investor preferences, expectations, and decisions. The result is that some companies, such as those in Exhibit 10–8, are favorites of institutions, which hold a very large percentage of their outstanding shares.

Exhibit 10–8   The 25 Nasdaq Companies With the Largest Institutional Holdings (December 31, 1990)

Symbol	Company Name	Shares Held by Institutions (Millions)	Total Shares Outstanding (Millions)	Percent of Institutional Holdings
TCOMA	Tele-Communications, Inc.	242.1	308.5	78.5
MCIC	MCI Communications Corp.	158.0	252.9	62.5
INTC	Intel Corp.	142.6	199.6	71.4
AAPL	Apple Computer, Inc.	80.4	119.8	67.1
TWFS	TW Holdings, Inc.	74.5	110.0	67.7
CMCSK	Comcast Corp.	57.2	66.4	86.0
MCAWA	McCaw Cellular Comm.	55.1	110.8	49.7
SUNW	Sun Microsystems, Inc.	51.5	98.4	52.3
NOVL	Novell, Inc.	49.2	67.4	72.9
RTRSY	Reuters Holdings PLC	45.2	57.9	78.0
RGEQ	Regency Equities Corp.	39.2	87.3	44.9
SAFC	SAFECO Corp.	37.3	62.9	59.2
STPL	St. Paul Companies, Inc. (The)	37.0	42.3	87.5
ORCL	Oracle Systems Corp.	37.0	131.9	28.0
USHC	U.S. Healthcare, Inc.	36.9	42.0	88.0
TLMD	Telemundo Group, Inc.	34.6	36.9	93.8
USBC	U.S. Bancorp	34.6	59.9	57.8
BMET	Biomet, Inc.	33.8	56.0	60.4
MSFT	Microsoft Corp.	33.4	113.7	29.3
STJM	St. Jude Medical, Inc.	32.6	47.0	69.5
SIAL	Sigma-Aldrich Corp.	31.2	49.6	62.8
CSFN	CoreStates Financial Corp.	31.1	54.3	57.3
LOTS	Lotus Development Corp.	31.1	42.5	73.1
MENT	Mentor Graphics Corp.	30.3	42.8	70.7
NOBE	Nordstrom, Inc.	30.1	81.7	36.8

Industry characteristics also affect the mix of institutional individual ownership. Nasdaq benefits from a broad diversity of companies in terms of industry types as well as size. Some industries experience more institutional interest than others, but nearly all major industry categories have a substantial institutional presence. Only 6 out of the 28 separate industry categories in Exhibit 10–9 have institutional shares below 25 percent, and only 7 of the categories have institutional shares above 50 percent. The mix of individual and institutional ownership shifts from time to time as industries become more or less attractive to institutions. For example, the commercial banking group is broken down into separate geographic categories because institutional interest is affected by differences in regional economic conditions that affect commercial bank performance.

Individual Stockholdings Remain Dominant

Despite the tremendous growth in institutional involvement in Nasdaq securities, individuals and others still hold about 60 percent of the value of Nasdaq stocks as direct shareholders. (See Exhibit 10–4.) Because the individuals/other category is a residual, there may be some holdings of small domestic institutions and non-reporting foreign institutions (e.g., those not included in available data bases). Nevertheless, in terms of quantity of stock held and number of shareholders, the trend for individual participation continues upward with substantial increases registered in bull markets and sharp declines occurring following bear markets. The net result is a smaller individual proportionate share of a much greater corporate equity total.

It is clear that the broad corporate industry and size diversity of The Nasdaq Stock Market results in and requires a substantially larger participation of individual investors as holders of Nasdaq stocks than is true of equities generally. While Nasdaq has many companies with market values exceeding $1 billion, it also has a large number of medium and small companies that are below the self-imposed market-value limits for investing set by many large institutions. Therefore, there will always be many Nasdaq companies with little or no institutional shareholdings.

Exhibit 10-9   Institutional Holdings of Nasdaq Stocks by Industry Group — December 31, 1990

Industry Group	Number of Stocks	Dollar Value of Holdings ($ Mils.)	Total Market Value ($ Mils.)	Percentage of Total Market Value
Electronic Components	93	$ 6,460	$10,676	60.5%
Property/Casualty Insurance	37	5,756	9,822	58.6
Printing & Publishing	39	3,376	5,828	57.9
Apparel	45	3,509	6,483	54.1
Telecommunications	75	13,111	25,151	52.1
Computer Manufacturers	137	8,221	15,953	51.5
Wholesale Trade	132	5,599	11,049	50.7
Medical Instruments & Supplies	101	4,746	9,487	50.0
Health Services	79	4,029	8,101	49.7
Computer & Data Processing Services	160	10,990	24,285	45.3
Machinery	92	2,184	4,840	45.1
Primary Manufacturing	117	4,100	9,332	43.9
Trucking & Transportation	92	3,898	9,032	43.2
Restaurants	50	1,531	3,693	41.5
Pharmaceuticals	99	3,733	9,342	40.0
Commercial Banks & Bank Holding Companies (West)	64	2,500	6,353	39.4
Communications Equipment	100	1,461	3,766	38.8
Electrical Equipment	60	788	2,145	36.7
Food Products	51	2,415	7,025	34.4
Savings & Loans	73	616	1,793	34.4

Industry Group	Number of Stocks	Dollar Value of Holdings ($ Mils.)	Total Market Value ($ Mils.)	Percentage of Total Market Value
Business Services	92	$1,558	$ 4,704	33.1%
Oil & Gas	124	1,403	4,277	32.8
Commercial Banks & Bank Holding Companies (Great Lakes)	88	4,381	13,465	32.5
Retail Trade	107	3,779	12,600	30.0
Instrumentation	97	656	2,284	28.7
Life Insurance	39	995	3,500	28.4
Commercial Banks & Bank Holding Companies (Midwest)	30	1,084	3,945	27.5
Commercial Banks & Bank Holding Companies (Northeast)	238	4,517	17,283	26.1
Commercial Banks & Bank Holding Companies (Southwest)	16	262	1,086	24.1
Electric, Gas & Sanitary Services	73	1,379	5,873	23.5
Construction	35	252	1,157	21.8
Commercial Banks & Bank Holding Companies (South)	109	1,740	8,312	20.9
Travel & Entertainment	52	191	1,101	17.4
Gold & Silver	27	68	462	14.7

Note: Includes securities assigned to a major industry category (MIC) code.

Data Source: Vickers Stock Research Corporation.

Many such companies, attractive to individual investors even when small, will experience increasing institutional demand as they grow in size.

Independent academic studies find stock liquidity provided in Nasdaq to be greater than that on exchanges, enhancing the attractiveness of Nasdaq companies of all sizes to institutional and individual investors.[7] However, with a high correlation between size of company (market) and liquidity, most liquidity derives from the characteristics of the company and its stock. The ability of The Nasdaq Stock Market to accommodate the liquidity needs of both institutional and individual investors and the capital needs of both large and small companies is one of Nasdaq's greatest strengths as a market.

This is reflected in the ability of the market to accommodate change in the mix of institutional and individual ownership. For rapidly growing companies that become attractive to institutions, the change in mix can be dramatic. Illustrative of such rapid changes is the experience of the Nasdaq/NMS companies in Exhibit 10–10. Between 1985 and 1990, some experienced a shift from almost 100 percent individual holdings to more than 67.6 percent institutional ownership. Such change is often accompanied by associated changes in the market characteristics of a company's stock. In particular, there is more block volume with greater price pressures, requiring more liquidity. Literally hundreds of Nasdaq/NMS companies have successfully accomplished this transition from individual to mixed ownership in Nasdaq/NMS.

Dependence of Small Companies on Individual Investors

Share ownership of small companies continues to be predominantly direct holdings by individuals. Only 28 percent of the market value of companies with capitalizations below $25 million is held by institutions. (See Exhibit 10–11.) For the most part, large institutions desire large equity positions in companies but not large proportionate holdings of outstanding shares. This excludes small-company shares from many portfolios, because it is very difficult to accumulate and liquidate such positions in

Exhibit 10–10 Nasdaq Securities With the Largest Gains in Institutional Ownership — 1985–1990

Symbol	Company Name	Gain in Percent Inst. Holdings	1990 Percent Inst. Holdings	1985 Percent Inst. Holdings	1990 Percent Block Volume	1985 Percent Block Volume	Market Value ($ Million) 12/31/90
SMLS	SciMed Life Systems, Inc.	82.2%	91.2%	9.0%	36.5%	5.7%	$ 414.4
MCCS	Medco Containment Services, Inc.	73.0	79.2	6.2	54.8	2.6	1,444.1
UNIH	United Healthcare Corporation	66.6	68.8	2.2	53.4	19.8	627.7
HINS	Hanover Insurance Company	60.6	88.6	28.0	61.3	41.2	546.7
SANF	Sanford Corporation	60.3	74.0	13.7	51.4	—	352.4
COST	Costco Wholesale Corporation	56.1	63.5	7.4	37.4	—	1,671.6
OCER	Oceaneering International, Inc.	55.4	74.5	19.1	54.0	25.2	262.8
SREG	Standard Register Company	54.9	86.4	31.5	56.8	9.7	255.7
MEDC	Medical Care International, Inc.	54.1	75.1	21.0	33.7	39.7	891.9
NREC	NAC Re Corp.	50.5	74.2	23.7	46.1	49.5	343.0
SPCO	Software Publishing Corp.	49.8	72.0	22.2	36.5	30.0	272.3
STJM	St. Jude Medical, Inc.	48.8	69.5	20.7	32.2	16.2	1,620.1
CNTO	Centocor, Inc.	47.1	70.6	23.5	30.0	32.3	619.7
DUFM	Durr-Fillauer Medical, Inc.	45.3	74.9	29.6	37.7	34.1	283.9
WSAU	Wausau Paper Mills Company	44.7	52.6	7.9	19.2	18.2	251.5
STRY	Stryker Corporation	43.4	67.8	24.4	20.8	29.8	740.6
BKLY	W.R. Berkley Corporation	40.4	83.5	43.1	54.3	46.9	443.4
IMNX	Immunex Corporation	40.1	55.8	15.7	28.5	26.0	430.6
CHIR	Chiron Corporation	39.5	55.9	16.4	24.9	26.8	714.7
AMGN	Amgen Inc.	38.5	52.4	13.9	24.7	18.5	2,437.5
GOSHA	Oshkosh B'Gosh, Inc.	38.4	70.4	32.0	37.9	4.3	290.7
SCAF	Surgical Care Affiliates, Inc.	38.4	41.1	2.7	32.2	26.6	483.3
INDQA	International Dairy Queen, Inc.	37.7	55.4	17.7	24.6	—	287.9
AAPL	Apple Computer, Inc.	36.5	67.1	30.6	49.2	45.9	5,151.0
TECU	Tecumseh Products Company	36.3	77.8	41.5	37.3	1.8	437.6

Exhibit 10–11   Distribution of Nasdaq/NMS Institutional Holdings by Market Value — December 31, 1990

Market Value ($ Millions)	Number of Stocks	Total Institutional Holdings ($ Millions)	Total Market Value ($ Millions)	Percentage of Total Market Value
$25.0 or less	1,080	$ 3,364	$12,016	28.0%
$25.1 to 50.0	411	3,550	14,730	24.1%
$50.1 to 100.0	336	7,258	24,273	29.9%
$100.1 to 250.0	344	19,469	54,231	35.9%
$250.1 to 500.0	126	19,257	42,605	45.2%
$500.1 to 1,000.0	70	23,308	49,277	47.3%
$1,000.1 or more	52	53,297	122,522	43.5%

Note: Includes only securities with institutional holdings.
Data Source: Vickers Stock Research Corporation.

---

small companies without substantial market impact costs. In the 1986 Wharton School study of institutions, three-quarters of the large institutions and almost two-thirds of the small institutions had formal or informal policies establishing minimum capitalizations for investment.

Optimization of Shareownership Goals

Each of the participant groups in the market, including issuers, intermediaries, and individual investors, have capital-raising or investment goals that are reflected in and facilitated by a quality market environment. The Nasdaq/NMS market has retained the inherent strengths and economic flexibility of the historically diverse, sprawling OTC market while adapting all of the best features of exchange markets.

Using state-of-the-art information and communications technology in an open competitive environment, the built-in flexibility of The Nasdaq Stock Market results in economically optimum markets for companies with all different shareownership mixtures. Nasdaq market facilities reflect quickly and accurately the anonymous forces of competition, and they enable issuers and investors, individual and institutional, to successfully implement their capital-raising and investment decisions.

Endnotes

[1] In the NASD's 1985 shareholder survey, conducted for the National Association of Securities Dealers, Inc. by Opinion Research Corporation, Princeton, N.J., approximately 18 percent of respondents reported that they owned only equity mutual funds. "NYSE Shareownership 1990" estimated the investor population to be 51.4 million persons.

[2] Statistical Abstract of the United States 1991, U.S. Department of Commerce, Bureau of the Census, U.S. Government Printing Office, Washington, D.C., 1990.

[3] *NYSE 1990 Fact Book* and "NYSE Shareownership 1990."

[4] These data are taken from the 1985 NASD shareholder survey, but there is no reason to expect dramatic changes in the demographics of shareownerships since then.

[5] *Recent and Prospective Trends in Institutional Ownership and Trading of Exchange and OTC Stocks*, Marshall E. Blume and Irwin Friend, University of Pennsylvania, May 1986.

[6] Comparisons of foreign holdings of stocks with equivalent total institutional holdings indicate that the proportion of the capitalization of a company held by foreign institutions is essentially the same for companies (Nasdaq/NMS or NYSE) with equivalent total institutional holdings.

[7] See Chapter 20 for a discussion of Nasdaq liquidity.

Chapter Eleven

William J. O'Neil, founder of *Investor's Business Daily*, is chairman and chief executive officer of William O'Neil & Co., Incorporated, an institutional brokerage firm, and O'Neil Data Systems, a computer services company. William O'Neil & Co. maintains an extensive research capability with historical information on more than 7,500 securities. Mr. O'Neil began his career as a broker with Hayden, Stone & Co.

Strategies for Investing in a New America

by William J. O'Neil
Founder
Investor's Business Daily

Today we live in a new America. Of the 100 best-performing companies in the stock market since the bottom of the 1987 market break, 75 are companies that had their first public offerings in the last 5, 10, or 15 years. The securities of almost all these entities are listed on The Nasdaq Stock Market.

These companies are part of a new business cycle in America. In the business cycle of the past, the economy moved up for three to four years and then typically plummeted into recession for a year. That traditional cycle still exists and revolves around the many large, old corporations with entrenched "maintainer" managements in what I call the "old America."

The powerful new cycle I'm talking about centers on the hundreds of small- to medium-sized innovative companies that create almost all of this nation's new products, services, inventions, and jobs. Every six months, a whole new group of entrepreneurial companies with innovative products and systems leaps to the head of the national parade. I call this the six-month entrepreneurial cycle of the "new America."

Many of these companies are not closely followed by Wall Street research departments. Most of the entrepreneurial corporations represented in the new America are headquartered in the West and the South, plus some northern cities such as Minneapolis. Old America lives off yesteryear's successes. New America, as represented by the kind of companies listed on Nasdaq, is creating new products, new services, and entirely new industries — from computer software to gene splicing.

Too many people are afraid to capitalize on the enormous number of investment opportunities and join in a successful partnership with our nation's finest business innovators and inventors. The reason: they have too little knowledge and therefore become easily discouraged.

In my view, there are just two reasons why people do not do well investing in the stock market:

- They don't know how to select the best companies.
- They don't know when a stock should be sold once they have invested in it.

Some research we performed years ago sheds light on how to overcome these problems. We conducted a study that covered seven or eight stock market cycles in which we examined every one of the outstanding performing stocks in each year. The study covers more than a 30-year time period.

We examined all of the fundamental as well as market or technical characteristics of each of these highly successful companies at an emerging point just before their common stock doubled or tripled in price. We then combined the vast number of variables studied to see which factors occurred with the greatest degree of frequency so they could be considered the common characteristics of America's most outstanding investments.

Characteristics of Top-Performing Companies

We discovered that, in cycle after cycle, nearly all of these top-performing companies had seven basic characteristics. We then developed a simple formula we call "CANSLIM." Each letter stands for one of the seven fundamental factors found to be essential for outstanding stock selection.

- **"C" stands for "current earnings per share."** The first and most important variable that causes a stock to sky-rocket in price is the percentage increase in current earnings per share in the last quarter versus the same quarter the year before. The higher the percentage increase, the better. The best stock in the market may show an earnings increase of 400 percent to 500 percent. The next best stock will display an increase of 100 percent to 200 percent or more in its recent quarterly earnings. And the most attractive stocks after that might show earnings up 35 percent, 40 percent, 50 percent, or 60 percent or more. So the percentage increase of earnings already out in the public's view is the single most important factor in superior stock selection.

We also learned that in all highly successful companies, this percentage increase showed an acceleration at some point in recent quarters. In other words, when a company's earnings have been increasing 20 percent for three or four quarters in a row and suddenly the earnings increase accelerated to 40 percent, 50 percent, or more, you had the classic example of an outstanding potential investment.

- **"A" stands for "annual earnings increase."** About 75 percent of the stock market leaders showed an increase in earnings on a year-to-year basis during the previous five years. In other words, each year's earnings tended to increase. In a few cases, reduced earnings for the year might be acceptable, as long as the following year they recouped and moved back into new high ground. It is the combination of having a good five-year growth rate in annual earnings plus the steady or accelerating increase in recent quarterly earnings that makes a truly worthwhile potential investment.

- **"N" stands for "new."** More than 95 percent of the organizations that showed strong current earnings and an annual earnings growth rate in recent years had developed a new product or new service or acquired new management.

We also discovered that the best time to buy these tremendous growth companies was when they emerged from a long price-consolidation phase just before the stock was getting ready to resume its price advance and make new highs.

To most investors, particularly those new to the stock market, this may seem paradoxical. Most people instinctively want to buy a stock that looks cheap. Buying stocks that are on their way down in price and are selling near their lows for the year may seem a good strategy. But it rarely ever works.

The reality is that a stock down substantially in price is generally down for a good reason — the company may be developing a problem. So while it's sometimes hard to understand, the price of most stocks is about what it should be. If a stock's price moves up in the next six months, this is because its earnings and fundamentals continue to grow and improve.

- **"S" stands for "shares outstanding or "supply and demand."** The number of shares of common stock in the capital structure of a company determines how much stock may be available in the marketplace.

Generally speaking, stocks of companies with less than 50 million shares outstanding are going to respond faster and move quicker in the market. Companies with enormous capitalizations (150 million shares or greater) will move slower because of their larger supply of stock. They will also tend to represent the older America we talked about earlier. There are some outstanding companies among larger-capitalization stocks. But it is a relatively small group of perhaps 15 to 20 companies compared with the universe of smaller-capitalization, younger entrepreneurial companies where you may find perhaps 200 different rewarding investment opportunities.

- **"L" stands for "leader" or "laggard."** Learn to locate and buy the true leaders in the market or an industry. The best performing stock in an industry may double in price while the fourth or fifth company in a group may go up only 10 percent or 15 percent.

One simple measurement that helps rule out most of the also-rans in the market is the relative price strength of a stock in an accepted rating system. If it falls below 70, that normally means a stock's performance is lagging and the stock should, in most instances, be avoided. I personally limit all of my new investments to stocks that rate 80 or higher on a relative price-strength basis.

Relative price strength is a simple measurement that monitors either the last 6 or 12 months of a stock's price and compares its price change for that period with the change in either the market averages or all other stocks. The approach is similar to that in baseball, where the relative leaders show batting averages around .300, and the laggards are the .100 and .200 hitters that are just not performing.

- **"I" stands for "institutional sponsorship."** This is important because about 50 percent of today's buying and selling action in the stock market is usually institutional. Institutions such as mutual funds, banks, and insurance companies are the overpowering forces that can move a stock price up substantially or cause it to drop precipitously. The stock doesn't need a large amount of sponsorship, but it is helpful to see that at least a few of the better performing institutions have purchased it in a recent quarter.

One source of information can be found in studying the actions of mutual funds. You can review top-performing funds and determine their 10 largest investment positions, as well as the largest new investments made in the last quarter plus the stocks most often sold. If, over a period of a few weeks, you notice several different funds have been selling out of certain stocks, it also may tell you which stocks you might want to avoid.

- **"M" stands for "market."** Our research shows that when the Standard & Poor's (S&P) 500 stock index or the Dow Jones Industrials Average goes into a correction, three of every four stocks will drop with the market averages. When the averages are in a major uptrend, most stocks will eventually follow.

Therefore, it is important to have a market analysis tool in your kit that tells whether you are investing in a bull or bear market, shows if the market is in an early stage of a move, and indicates the market's true condition and status. For many years, I've used as my primary market analysis tool the actual day-by-day performance of the Dow Jones Industrials 30-stock average.

The United States stock market is on an uptrend most of the time. It is only during shorter time periods that we have the difficult bear markets or intermediate-term market drops of 8 percent to 15 percent. Yet, you need to recognize these more severe adjustment periods and perhaps sell a few of your stocks to hedge and protect yourself.

Why You Should Buy .300 Hitters

My investment philosophy is to buy top quality. An illustration might demonstrate why.

Suppose you managed a big league baseball team and wanted to recruit new players or make some trades to improve your team. Would you invest in as many .100 hitters as you could find or would you try to sign as many .300 hitters as possible? The .100 hitters will cost less in salary (their P/E will be much lower). Are they really undervalued? How many ball games will you win if you have a lineup of all .100 or .200 hitters? Are the .300 hitters so overvalued that you would never want to have any .300 hitters on your team? No.

The reality of any open marketplace is that everything sells somewhere around what it is worth at the time. And as long as the investment continues to deliver, those values will be maintained and even improved. You'll always win many more ball games with .300 hitters than you will ever win with .100 and .200 hitters even though you can get the poor hitters cheaper. So why shouldn't you go first class and be a partner and shareholder in the very best companies in America, the ones with the greatest managements, the greatest products, and the greatest earnings percentage increase in growth?

Don't worry if you can't buy 100 shares or more of a stock. You should look at how many dollars you are investing, buy into the very best company possible, and not be concerned with the number of shares you purchase.

Average Up, Not Down

Another one of my rules is never to buy more of a stock if its price has declined from my initial purchase price. Called "averaging down," this can get you in a great deal of trouble if your stock selection is wrong. We all make mistakes in our stock selection. The object is not to compound our mistakes.

It is usually far better to average up. The proper way to average up, I believe, is as follows: Let's assume your game plan is to limit your portfolio to four stocks. That means each one of the four full positions will amount to a 25 percent commitment of your total investment money. When you make an initial buy of a stock, do not commit all of the 25 percent at once. Start with half that amount. Only after your stock has advanced at least 2 or 3 percent from your first purchase price and still looks strong should you consider making a second or follow-up commitment. This second follow-up buy could involve a little less money, perhaps 30 percent of a normal full position.

If the stock is still showing powerful progress, has active volume demand, and is up another 2 to 3 percent a week or so later, you could follow up with your third and last commitment of an even smaller amount of money, say 20 percent. This will get you to a normal full commitment for one stock. Since you plan to own four stocks, this amounts to a 25-percent position in one stock purchased three different times. In each case, the stock showed some small indication that you were possibly right in your selection by advancing in price before you made a further buy.

You will note that I suggest averaging up but with lesser sums of money so the average cost does not get too high. You definitely do not want to continue to average up once a stock is up more than 5 percent or so from a proper beginning buy point. Otherwise, you could get emotionally carried away and keep chasing a stock too far up the line as it leaps ahead in price. This creates the danger of an extended price situation. Stocks that are excessively extended in price eventually go through a normal correction (declining) process.

Do You Know When to Sell?

Now that you have a headstart toward selecting potentially sound investments, it's worth taking a look at the second area where most investors encounter problems — protecting the money in their accounts. Here, a good defense becomes essential. Your first objective should be to minimize your losses if you make a poor selection and your stock declines below the price you paid for it.

I try to limit every loss to 7 percent or 8 percent below the actual price paid . . . without exception. If you correctly cut all your losses quickly — without hesitating, vacillating, or getting emotional — this should protect you against the serious large losses that can and do happen to most investors. Be like the football team that has such a strong defense that it stops opponents from making first downs. If they cannot make much yardage against you, how can they beat you?

If you let a stock go down 50 percent in price, you must make 100 percent on the next one you buy just to break even. Most people are not good enough to make 100 percent on their stocks. Therefore, if they make a mistake, they should face up to it, correct it, and go on to the next thing.

This rule has saved my neck during many market cycles. One time I sold a stock at $90 a share and watched it go to $1. At the time, I had no idea any stock could drop that far. If I had not sold it, the loss would have been crushing.

If you are a new investor, you should sell about half to two-thirds of the stocks that run up in price and show a worthwhile profit after you buy them. These should be sold when they are up 25 percent to 30 percent. My theory here is simple: A bird in hand is worth two in the bush. Some stocks will rise 30 percent and fall back to where they started. It doesn't hurt to nail down a few profits.

For longer-term investment, you may decide to hold one out of three stocks that show a 30 percent or so increase in price. These few "long pull" stocks should be the ones that you know the most about, feel are the true leaders, and have acted stronger than your other positions. Only time and experience will help you decide which stocks to sell and which to hold.

Monitor Your Portfolio

All serious investors need to track the performance of their portfolios, as well as market trends. I monitor my stocks by turning to the Nasdaq stock tables of our newspaper, *Investor's Business Daily*, which runs the stock tables through a computer to calculate the three unique measurements:

- **EPS (Earnings Per Share) Rank.** Since the percentage increase in earnings per share is the most important factor that causes stocks to perform well, we measure the last five years' annual earnings growth rate of a stock and the percentage increase in recent quarters, combine the two, and compare the result with that of all other stocks in the market. This number is then placed on a scale of 0 to 99, with 99 being the highest, to create the EPS rank for a company. I restrict all of my new investments to companies that show an EPS ranking of 85 or higher because I want to operate in the top 15 percent of companies in America in terms of their proven record of earnings increase. (See Exhibit 11–1.)

- **Relative Price Strength.** We take each Nasdaq stock's current price, compare that with its price one year ago, and compare this percentage change with the percentage change for all other stocks in the market. The result is then put on the same simple 0-to-99 scale. I consider only stocks that rank 80 or higher, meaning they are in the top 20 percent of companies in America in relative price ac-

Exhibit 11–1

NASDAQ National Market

"Home of Tomorrow's Market Leaders"

EPS Rnk	Rel. Str.	52-Week High	52-Week Low	Stock Name	Closing Price	Chg.	Vol.% Change	Vol. 100s	Grp. Str.	Day's Price High	Day's Price Low
67	26	1¾	3/16	Eastco Indusl	7/16	....	−96	35	..	7/16	7/16
14	38	10¼	6¼	Eastern Bncp	7¾	....	−87	4	29	7¾	7¾
71	16	7⅜	3¼	Eastern Envtl	4⅛	− ⅛	−60	139	14	4⅜	4⅛
17	6	4¼	1 3/16	EastlandFincl	1⅞	....	−96	5	..	1⅞	1⅞
69	99	12⅛	1	Ecogen Inc	9½	+ ¼	−64	544	..	9½	9¼
85	72	18	7	Egghead Inc	13½	− ¼	−15	1371	59	13¾	13¼ k
15	81	**8⅛**	3½	El Paso Elec	8	− ⅛	+353	5397	..	8⅛	7⅞
75	81	**21**	11⅜	Elbitg	19⅛	....	−28	542	13	19¼	18⅞
21	14	3⅛	¼	Elcotel	7/16	− 1/16	−72	40	..	½	7/16 k
28	32	13½	6½	Eldec Corp	9	+ ½	−89	13	19	9	8½
71	49	9	3⅛	Electro Sctfc	5½	....	+209	541	..	5½	5¼
9	**72**	**44¾**	**4⅝**	**Electrlux AB**	**41¼**	**+1¾**	**+45**	**109**	**7**	**41¼**	**40½**
92	96	**13⅛**	3½	Electmag Sc	12	− ¼	−97	25	..	12⅛	12
97	90	23⅞	6⅛	Elctrnc Arts	21¼	+ ½	−28	877	23	21¼	20½
23	83	11	1½	Electrnc Data	4¼	− ⅛	0	110	7	4⅜	4¼
94	93	11½	4¾	Elctrnc Telcm	9½	....	−99	1	19	9½	9½
97	52	**16½**	12	Ellwd Fd Svg	15¼	+ ½	−60	4	..	15¼	15¼
48	88	**11⅞**	5½	ElronElctrnc	11¾	+ ¼	−5	116	18	11¾	11⅝
88	**95**	**N H**	**16½**	**EmployeeBnf**	**44¾**	**+1½**	**+45**	**1459**	**30**	**45¼**	**42¾**
85	52	7⅜	1¼	EmplyrCslty	3⅝	....	−39	153	..	3⅞	3⅝
84	79	11¼	4¾	Emulex Corp	8½	....	−94	57	14	8¾	8½
69	78	**17**	8¼	EnClean Inc	16¼	+ ½	−90	30	24	16¼	16¼
25	91	4⅛	7/16	EncoreCmptr	1¾	+ 3/16	−46	1881	..	1 13/16	1½
37	28	19¼	15¼	Energynorth	15¾	− ⅜	−87	2	18	16¼	15¾
81	75	26	11¾	Energy Ventr	20	−1½	−88	16	65	21	20
75	58	**4⅜**	2¾	ENEX Resrce	4	+ ⅛	+100	80	10	4	3½
94	14	7¼	1⅞	EnginrdSprt	3	....	−92	10	17	3	3
39	92	2 3/16	13/16	Engin Measr	1¾	....	−97	4	..	1¾	1¾
48	84	11½	5⅝	Engraph Inc	10⅛	− ¼	−97	13	27	10⅜	10⅛
54	93	3½	¼	EntronicsCp	2	+ ⅛	−62	23	..	2	1⅞
94	29	21½	13	Env Elements	14½	− ¼	−21	375	14	14¾	14¼
79	91	5½	1⅞	EnviroqCp	4¼	− ½	−70	13	11	4¼	4¼ k
44	71	19¾	5½	EnvirosafSvc	12	− ¾	−78	20	17	12	12
58	55	6½	1¾	Envirosource	3½	− ½	−16	125	..	3 13/16	3½
2	38	**12½**	**N L**	EnvoyCp	12¼	+ ½	....	1.1m	..	12¼	11⅜
12	67	12⅝	3	Enzon Inc	9¼	− ¼	−81	277	..	9½	9¼
71	78	31½	13½	Equitbl IA B	26¾	− ¾	−87	22	9	27¼	26¼
4	38	13/32	**N L**	Equitex Inc	3/32	....	−95	385	..	3/32	1/16
71	14	7¼	4⅜	Equity Oil	4⅝	− ⅛	−75	49	36	4⅞	4⅝
75	**13**	**47½**	**27¾**	**Ericsson LM**	**30¾**	**+1¼**	**−49**	**1441**	**13**	**30¾**	**29¾**
50	70	**61¾**	41	ErieLackawn	60¾	− ¾	0	14	..	60¾	60¾
24	**69**	**N H**	**4 3/16**	**ERLY Inds**	**7⅝**	**+ ⅜**	**−70**	**13**	**8**	**7⅝**	**7⅜**
8	**68**	**N H**	**17**	**Essex County**	**23**	**+1**	**−75**	**2**	**12**	**23**	**22**
28	23	33¼	14	Evans&Suthr	18¾	− ½	−61	139	12	19¼	18¾
37	74	2⅜	½	Evans Inc	1½	....	−68	7	..	1½	1½ k
14	66	10½	2⅝	EverexSystm	5 1/16	− 1/16	−92	220	..	5⅛	5 k
73	69	25⅞	6⅝	Exabyte	18⅝	− ⅛	−53	1761	14	18⅞	18½
89	97	21⅜	5¾	Exar Corp	19¼	− ¼	−94	37	13	19½	19¼
8	84	**18½**	7¼	Excalibur Tch	17⅜	− ⅛	−60	52	..	17¾	17
23	25	8⅜	2½	Excel Bancrp	4¼	+ ⅛	−86	18	..	4¼	4⅛
53	77	2⅛	⅜	EXECUTONE	1 1/16	− 1/16	−90	95	18	1⅛	1
21	67	11¼	6½	ExideElectr	9½	+ ¼	+60	290	..	9½	9¼
78	**78**	**29½**	**14**	**ExpeditorIntl**	**27¼**	**+1⅛**	**−93**	**13**	**16**	**27¼**	**27¼**

— F —

EPS Rnk	Rel. Str.	52-Week High	52-Week Low	Stock Name	Closing Price	Chg.	Vol.% Change	Vol. 100s	Grp. Str.	Day's Price High	Day's Price Low
62	43	15	8½	F&M Fnl Svcs	11¼	− ¾	+31	17	10	12	10¾
92	**85**	**29¾**	**8¾**	**FHP Intl Corp**	**22⅞**	**+1⅜**	**−13**	**2296**	**20**	**23**	**21¼ o**
43	94	14	4	FNB Rochstr	11⅛	− ⅛	**+109**	317	12	11¼	10½
61	79	**14¼**	7½	FNW Bancorp	13¼	+ ⅛	−91	12	13	13¼	13¼
43	38	5¼	1⅝	FSI Intl	3¼	....	+174	85	..	3½	3¼
99	61	30	14	Failure Grp	22¼	− ¾	−29	228	26	23	22¼
4	10	4⅝	**N L**	FairfldCntyBc	1¼	+ ¼	+45	61	..	1¼	½
4	7	5¼	1¾	Fairfld Fst Bk	2¼	−1	+25	10	..	2¼	2¼
69	18	7½	2½	FalconOil&Gs	3	− ⅛	−80	2	10	3	3 k
76	74	**6⅜**	4	Falcon Prods	6⅛	....	+62	47	11	6⅛	5⅝ k
46	80	2	7/16	Family Stk Hs	1¼	+ ⅛	−78	42	99	1¼	1
20	7	2	3/16	Famous Rstrt	7/16	+ 1/32	+184	341	..	7/16	⅜
50	56	7¼	3½	Faradyne Elc	5 3/16	+ 3/16	+145	76	9	5¼	5 k
88	84	**13½**	6	Farm&Home	12⅝	+ ⅝	−49	18	35	12⅝	12¼
79	63	**102**	79	Farmer Bros	96	....	−67	2	9	96	96
62	63	16⅛	7½	Farr Co	12½	+ ¼	−87	14	13	12½	12¼
90	52	28¾	12⅜	Fastenal Co	22¾	− ½	−95	31	34	23½	22½
2	38	**14**	12½	Fedfirst Bncs	13	....	−99	3	..	13	13
94	70	13⅜	4	Ferrofluidics	9⅞	+ ⅜	−23	117	..	10¼	9½
24	54	12⅞	5½	Fibronics Intl	9⅛	....	−80	114	20	9¼	9
36	74	**20½**	13½	Fidelity Bnc	19½	− ⅛	+4	165	13	19¾	19¼
54	49	**7¼**	5	Fidelity Svgs	7	+ ¾	+614	50	8	7	6¾
90	**88**	**N H**	**23¼**	**FifthThirdBcp**	**50**	**+ ½**	**+100**	**981**	**16**	**50**	**49**
92	**99**	**N H**	**3 7/16**	**FiftyOffStores**	**19**	**+ ⅜**	**+11**	**2021**	**32**	**19⅜**	**18⅜ k**
37	43	25½	10½	Figgie Intl A	16⅛	+ ⅝	−23	391	..	16¼	15½
37	11	35½	15	Figgie Intl B	19	−1	−76	8	10	19	17½
59	83	21½	5	FileNet Corp	15¼	− ⅛	−85	111	40	15¾	15
48	**38**	**N H**	**15**	**Filenes Bsmt**	**18⅝**	**+ ¾**	**−60**	**1895**	**..**	**18¾**	**17½**
79	67	**36¼**	26	Fincl Trust Cp	33½	−1½	−80	2	9	33½	33½
89	81	**26⅛**	14⅝	First AL Bcshr	24¾	+ ¼	−80	160	11	24¾	24½
63	81	**6½**	3⅛	Frst Am Banc	6½	+ ¼	−71	22	4	6½	6½
48	71	15⅝	4⅞	FrstAm Cp TN	11⅝	+ ¼	−80	114	..	11⅝	11⅜
14	43	13¼	6½	First Am Finl	9½	....	−24	48	..	9¾	9½
14	62	11¾	5¼	FstAmrFinCA	9½	+ ½	−53	20	..	9½	9½
41	20	15	11½	FirstBncp NC	12½	....	−33	2	13	12½	12½
67	59	**27½**	16½	FirstBncp OH	25¾	....	**+96**	135	9	25¾	25¾
84	78	17¾	9½	FirstColonial	15¾	+ ¼	−98	3	11	15¾	15¾
69	68	**22¾**	12½	FtCommerce	21¾	+ ¼	−91	9	12	22⅛	21¾
89	59	10⅜	5¼	FstCmrclBcp	8	− ⅜	−96	5	6	8½	8
73	24	18⅞	14¾	FtCmrcl Bcsh	15½	....	−97	1	8	15½	15½
87	**81**	**N H**	**14½**	**Frst Commcl**	**23½**	**+1¼**	**−54**	**36**	**9**	**23½**	**23¼**
84	40	17½	11¾	FstCmntyBcp	15⅛	+ ⅜	−62	15	10	15⅛	14⅝
69	50	4⅝	¾	FtConstitnFnl	1¾	....	−92	30	..	1⅞	1¾
14	14	24¼	9¾	FstEastrn PA	13¾	+ ¼	−91	10	..	13¾	13¾
11	12	4½	1½	FstEssex Bcp	2½	+ ¼	−40	70	..	2½	2¼
94	**83**	**13¼**	**4¼**	**FstFedlCap**	**12½**	**+1**	**−81**	**9**	**..**	**12½**	**11½**
46	45	17½	8⅞	FirstFed Mich	13⅝	....	−54	143	12	13⅝	13⅜
89	64	**15½**	9¼	First Fed MI	15½	+ ¾	−89	2	10	15½	15½
23	49	7¾	4	FstFd EHartfd	6¼	− ¼	0	20	10	6¼	6¼
48	23	9¼	5¼	FstFd PrtRico	6½	....	−68	11	..	6¾	6½
54	20	13	8	FtFdSv Charlt	9½	+ ¼	−94	1	10	9½	9½
67	45	10¾	8	FtFd LaGrnge	9¼	+ ¼	−83	1	9	9¼	9¼
65	66	**11**	7⅜	FstFideltyWV	10¾	+ ½	**+860**	96	8	10¾	10¼
96	75	**18**	9¾	First Fincl Cp	16½	+ ¼	−79	41	9	16½	16¼
62	45	12¼	8	FstFncl Hldgs	9¾	− ¾	−89	5	5	10½	9¾
18	12	25¼	7¾	FirstFlaBnks	11⅜	− ⅜	−49	166	..	11¾	11⅜
78	40	12¾	7¼	Fst Harrisbrg	9¼	+ ½	−56	4	12	9¼	9¼
82	76	**28**	14½	Frst Hawaiian	27½	− ¼	−89	67	11	27¾	27

tion in the last year. It is not enough for a stock to have just one of these high-ranked measurements. They should have both a high EPS rank and a high relative-price strength.

- **Volume-Percentage Change.** This allows you to track the flow of institutional money into and out of a Nasdaq stock. If your stock is down 2 points for the day and its volume-percentage change shows +500, for example, that means the stock sold off on 500 percent more volume than the stock normally trades.

This table, which monitors every stock's average daily volume on a running 10-week basis, also tells you whether the daily buying or selling of a stock is less than normal. Suppose your stock is down 2 points for the day, but the volume-percentage change column displays a -50. This means no major selling is occurring in your stock. This is key information you need to know.

The Nasdaq stock tables show in boldface print every stock that is up 1 point or more or making new price highs. Stocks down 1 point or more or making new price lows for the year are underlined. I scan these tables quickly each day, primarily to look at the stocks that are boldfaced. It takes only a couple of minutes but keeps me aware of any unusual action that may suddenly occur in a new stock.

I also look at the list of 100 stocks with the greatest percentage rise in volume. The computer selects every stock that trades a large percentage increase above its average daily volume level and prints this list for your analysis. The stocks that have both a high EPS and relative strength rank are boldfaced.

I scan the 30 most active stocks in the Nasdaq tables, as well as the 15 biggest percentage gainers in price. This latter list concentrates on higher-priced stocks that institutional buyers may consider.

Investor's Business Daily publishes a variety of other Nasdaq information, some of which is shown in Exhibits 11–2, 11–3, 11–4, and 11–5.

Exhibit 11–2

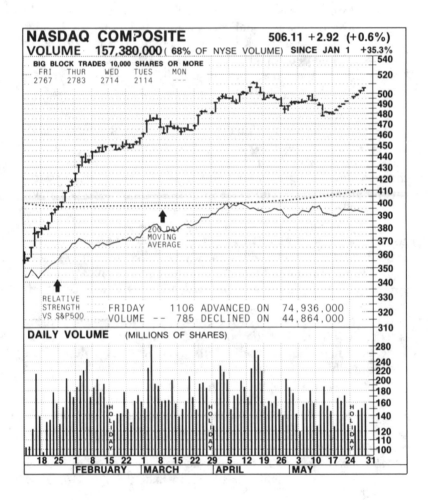

Exhibit 11–3   30 Nasdaq Stocks Displayed in *Investor's Business Daily* on January 18, 1991

Stock Name	Closing Price on 1/17/91	Close Price on 5/30/91	Percentage Change
AST Research	40	47	17.5
Aldus Corp.	33	53 1/4	61.4
Amgen	65 1/2	126 5/8	93.3
BMC Software	34 3/4	39	12.2
Biomet	19 3/8	28 3/4	48.4
Borland	38 1/8	51 3/8	34.8
Cisco Systems	49	65 1/4	33.2
Concord Computing	33	55 1/2	68.2
Costco	53 1/4	88 1/2	66.2
Cybertek	13 1/4	10 1/2	— 20.8
Dell Computer	20 1/4	25 1/4	24.7
Digi International	22	37 1/4	70.5
First Alabama	18 3/4	24 7/8	32.7
Fuller	31 1/4	48 7/8	56.4
General Kinetics	14	20	37.9
HealthCare Compare	19	42 1/4	122.4
Invacare	22 1/4	33 1/4	49.4
LDDS Communications	20 1/4	26 1/4	29.6
Legent Corp.	30 1/4	30 3/8	.4
Linear Technology	13 1/2	22 3/4	68.5
McCormick & Co.	27	38 1/2	42.6
Microsoft Corp.	84	110 1/4	31.3
Minntech Corp.	17	25 1/2	50.0
Novell Inc.	37 7/8	57 1/4	51.2
Smithfield Foods	22 1/4	47 1/4	112.4
Synoptics	28 1/2	37	—3.9
T^2 Medical	30 3/4	49 1/4	60.2
Vencor Inc.	18	39 1/4	120.8
Vicor Corp.	18 1/4	40 1/2	121.9
Vital Signs Inc.	15 3/4	18 1/4	15.9
Average Percentage Change from Nasdaq Display			50.3
Dow Jones Industrial Average	2508.91	3000.45	19.6%

Exhibit 11–4 *Investor's Business Daily* Earnings Reports

AUTODESK INC		ACAD 55¼
Computer-Software		Eps 91 Rel 66
Quar Apr 30:	1991	1990
Sales	$69,461,000	$55,195,000
Net Income	15,666,000	13,449,000
Share earns:		(OTC)
Net Income	0.63	0.55
% Change	**+15%**	

BOSTON ACOUSTICS INC		BOSA 32
Audio/Video Home Prod		Eps 95 Rel 85
Quar Mar 30:	1991	1990
Sales	$8,118,474	$7,706,233
Net Income	1,251,978	1,012,044
Avg shares	2,070,541	2,029,856
Share earns:		(OTC)
Net Income	0.60	0.50
% Change	**+20% ★**	
12 months:		
Sales	29,781,387	26,453,728
Net Income	4,218,499	3,443,380
Avg shares	2,055,703	2,023,574
Share earns:		
Net Income	2.05	1.70
% Change	+21%	

CISCO SYSTEMS INC		CSCO 31¾
Computer-Peripheral Eq		Eps 99 Rel 93
Quar Apr 28:	s1991	s1990
Sales	$49,707,000	$17,851,000
Net Income	11,646,000	3,825,000
Avg shares	31,411,000	29,114,000
Share earns:		(OTC)
Net Income	0.37	0.13
% Change	**+185% ★**	
9 months:		
Sales	126,417,000	47,993,000
Net Income	29,967,000	9,274,000
Avg shares	31,125,000	26,760,000
Share earns:		
Net Income	0.96	0.35
% Change	+174%	

s–Share data reflect a 2–for–1 stock split on March 15, 1991.

NORDSTROM INC		NOBE 41¼
Retail-Apparel/Shoe		Eps 85 Rel 89
Quar Apr 30:	1991	1990
Sales	$610,603,000	$555,038,000
Net Income	25,657,000	13,169,000
Avg shares	81,739,858	81,617,491
Share earns:		(OTC)
Net Income	0.31	0.16
% Change	**+94% ★**	

Exhibit 11–5 66 Nasdaq New Highs With Closing Prices

(**†See graphs on page 12**) (Common stocks over $2 only)

†Advo System Inc	21⅛	Hingham Inst Svngs	5¼
Ameritrust Corp	21⅝	I N B Financial Corp	27¼
†Assoc Banc Corp	27	Image Retailing	2
AMCORE Financial	15	†Immucor Inc	23¼
†Basic Petroleum Intl	27	Immulogical Pharmtl	10½
Big B Inc	14⅛	†Information Resourc	22⅞
Centennial Bancorp	6⅝	Intl Absorbents	2⅞
†Central Bancshares	24½	†Isomedix Inc	20⅝
†Collective Bancorp	12⅛	Macmillan Bloedel	17½
†Colorado Natl Bkshr	18⅝	†Mark Twain Bancs	18¾
Cooper Developmnt	2¾	N A I C Grth Fd	14¾
†Costco Wholesale	43	Neolens Inc	5 3/16
†Coventry Corp	18¼	†New York Bancorp	14¼
Dairy Mart Cnvnce B	9½	†O E S I Power Corp	14¾
Datascope Corp	66¾	Optical Coating Lab	8
†Datron Systems Inc	14¾	†Osmonics Inc	20¾
Digital Biometrics	12⅜	†Pioneer Federal Bcp	19½
†Dollar General Corp	15¾	Puritan-Bennett	34½
Dress Barn Inc	13½	Security FSB MT	7⅝
Dynamic Oil Ltd	3	Shared Medical Sys	22⅜
E R L Y Industries Inc	7⅝	†Stephan Company	16¼
†Employee Benefit	44¾	Sylvan Foods Hldgs	9⅜
Envoy Corp	12¼	T J Systems Corp	2½
Essex County Gas	23	†Tech Data Corp	14
†Fifth Third Bancorp	50	†Thorn Apple Valley	39¼
†Fifty Off Stores Inc	19	†U S Healthcare Inc	35¼
Filenes Basement	18⅝	Ultra Pac Inc	7⅝
Fingermatrix	2 7/16	Untd New Mexico Fnl	11¾
†First Commercial Cp	23½	US Facilities Corp	9⅝
Future Commctns	5¼	Value Merchants	18¼
Galileo Electro Optc	6¾	†Vicor Corp	37½
†Gambro AB Adr	33⅝	†Washgtn Fd Bk Or	16¼
†Healthcare Compre	38	†Wstn Bk Coos Bay	14¼

Nasdaq Offers Growth Companies

The Nasdaq Stock Market contains hundreds of top-quality young companies whose securities trade in large volume. In fact, I believe Nasdaq has the best growth companies in this country today.

One reason I buy Nasdaq stocks is that I do not have to worry so much about pesky program trading, which tends to be concentrated in Dow Jones and S&P-listed securities. Program trading causes excessive volatility up and down in the market averages during most trading days.

Anyone can learn to invest better. If you will prepare, do a little research and study, have courage, patience, and confidence, you should definitely go after it. Good luck with your investing in The Nasdaq Stock Market and the new America.

Chapter Twelve

Edward J. Mathias joined T. Rowe Price Associates Inc. in 1971 and is a managing director and a member of its management committee. Earlier, he managed the New Horizons Fund, a small-company growth fund. He serves on the NASD's institutional investor committee.

Nasdaq:
The Home of Emerging
Growth Companies

by Edward J. Mathias
Managing Director
T. Rowe Price Associates Inc.

The Nasdaq Stock Market provides a home for many of the most innovative, dynamic companies in the U.S. economy. Included are companies operating in rapidly growing areas such as technology, biotechnology, health care, finance, consumer, and business services. The availability of venture capital and the rise in initial public offerings (IPOs) in the 1980s expanded this universe dramatically, in terms of the number of companies and their market capitalization. An abundance of opportunities, together with attractive stock valuations for small growth companies, suggests favorable investment returns during the 1990s. Emerging growth companies list predominantly on The

Nasdaq Stock Market and represent an important segment of that market.

The Dynamic Sectors of the U.S. Economy

The U.S. economy's growth rate appears to be slowing as we enter the final decade of the 20th century. The annual rate of real Gross National Product (GNP) growth from 1970 to 1990 was 2.9 percent, down from 3.5 percent during the 1950 to 1970 period. Although the U.S. economy is expanding more slowly than in prior periods, there still exists numerous industries and market niches that offer dynamic growth potential.

Some of these growth sectors are tied to the rapid spread of electronic technologies throughout our society. Others are related to the growth of biotechnology, pharmaceuticals, specialized medical devices, and outpatient health services. Beyond these areas, rapid growth is occurring in such diverse industries as computer software, warehouse club retailing, cellular telephones, and pollution control. In nearly all of these industries, Nasdaq companies are playing major roles. Whether in services, health care, or technology, newer companies are creating market niches, new industries, and jobs by meeting consumer and business needs in areas that more mature companies have left unexploited.

Smaller companies are in the forefront of economic opportunity. According to U.S. government data, small to medium-sized companies created most of the nation's new jobs during the past 10 years. These companies are typically managed by founders who embody the entrepreneurial drive for success, investing personal wealth and "sweat equity" into their nascent businesses.

Venture capital organizations provide a formalized multi-billion dollar channel for both startup and expansion capital for young private companies. As they outgrow the venture capital community's funding resources, young companies turn to the public market where investors' funds are attracted by the prospect of significant long-term capital gains. The vast majority of the young companies going public do so via Nasdaq, and they constitute the raw material for growth stock investors seeking a stake in the most rapidly growing industries.

Profiles of High Growth Leaders

There are numerous examples of Nasdaq companies that have led revolutionary changes in their industries and generated extraordinary investment results. The following representative examples describe companies on the leading edge of three fast-growing sectors: technology, biotechnology, and health care. The examples also attest to the returns achieved through early recognition of such situations.

Technology can be divided into two categories: hardware and software. Hardware encompasses actual equipment — personal computers, workstations, and printers; software consists of the programs that run the equipment. Major hardware success stories include Apple Computer and Sun Microsystems, while Microsoft and Oracle Systems are two leading firms in the software segment. All initially listed on Nasdaq and continue to trade there.

Apple Computer makes user-friendly personal computers with proprietary operating systems such as Macintosh. The company now enjoys a 17 percent share of the personal computer market and is also a major factor in laser printers, system software, networking products, and scanners. Apple's sales have grown rapidly from $118 million in 1980 to $5.6 billion in 1990. And since coming public in 1980, the stock has risen threefold.

Sun Microsystems produces high-performance computer workstations, specialized computer networking equipment, and peripherals. Sun's workstations have revolutionized computing in the engineering, scientific, and technical fields. The company's success can be measured by its extraordinary growth of revenues from $9 million in 1983 to $3.2 billion in fiscal year (ending June) 1991, a compound growth rate of more than 100 percent per year. The stock has also been rewarding, again more than tripling during the initial five years the company has been public.

Microsoft is a pre-eminent personal computer software company. It developed both of the industry-leading operating systems — MS-DOS and OS/2 — as well as the popular Windows graphics applications software package. Microsoft has enjoyed explosive growth, with sales rising from $24 million in 1982 to $1.2

billion in 1990. In five years, Microsoft stock has risen to more than 11 times its initial offering price.

Oracle Systems designs software used in data-base management, applications development, and other areas of interest to computer professionals. A relational data-base management system (named "Oracle") is the company's principal product and has been the catalyst for Oracle's phenomenal sales growth from $1 million in 1981 to $971 million in 1990. Before a setback in 1990, the stock had risen nine times from its IPO price established in early 1986.

In the biotechnology arena, small companies achieve many of the important research and development breakthroughs. Amgen, a leader in recombinant DNA technology, is one of Nasdaq's largest biotech firms. The company's first product, EPOGEN, stimulates red blood cell production in anemia patients. Amgen is developing other human pharmaceutical products and appears on the threshold of several years of rapid growth. Yet Amgen is not alone. There are literally dozens of smaller biotech companies with promising futures trading on Nasdaq. Among them are Immunex, Collagen, Genzyme, and Chiron. In many of these cases, the companies' bright prospects have been reflected in rapid stock price gains over time. Amgen stock, for example, has risen more than 20 times from its IPO price of $6.59 per share.

The health care industry is similarly well represented in Nasdaq by innovative and rapidly growing companies. Two of the most successful are St. Jude Medical and Medco Containment Services.

St. Jude Medical is the world leader in mechanical heart valves and has augmented its cardiovascular product development effort by acquiring companies with tissue heart valves, intra-aortic balloon pumps, and centrifugal blood pump systems. St. Jude's sales have grown at a compound rate of 33 percent since 1982 to $175 million in 1990, while its stock has risen at an almost identical 34 percent rate during the same period.

Medco Containment is America's leading provider of prescription drug mail-service programs, which help contain the spiraling cost of employer-funded health plans. This innovative company has traded on Nasdaq for more than six years, during which time it has grown to $1 billion in revenues and enjoyed a 600 percent stock price rise.

These are but a few of the many examples of exciting small companies that have grown at extraordinary rates for an extended period. They offer demonstrable evidence that the long-term growth of sales and earnings produces good long-term investments. Such companies are not easy to uncover at the beginning of their growth spurt, and admittedly many stumble along the way. However, as these examples suggest, attractive opportunities exist and diligent research into America's most fertile and dynamic industries can produce extraordinary investment results.

The Expansion of the Nasdaq Universe

As a result of a surge of entrepreneurial activity, the number of Nasdaq companies expanded rapidly during the past decade. From 2,894 companies in 1980, Nasdaq grew 43 percent to 4,132 companies in 1990. The market capitalization of these companies grew 155 percent, from $122 billion in 1980 to $311 billion in 1990. Similarly, trading volume increased from 6.7 billion shares in 1980 to 33.4 billion in 1990. This fourfold increase in trading volume reflects the growing activity in the Nasdaq market.

At the same time, Nasdaq provided a trading home for the hundreds of companies that took advantage of a robust IPO market during the 1980s to raise capital. During the peak year of 1983, 637 offerings raised in excess of $11 billion in equity. Uncertainty in the stock market and the economy has depressed IPOs since 1987 (see Exhibit 12–1), but the level of new-issue offerings is likely to increase during the 1990s as market conditions permit.

IPO volume is expected to increase in the coming years given the large number of privately held companies that are reaching sufficient size and maturity to be public. Many of these private companies were formed during the venture-capital boom of the mid and late 1980s. From 1983 through 1989, more than $21 billion was committed to private venture capital firms, just one of several sources for private company funding. (See Exhibit 12–2.)

Exhibit 12–1   Nasdaq Initial Public Offerings: 1980–1990

Year	Number of Offerings	Dollar Value of Offerings ($ Billions)
1980	128	$1.08
1981	333	3.01
1982	110	1.15
1983	637	11.21
1984	304	2.77
1985	294	4.00
1986	570	9.65
1987	402	6.11
1988	159	2.13
1989	148	2.16
1990	135	2.38

Exhibit 12–2   Capital Commitments to Independent Private Firms

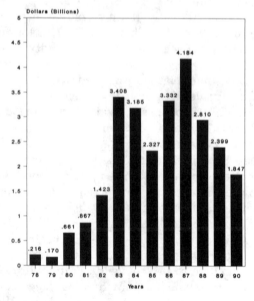

Data Source: *Venture Capital Journal.*

Usually, it takes five to seven years for the average success-ful company to attain profitability and become a candidate for a public offering. A large number of companies founded in the mid 1980s are now reaching that point, and represent an encouraging pipeline of opportunity for new public offerings in the years ahead. Most will surely choose to list on Nasdaq, thus providing ample new raw material for investors in emerging growth stocks.

Opportunities in Growth Stock Investing

Growth stock investing is a well accepted and proven approach for achieving superior investment results. Origi-nally developed by T. Rowe Price Associates in the 1930s, the theory states that superior investment returns can be achieved by owning the stocks of companies that increase their revenues and earnings at a rate faster than inflation and the general economy. A secondary consideration was that this growth would permit above-average increases in the company's dividend. Products, companies, and industries have life cycles, consisting of introduc-tion (or infancy), growth, maturity, and decline. The most oppor-tune time to invest is in the early stages of a company's life cycle.

Growth stock investing can be extremely rewarding if exe-cuted properly and pursued with long-term horizons. Significant rewards accrue to investors who identify companies in the early stages of growth. During this period, the company's earnings will increase faster than will those of the average company. Since stock valuations are generally a function of the level of earnings and dividends, earnings growth typically drives stock prices higher and provides capital gains for the stockholder.

In addition to the potential for superior earnings growth, several other factors favor investors in emerging growth stocks:

- Historical studies of stock market returns by Roger Ibbotson and Rex Sinquefield demonstrate that small-capitalization stocks tend to outperform large-capitaliza-tion stocks by a wide margin over the long run.

- Emerging companies generally receive less attention from Wall Street, thus creating opportunities to be early in identifying such situations.

- Small stocks also tend to have a lower percentage of their outstanding shares in the hands of institutional investors. As a company matures and attracts such investors, it tends to sell at a higher valuation.

- Most emerging growth companies are owned heavily by their managements. These managers think and act like owners, intent on building shareholder value.

The convergence of these factors can make successful emerging growth companies extraordinary investments. The previous examples of Apple Computer, Sun Microsystems, Microsoft, Medco Containment, and St. Jude Medical are instructive. In this respect, prices of these stocks have grown at compound rates from 15 percent to 34 percent over long periods. Most of these gains reflect the growth in earnings of the companies, but increasing visibility among institutional investors also produces premium valuations relative to smaller, less well-known situations. While these examples are not typical of all small companies, they demonstrate the potential that can be realized by successfully applying the growth stock theory of investing to Nasdaq's emerging growth companies.

The Mutual Fund Approach to Investing in Small-Cap Growth Stocks

Individual investors with long time horizons and the willingness to assume above average risk may wish to invest part of their assets in small growth companies. They may not, however, have the time or expertise to identify appropriate investment candidates or the resources to achieve adequate diversification in this sector. These investors often consider the various mutual funds that concentrate on small companies.

Today's investor has a wide range of options because professional investment managers' styles and strategies differ. Some buy and hold their stocks for long periods of time. Others trade the portfolio frequently. One portfolio manager may focus on earnings growth, while another is more sensitive to the price-to-earnings (P/E) multiple of a stock. Portfolios can be diversified across a hundred names, or be highly concentrated. For these reasons, it is essential to study a fund's prospectus and recent shareholder reports to ensure that a particular fund meets one's investment objectives.

The mutual funds listed in Exhibit 12–3 are invested primarily in small-cap stocks and thus have large exposure to Nasdaq. The list is drawn from Lipper Analytical Services data covering funds in the small company growth sector.

Exhibit 12–3   The 25 Largest Small-Company Growth Funds

Fund	Assets ($ Millions)
T. Rowe Price New Horizons Fund	$856
Acorn Fund	770
Fidelity OTC	619
DFA US 9-10 Small Co.	566
Pennsylvania Mutual	548
Keystone S-4	493
Nicholas II	355
Scudder Development	310
Janus Venture	277
Alliance Quaser	263
Vanguard Explorer	238
Over-the-Counter Securities	215
Amer. Cap. Emerging Growth	213
Calvert - Ariel Growth	208
Kemper Summit Fund	206
Putnam OTC Emerging Growth	184
Vanguard Extended Index Fund	179
Mass. Fin'l Emerging Growth	169
IDS Discovery Fund	150
Royce Value Fund	148
USAA Mutual: Aggressive Growth	135
WPG Growth	117
Eclipse: Equity Fund	108
Lord Abbett Development Growth	106
Dreyfus New Leaders	102

Data Source: Lipper Analytical Services, December 1990.

The 1990s Will Be a Period of Opportunity

The performance of emerging growth stocks is a cyclical phenomenon. At T. Rowe Price Associates, we believe that these stocks are poised at the beginning of a new phase of superior performance. The primary underlying reason is low relative valuation. At the end of 1990, the average, 12 months-forward P/E ratio of the T. Rowe Price New Horizons Fund's companies, a broadly based universe of small growth companies, was roughly equivalent to the P/E ratio of the Standard & Poor's 500 stock index. Exhibit 12–4 displays the fund's relative valuation over the last 30 years. Exhibit 12–5 shows that the fund outperformed the market (as represented by the S&P 500) in each of the five-year periods following periods of low relative P/E ratios.

The emerging growth sector of the market has significantly lagged the S&P 500 during the 1980s, much of which can be attributed to the decline in the relative P/E multiple noted above. Several factors contributed to the strong performance of S&P 500 companies.

- The rise of indexing among large institutional investors created artificial demand for stocks comprising the S&P 500 index.

- Increased foreign investment in the U.S. market was directed primarily into the stocks of large and familiar multinational firms rather than smaller, dynamic growth companies.

- The takeover craze of the 1980s diverted attention away from growth stocks and on to likely targets of corporate raiders. More attention was focused on potential leveraged buyouts and corporate breakups of mature companies with underutilized assets than on companies that were generating internal growth through skillful management.

- The increased amount of debt leverage taken on by large corporations resulted in higher earnings for the S&P 500 during the benign economic environment following the 1981–1982 recession. The gap narrowed between large

Exhibit 12–4   T. Rowe Price New Horizons Fund

(P/E Ratio of the Fund's Portfolio Securities Relative to the "S&P 500" P/E Ratio — 12 Months Forward)

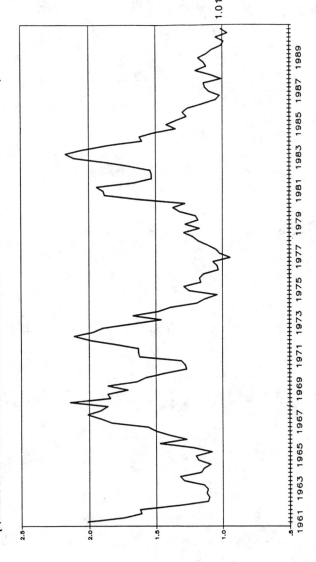

This chart is intended to show the history of the average (unweighted) P/E ratio of the fund's portfolio companies compared with the P/E ratio of the "S&P 500" Index. Earnings per share are estimated by the fund's investment advisor from each quarter's end.

Data Source: T. Rowe Price Associates, Inc.

Exhibit 12-5 New Horizons Fund (NHF) — Performance Following Periods of Low Relative P/E Ratios

Quarter	Relative P/E	1-Year Performance		3-Year Performance		5-Year Performance	
		NHF	S & P 500	NHF	S&P 500	NHF	S&P 500
'62 2Q	1.11	17.2 %	31.2 %	29.2 %	69.2 %	211.0 %	94.8 %
'62 3Q	1.10	12.8	31.7	43.7	75.8	241.8	101.9
'62 4Q	1.12	9.7	22.8	60.6	60.9	255.2	79.3
'63 1Q	1.11	5.0	22.5	64.3	47.1	209.7	58.9
'63 2Q	1.14	1.5	21.5	65.4	34.1	274.5	68.4
'64 2Q	1.14	8.6	6.2	161.4	22.2	261.1	40.2
'64 3Q	1.09	25.6	10.2	198.7	26.6	254.8	29.8
'65 2Q	1.08	50.1	4.0	239.9	30.5	134.9	1.9
'74 3Q	1.13	39.3	38.1	71.8	72.9	178.3	118.1
'74 4Q	1.04	39.6	37.2	74.8	57.9	186.3	99.7
'76 1Q	1.14	-9.9	-0.2	43.5	14.3	187.7	69.9
'76 2Q	1.03	3.4	0.6	53.7	14.6	200.4	62.1
'76 3Q	1.04	8.3	-4.0	75.4	21.0	154.6	42.7
'76 4Q	1.07	12.7	-7.2	84.6	17.4	168.1	47.8
'77 1Q	0.94	23.9	-4.6	79.0	21.6	153.5	48.0
'77 2Q	1.02	33.6	0.2	94.8	33.6	126.7	42.5
'77 3Q	1.05	42.8	12.0	142.3	52.8	147.7	63.4
'77 4Q	1.11	20.8	6.6	158.1	67.5	192.1	93.5
'86 3Q	1.05	29.5	43.4	39.8	67.1	—	—
'86 4Q	1.02	-7.2	5.3	33.5	61.5	—	—
'87 1Q	1.10	-16.3	-8.3	7.4	29.1	—	—
'87 2Q	1.13	-6.5	-6.9	20.5	30.7	—	—

Quarter	Relative P/E	1-Year Performance		3-Year Performance		5-Year Performance	
		NHF	S & P 500	NHF	S&P 500	NHF	S&P 500
'87 3Q	1.14	−15.4	−12.4	−15.3	5.8	—	—
'87 4Q	1.01	14.0	16.6	30.0	48.7	—	—
'88 1Q	1.09	9.2	18.1	—	—	—	—
'88 3Q	1.12	27.6	32.9	—	—	—	—
'88 4Q	1.14	26.2	31.6	—	—	—	—
'89 1Q	1.12	17.5	19.2	—	—	—	—
'89 2Q	1.12	16.8	16.5	—	—	—	—
'89 3Q	1.08	−21.5	−9.2	—	—	—	—
'89 4Q	1.01	−9.6	−3.1	—	—	—	—
No. of Periods NHF Outperformed S & P 500		14 out of 31		14 out of 24		18 out of 18	

companies' normally slower earnings growth rate and that of emerging growth companies, and as a consequence their relative stock prices were affected as well.

Today, many of these factors have recently diminished or even reversed. The trend toward indexing the S&P 500 appears to have peaked. Leveraged buyout volume has fallen to a fraction of its previous high as a result of the collapse of the junk-bond financing market. International investors, particularly Europeans, seem likely to show more interest in small companies if their relative performance improves. Finally, the extra debt leverage taken on by large companies is proving to be a drag on earnings during a period of slow economic growth.

Taken together, these changes have created an extraordinary investment opportunity in small-cap growth stocks. Emerging growth investors participating in this expected surge can buy public companies either directly or through specialized mutual funds at what seem to be attractive prices. In addition, a large new supply of private companies, many venture-capital backed, is coming public and trading on Nasdaq. A combination of attractive growth industries and reasonable stock valuations creates a highly favorable environment for long-term investors. Those seeking such opportunity will naturally look to The Nasdaq Stock Market as the primary source for emerging growth companies.

Chapter Thirteen

Alfred (Pete) Morley currently is senior advisor to the Association for Investment Management and Research (AIMR), the successor organization to the Institute of Chartered Financial Analysts and the Financial Analysts Federation (FAF). He became chairman and chief executive officer of FAF in 1986. He later assumed the same position with the newly formed AIMR. He also has served as chairman and chief executive officer of Wainwright Securities, Inc.

Nasdaq Equities in Investment Portfolios

by Alfred C. Morley
Senior Advisor
Association for Investment Management and Research

Today's investor, both individual and institutional, can choose from a huge array of security issues when developing an investment portfolio. Not too many years ago, investment literature referred only to stocks, bonds, and cash equivalents as generic elements of a portfolio. In the current, much more dynamic environment, those generic elements have been subdivided into a galaxy of specific types of stocks, bonds, and cash equivalents. To this long list has been added a host of other asset classes, including options, futures, and other derivative products; equity real estate; venture capital; oil and gas drilling programs; and on and on.

In a sense, there is increasing competition between and among asset classes and subclasses as investors design portfolios for particular purposes and objectives. However, there also is increasing awareness of how specific asset classes and subclasses can contribute to achievement of those purposes and objectives, fueled by still expanding wealth available for investment from both domestic and international sources.

Nasdaq Equities

Nasdaq issues have been, are, and undoubtedly will continue to be an asset class receiving growing long-term attention from investors for inclusion in their portfolios.

It is estimated that, as of the end of 1990, the market capitalization of all U.S. common stocks totaled close to $3.4 trillion. Of this amount, 137 stocks (each with a market capitalization above $5 billion) accounted for about 54 percent, 429 (each with capitalization between $1 billion and $5 billion) added more than 28 percent, and somewhat over 5,800 other issues comprised the remainder of less than $1 trillion. The spread of all issues by market capitalization size is shown in Exhibit 13–1.

The perception in some quarters is that "Nasdaq" is synonymous with "small cap stocks." The fact is that the market capitalization of Nasdaq issues ranges over the entire spectrum depicted in Exhibit 13–1, with representation in each of the five size categories shown. As of year-end 1990, for instance, the Nasdaq National Market (Nasdaq/NMS) had 2,390 domestic common stocks with an aggregate market capitalization of $287.5 billion, representing 37.5 percent and 8.5 percent, respectively, of the totals recorded in Exhibit 13–1. While heaviest representation of Nasdaq issues is in the market-capitalization size of $500 million and less, many of these companies have above-average growth characteristics. Also, among Nasdaq issues with market capitalization in excess of $500 million are some of the most successful companies in the United States, including MCI Communications, Intel, Microsoft, Apple Computer, and Nordstrom.

Another perception in some quarters is that "Nasdaq" is synonymous with "high tech" stocks. The fact is that issues on Nasdaq cover a complete range of industry groups participating in every major segment of the U.S. economy. This clearly is indicated in Exhibit 13–2.

Exhibit 13–1   Domestic Equity Market Capitalization — As of December 31, 1990

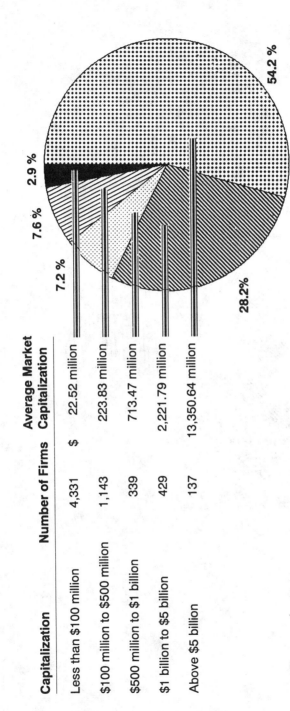

Capitalization	Number of Firms	Average Market Capitalization
Less than $100 million	4,331	$ 22.52 million
$100 million to $500 million	1,143	223.83 million
$500 million to $1 billion	339	713.47 million
$1 billion to $5 billion	429	2,221.79 million
Above $5 billion	137	13,350.64 million

Total Domestic Equity Market Capitalization $3,377 billion

Data Source: Media General Financial Services & National Association of Securities Dealers.

Exhibit 13–2   Distribution of Nasdaq Companies by Industry Group — As of December 31, 1990

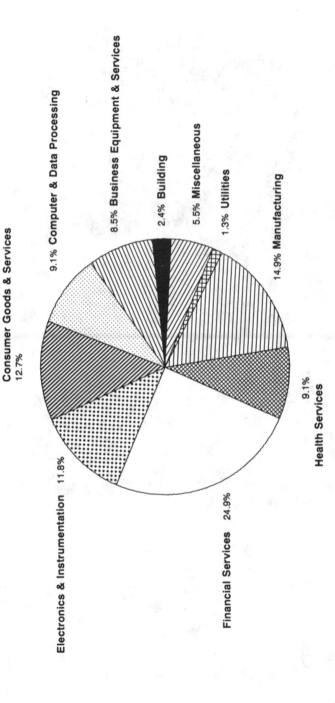

Consumer Goods & Services
12.7%

9.1% Computer & Data Processing

8.5% Business Equipment & Services

2.4% Building

5.5% Miscellaneous

1.3% Utilities

14.9% Manufacturing

9.1%

Health Services

Financial Services   24.9%

Electronics & Instrumentation   11.8%

Data Source: Institutional Brokers Estimate System & Media General Financial Services.

Also noteworthy is that The Nasdaq Stock Market offers investor access to the international economy through its listings of almost 300 foreign securities, including nearly 90 American Depositary Receipts (ADRs), far more than on either the New York or American stock exchanges.

Nasdaq is a large and diverse market that should be considered by investors in constructing investment portfolios to meet almost any purpose and objective.

The Portfolio Management Process

An investment portfolio is the vehicle by which investors, both personal and institutional, aggregate their wealth in the form of securities. Construction and management of an investment portfolio is a dynamic process essentially involving the following steps:

1. An investor's objectives, preferences, and constraints are identified and specified to develop explicit investment policies.

2. Strategies are developed and implemented through the choice of optimal combinations of financial and perhaps other assets in the marketplace.

3. Market conditions, relative asset values, and the investor's circumstances are monitored.

4. Portfolio adjustments are made as appropriate to reflect significant change in any or all of the relevant variables listed previously.

Among investor objectives, preferences, and constraints to be evaluated are current income desires; the required rate of growth in principal relative to portfolio objective, inflation, and other benchmarks; degree of risk aversion; liquidity needs; time horizon (i.e., the likely life of the portfolio); and tax and regulatory considerations, including the Employee Retirement Income Security Act. Obviously, such portfolio characteristics will vary widely among the multitude of different types of investors, ranging from a very conservative stance for, say, an elderly widow having no direct heirs, to a much more aggressive approach for, among others, a young couple with a long time horizon and willingness to assume greater risk for potentially greater rewards.

Once the framework of the portfolio is designed, the next step is to select classes and subclasses of securities meeting the determined needs of the portfolio. Broad classifications available include common stocks, corporate and government bonds, money-market instruments, equity participation in real estate, options, and other derivative securities, venture capital commitments, etc. Within each of these classifications is an almost endless array of more specific selections. For example, in the common-stock segment of the portfolio, one can consider such factors as small capitalization versus large capitalization, low versus high price-to-earnings ratios, domestic versus foreign, growth versus defensive, and, of course, any combination of these and many other specific categories.

Asset allocation — that is the selection of security classes and subclasses — is the most important process in constructing a portfolio. It is asset allocation, not individual security selection, which largely will determine the performance of a portfolio relative to objectives.

Both security market and investor conditions change with time, and these changes must be reflected in appropriate modifications of portfolio content on an ongoing basis. This dynamic process can be as loose or as disciplined, as quantitative or as judgmental, and as simple or as complex as the portfolio manager wishes it to be, but always within the investor's stated objectives, preferences, and constraints.

All financial securities, and thus a portfolio of securities, inherently are risky assets and are subject to two basic forms of risk. Systematic risk results from the impact of changes in macro variables. For example, if the economy performs well and/or the political environment is favorable, investment returns usually are positive, and vice versa. The portfolio manager can do little to control systematic risk unless moving from a fully invested to a total cash position and reversing the procedure exactly in line with macro cycles. Evidence strongly suggests that few, if any, portfolio managers have this capability with consistency. However, appropriate asset allocation often minimizes the influence of systematic risk.

Unsystematic, or unique, risk is that directly associated with an individual security and is influenced by, among other factors, changes in company earning power, competitive position, balance-sheet strength, and management effectiveness. The combination of diversification within individual asset classes and the overall asset-allocation process are tools used to reduce the impact of unsystematic risk.

Obviously an overly extensive level of diversification could result in a large group of stocks more or less performing in line with the market average. On the other hand, very limited diversification likely will not do much to minimize unsystematic risk. Various studies indicate 10 to 25 individual securities spread across several industries might be the optimal level of diversification to control of unsystematic risk. However, depending on portfolio size, many portfolio managers typically have a greater number of individual holdings.

Performance Provides Insight

Past performance is not necessarily an indication of possible future returns. Nevertheless, historical data are useful in analyzing returns during various stages of business and market cycles. Assuming continuation of a well-functioning capitalistic economy, historical data provide insight to potential during similar cyclical stages in coming years. First, one can look at returns for major asset classes during an extended period of time.

As used in Exhibit 13–3, common stocks are defined as the S&P 500 index, and small company stocks represent the fifth capitalization quintile (as measured by market capitalization, those stocks ranked in the bottom 20 percent of all issues) of stocks on the New York Stock Exchange for 1926 to 1981 and, thereafter, the performance of the Dimensional Fund Advisors Small Company Fund (a market-value-weighted index of small stocks as defined above, plus certain American Stock Exchange and Nasdaq-listed low-capitalization issues). The Nasdaq Composite Index is not included in the exhibit (but is referred to in subsequent tabulations) because it was not started until 1971.

Exhibit 13–3   Annual Returns — 1926–1990

	Geometric Mean	Arithmetic Mean	Standard Deviation
Common Stocks	10.1%	12.1%	20.8%
Small-Company Stocks	11.6	17.1	35.4
Long-Term Corporate Bonds	5.2	5.5	8.4
Long-Term Government Bonds	4.4	4.9	8.5
Intermediate-Term Government Bonds	5.0	5.1	5.5
U. S. Treasury Bills	3.7	3.7	3.4
Inflation	3.1	3.2	4.7

Data Source: *Stocks, Bonds, Bills, and Inflation Yearbook,* Ibbotson Associates, Chicago (annually updates work by Roger G. Ibbotson and Rex A. Sinquefield). All rights reserved.

Based on the historical rates of return of the asset classes provided in Exhibit 13–3, the small-company-stock category performed best. But with that reward came a substantial level of risk as measured by standard deviation. However, merely as an example, had the equity portion of a given portfolio been composed of 75 percent common stocks and 25 percent small-company stocks for the 1926 to 1990 period, the average annual compound return would have approximated 13 percent with a standard deviation of 24 percent. In other words, prudent diversification into small-company stocks added measurably to return at a reasonably tolerable higher level of risk, versus a 100 percent S&P 500 equity portfolio.

As indicated in Exhibit 13–4, average annual returns for the various asset classes have fluctuated considerably, both on an absolute basis and relative to each other, during specific past time periods.

As noted in Exhibit 13–4, performance of small-company stocks and the Nasdaq Composite Index in recent years has been less favorable than previously and has fallen below that of com-

Exhibit 13–4   Compound Annual Returns for Five-Year Holding Periods

Holding Period	Common Stocks	Nasdaq Composite Index	Small-Company Stocks	Long Govt. Bonds	Interm. Govt. Bonds	Treasury Bills	Inflation
1976-80	14.0 %	21.1 %	37.4 %	1.7 %	5.1 %	7.8 %	9.2 %
1977-81	8.1	14.9	28.9	(1.1)	4.4	9.7	10.1
1978-82	14.1	17.2	29.3	6.0	9.6	10.8	9.5
1979-83	17.3	18.8	32.5	6.4	10.4	11.1	8.4
1980-84	14.8	10.4	21.6	9.8	12.4	11.0	6.5
1981-85	14.7	9.9	18.8	16.8	15.8	10.3	4.9
1982-86	20.0	12.2	17.3	21.6	17.0	8.6	3.3
1983-87	16.5	7.3	9.5	13.0	11.8	7.6	3.4
1984-88	15.4	6.5	6.7	15.0	11.5	7.1	3.5
1985-89	20.4	13.0	10.3	15.5	11.4	6.8	3.7
1986-1st quar. 1991	15.4	7.8	5.5	10.6	9.2	6.8	4.1

Data Sources: The Nasdaq Stock Market; *Stocks, Bonds, Bills, and Inflation Yearbook,*™ Ibbotson Associates, Chicago (annually updates work by Roger G. Ibbotson and Rex A. Sinquefield).

mon stocks in general, a trend that continued in 1990 but reversed in the first quarter of 1991. The only other recent five-year period when such returns fell below the S&P 500 average occurred in the early 1970s. During recent 10-year and 20-year holding periods, Nasdaq Composite and small-company-stock performance consistently exceeded that of stocks in general, and thus portfolios with long time horizons and ability to tolerate above-average risk would have benefited measurably from the inclusion of a component of Nasdaq and small-company stocks.

The Nasdaq Composite Index recovered sharply in the first quarter of 1991, both on an absolute basis and relative to the S&P 500. Will this more favorable trend in returns continue in the future? An unqualified response to this question would not be prudent. However, whether measured in an absolute sense or relative to the overall market, such ratios as price-earnings multiple, price-to-book, and price-to-expected growth rate for Nasdaq issues currently do not seem high when compared with experience of recent years. This is illustrated by data contained in Exhibit 13–5.

Exhibit 13–5 shows that, from 1985 through 1990, generally above-average growth was recorded in total assets, shareholder equity, revenues, and net income, although the year-to-year rate varied. For a number of external and corporate reasons, 1986 to 1987 proved a rather difficult period. Also noteworthy is that, in most recent years, the return on equity and the return on sales compare favorably with those of preceding years, while for 1990 the P/E and the price-to-book ratios were below peaks of other periods.

Any asset class or subclass has times of overvaluation and undervaluation. Based on the data in Exhibit 13–5 it appears that Nasdaq stocks are undervalued relative to the past and relative to some other classes of common stocks even after considering price recovery in the first quarter of 1991. As such, they possibly are strong candidates for inclusion in a portfolio with objectives, including a long time horizon, acceptable to this class of asset.

Exhibit 13–5   Profile of Typical Nasdaq-100® Company[a]
(Dollar Amounts in Millions)

	1985	1986	1987	1988	1989	1990
Nasdaq-100 Index Profile	265	283	313	355	448	401
Total Assets	$650	$589	$719	$875	$1,115	$1,020
Shareholder Equity[b]	291	308	318	334	396	419
Revenues	750	685	778	932	1,030	1,154
Net Income	32	23	19	42	44	59
Market Value[b]	637	721	777	881	1,164	1,088
P/E Ratio[c]	19.9	31.4	41.8	21.0	26.4	18.5
Return on Equity[d]	11%	8%	6%	13%	11%	14%
Return on Sales[e]	4%	3%	2%	5%	4%	5%
Price-to-Book Ratio[f]	2.2	2.3	2.4	2.6	2.9	2.6

---

[a] The Nasdaq-100 accounts for approximately one-third of total Nasdaq/NMS market value.
[b] At year's end.
[c] Market value divided by net income.
[d] Net income divided by shareholder equity.
[e] Net income divided by sales.
[f] Market value divided by shareholder equity.

Data Source: Nasdaq Fact Books.

Portfolio Trading Costs

Assume that ABC Company, a Nasdaq-listed stock, is being considered for inclusion in the equity segment of a given portfolio because the issue meets the investor's objectives, preferences, and constraints. Before it is purchased, the stock's acquisition cost and liquidity must be considered. In this context, acquisition cost and liquidity pertain to the Nasdaq stock's marketability, a key factor in considering stocks of all types and sizes for inclusion in a given portfolio.

For the most part, liquidity is not a problem in selecting Nasdaq issues for inclusion in the equity segment of a given portfolio. Approximately 4,000 individual securities are in The Nasdaq Stock Market. Each has an average public float of around 7 million shares, a market capitalization of about $78 million, and 10 market makers. These are arithmetic averages that are heavily influenced by the inclusion of a substantial number of companies with comparatively small floats and capitalizations.

More indicative of marketability of Nasdaq issues is that about one third of Nasdaq market value is concentrated in the Nasdaq-100 group, the 100 largest issues that include such well-known and accepted names as Apple Computer, Intel, MCI Communications, and Nordstrom. Each of these companies has an average public float of in excess of 36 million shares, a market capitalization over the $1 billion level, 26 market makers, and an annual trading volume of about 73 million shares, of which close to 50 percent is of block size.

Portfolio Composition

The typical life cycle of a company begins with early development, which is characterized by relatively rapid revenue growth but usually with negative profit margins until sales reach a critical mass. Next is a phase of rapid expansion, when revenue increases continue to be strong and are accompanied by considerable profit-margin improvement, thus resulting in significant gains in earnings. This is followed by a period of mature growth, typically a timeframe of a declining rate of sales growth and general leveling of profit margins. Finally, the company enters a phase of stabilization or decline during which, under a worst-case scenario, it might experience drops in both sales and margins.

A host of corporations in the stages of early development and rapid expansion list their securities on Nasdaq, thus providing portfolio owners with opportunities for participation in economic gains that could well exceed the average. In taking such an approach, the investor must exercise patience because corporate success in reaching a particular objective often takes longer than

expected; be willing to assume a fairly high degree of risk because the rate of progress may not always be at a high rate and
may be disappointing at times; and have a reasonable level of
diversification within this segment of the portfolio to guard
against possible severe disappointments or even failure.

Inherent in all of this is one of the basic principles of portfolio management — portfolio adjustments should be made to reflect a significant change in an investor's objectives, preferences,
and constraints, as well as changes in market conditions and relative asset values.

Portfolio Implementation

Inclusion of Nasdaq stocks, and any other security
issue, is dependent on portfolio objectives, preferences, and constraints. Once these parameters have been determined, individual
securities can be selected. For large institutional accounts, in-
house management and/or outside investment advisors may
identify those specific issues that meet portfolio parameters. Another approach is to evaluate mutual funds and commingled accounts specializing in investing in such stocks. This approach,
particularly applicable to Nasdaq stocks and to small-capitalization stocks in general, is used by both institutional and individual
investors.

A recent study conducted by Cambridge Associates identified no fewer than 98 money management organizations in the
United States offering mutual funds, commingled accounts,
and/or separate accounts emphasizing small-company stocks.
This universe was divided as follows: 56 with a "growth" management style, 27 using a "value" approach, 9 classifying themselves as "opportunistic," and 6 offering a "diverse" fund. Many
of these organizations, and others, manage publicly traded mutual funds, thus providing easy access by individual and institutional investors alike to include Nasdaq or small-company stocks
in their portfolios.

PART IV

Market Making:
Where Competition and
Technology Meet

Chapter Fourteen

John L. Watson, III. Since 1985, John L. Watson, III, has been president of the Security Traders Association, an international organization representing 7,000 members. Previously, Mr. Watson was with Robinson-Humphrey/American Express in Atlanta, Georgia for 28 years. He served as executive vice president and director of capital markets and was a member of the board of directors and the executive committee.

Market Makers: The Hallmark of the Nasdaq Market

by John L. Watson, III
President
Security Traders Association

Market makers or traders perform a unique role within the securities industry.

Successful market makers possess the innate ability to make rapid-fire decisions in an extremely fast-paced environment. They decide if they should buy or sell hundreds of thousands of dollars worth of securities in seconds. They are confronted with similar decisions time and time again throughout the market hours.

The ingredients for being a good market maker include a quick mind, nerves that can stretch but not break, an ability to size up a situation by weighing untold numbers of facts, a calmness and sureness under fire, and an intellect attuned to those needs.

SEC Regulates Market Makers

Market making is a separate, regulated segment of the securities industry, and its participants are held to specifically high standards of conduct.

The Securities Exchange Act of 1934 defines a market maker as "any specialist permitted to act as a dealer, any dealer acting in the capacity of a block position, and any dealer who, with respect to a security, holds himself out (by entering quotations in an inter-dealer communications systems or otherwise) as being willing to buy and sell such security for his own account on a regular or continuous basis."

The SEC has expanded this definition to include: "a dealer who, with respect to a particular security, (i) regularly publishes bona fide, competitive bid and offer quotations in a recognized inter-dealer quotation system; or (ii) furnishes bona fide competitive bid and offer quotations on request; and (iii) is ready, willing, and able to effect transactions in reasonable quantities at his quoted prices with other brokers and dealers."

Thus, firms making markets in Nasdaq securities are expected to stand behind their quotations and execute transactions at published prices. In addition, the SEC's rules also contain special capital requirements for market makers.

These special criteria assure continued "fair competition among brokers and dealers, among exchange markets, and markets other than exchange markets."

NASD Registration

Nasdaq market makers must also adhere to certain NASD rules and regulations.

Any broker-dealer seeking to act as a market maker must first register with the NASD. Registration must also be granted separately for each security for which the market maker desires to make markets. If the security is a designated Nasdaq National Market System (Nasdaq/NMS) security, the market maker must also be registered in that security on the NASD's Small Order Execution System (SOES).

In addition to these fundamentals, NASD rules impose parameters on the manner in which a market maker must perform its functions. These requirements ensure the integrity of the market and provide for liquidity. This is accomplished in several ways.

First, for each security in which a market maker is registered, it must be willing to buy and sell that security for its own account on a continuous basis and must enter and maintain two-sided quotations for it. If the market maker is registered in SOES, it must display the size for each quotation within NASD-specified limits. That is, the market maker must indicate the number of shares of a particular security that it is willing to buy and sell at the price it displays on the Nasdaq screen. This amount must not be less than the maximum amount eligible for execution on SOES as determined from time to time by the NASD.

The NASD requires a market maker to stand behind its quotations by honoring an order received for at least a normal trading unit. For example, if the normal trading unit for a particular security is determined to be 1,000 shares, then the market maker must be ready, willing, and able to execute a buy and sell order for at least 1,000 shares at its quoted price.

Market makers are expected to assure that their quotations are reasonably related to the prevailing market and to keep them current and in line with the prevailing market. Finally, market makers are prohibited from entering quotations into the system that exceed maximum allowable spreads between the bid and asked prices as determined and published by the NASD from time to time.

The NASD also has set limits on market-maker activity in "locked" and "crossed" markets. A "locked" market occurs when a bid quotation is equal to the asked quotation of another market maker. A "crossed" market occurs when the asked quotation is less than the bid quotation of another market maker. A market maker is charged with assuring that it does not lock or cross a market. If it does do so, it is obligated to execute transactions at its quotations as displayed at the time of the receipt of the order, even if the transaction results in a loss to the market maker.

1987 Crash Brings Changes

Prior to October 1987, market makers that were registered in a particular security could withdraw from making a market in that security and suffer only the slight inconvenience of not being able to quote that security for two days. Following the market crash in October 1987, the NASD, on the recommendation of the market makers themselves, directed that any unexcused withdrawal from Nasdaq for a security would bar the market maker from re-entering the system for that security for 20 business days. This prerequisite made withdrawal a matter of considerable substance and enforced the NASD's high standards for market makers' continuous performance.

Another enhancement of the system to result from the 1987 crash was the decision to make the use of SOES mandatory for market makers in Nasdaq/NMS stocks. Under this rule, a market maker is required to operate in SOES and stand ready to have its quotations acted on to the full extent of its obligations as set from time to time by the NASD.

Path to Modern Market Making

The modern market making inherent in these requirements has deep if somewhat diverse roots. Market making is as old as commerce itself. Whenever a group of traders dealing in the same merchandise come together in the same marketplace, there's a give and take to offer the consumer the best price. The more traders you have offering the same product — be it fur pelts or a biotechnology stock — the more competitive the pricing of a product.

In the pre-Nasdaq over-the-counter (OTC) market of the 1930s and 1940s, broker-dealers buying and selling OTC securities faced no restrictions other than general fraud concepts. Trading transactions were handled by telephone between the buying and selling broker-dealers. They were linked only through a daily publication that listed the previous day's prices at which interested broker-dealers (identified by name and phone number) were willing to buy and sell 100 shares of particular securities.

Actual transactions in the OTC market were cumbersome then. An investment firm interested in effecting a trade for a customer was required to call at least three other broker-dealers to ascertain a sense of the market and then to negotiate the actual transaction.

Although this fulfilled a dealer's obligation to test the market, the likelihood that the calls would be made only locally meant that there was always the risk the customer may not have received the best available price nationwide for the security. Moreover, the customer or his or her broker-dealer had no way of knowing whether other transactions had taken place at the same or different prices.

There also were no special requirements for a broker-dealer to become a market maker. So long as it was duly registered with the SEC and observed the general capital requirements, the securities firm was able to enter quotations and make markets.

After World War II, an influx of unsophisticated first-time investors came into the financial markets. All the markets expanded tremendously, securities firms grew, and new ones were formed. As the number of customers and the resulting trading volume soared, the trading community soon realized that the nature of the fast-expanding marketplace was outpacing the mechanics of trading.

To modernize the system, the industry looked toward automation and the computer. Realizing the dramatic need to alleviate the crunch of business and assure the competitiveness of the marketplace, the NASD in 1971 introduced Nasdaq, a new method of trading securities that was to transform the entire securities industry forever. Nasdaq enabled any NASD member to display on a computer screen all up-to-the minute bid and ask quotations for any Nasdaq security.

It was not long before Congress and the SEC saw the effect of Nasdaq and the electronic age on U.S. securities markets. The result was the Securities Acts Amendments of 1975, which mandated the development of a national market system providing, among other things, "fair competition among brokers and dealers." Since that time, the NASD has been extraordinarily successful in working with the SEC to build and enhance The Nasdaq Stock Market to reflect the sophistication demanded by the statute.

World Recognizes Electronic Trading

The electronic trading market as epitomized by Nasdaq market makers is recognized worldwide as the system of the future. Today, The Nasdaq Stock Market represents an enlightened era in the securities industry. Investors can have the confidence that their transactions on Nasdaq are receiving the best execution through market makers that are financially responsible and that are required to adhere to high standards of professional accountability.

Small firms can compete on an equal footing with larger broker-dealers no matter where they are located, whether they be regional or national, and whether they are full-service or limit their operations to defined areas, such as bank stocks or other special situations.

The NASD supervises both The Nasdaq Stock Market and the market makers in it to ensure business is conducted under the best possible circumstances. Specifically, among other things, the NASD seeks to assure that trading is conducted on the standard of a level playing field. It has the authority to halt trading in any security in the event of any impending material news to be announced by the issuer. This assures that everyone has the same information on which to base investment decisions.

Competitive Environment

One of the more beneficial aspects of the market-maker system is its competitive environment. Each market maker is in competition with the other market makers. In some instances, more than 40 market makers compete in making markets in a stock. (See Exhibit 14–1.)

This continuous rivalry ensures that the markets for the Nasdaq stocks are always the best they can be. On an exchange, only one specialist is responsible for the maintenance of a market. It is his decision alone that defines the market for a stock on the exchange and, if he is wrong, then the market and investors suffer the consequences. The Nasdaq market maker's commitment to open and continuous markets is virtually absolute. If it is regis-

---

Exhibit 14–1   Average Number of Market Makers of Nasdaq National Market Companies by Industry Group

December 31, 1990

Industry Group	Market Value of Common Stock (Millions)				
	$1-49	$50-249	$250-999	$1,000+	Total
Overall	8.5	13.4	18.8	28.6	11.0
Building	7.7	13.4	14.2	12.5	10.1
Business Equipment and Services	9.3	14.7	17.7	NA	11.5
Computers and Data Processing	11.0	18.8	29.1	44.7	16.1
Consumer Goods and Services	9.4	15.2	17.6	33.8	12.3
Electronics and Instrumentation	9.5	15.4	22.5	40.2	12.2
Financial Services	6.5	10.2	14.6	22.4	8.1
Health Services	11.0	16.2	22.3	29.3	14.3
Manufacturing	9.0	12.1	15.8	19.3	10.4
Utilities	5.6	9.3	14.0	NA	8.2
Miscellaneous	7.6	10.7	17.5	17.3	10.0

Data Source: Media General Financial Services.

---

tered in a particular security, it is expected to trade that security throughout the day. The Nasdaq market maker cannot delay openings as an exchange specialist is able to do.

Six Groups of Firms

In broad terms, market-making firms can be divided into six groups:

1. **Exceptionally large firms,** many times spoken of as "wire houses," have hundreds of offices and thousands

of salesmen and usually are well capitalized. They generally make markets in anywhere from 500 to 2,500 securities and have very large trading departments.

2. **Wholesale firms** are a group of specialty firms head-
    quartered in New York's metropolitan area that do the
    majority of their trading with other firms and institu-
    tions. They trade 1,000 to 5,000 securities, with some con-
    centrating on smaller inactive stocks, some on new
    issues, and others on the large volume stocks.

3. **Regional firms** generally limit their activities to a certain
    area of the country for retail sales, research, and under-
    writing. They trade 100 to 400 securities, usually of local
    companies.

4. **Investment banking firms**, most of which are in New
    York City, are heavily weighted toward trading in the
    large stocks or the "blue chips" of Nasdaq. Much of their
    business is with institutions, and their trading is in secu-
    rities for which they were bankers.

5. **Local firms** are the smallest category. These trading de-
    partments may have only one or two traders that special-
    ize in 10 to 50 securities.

6. **Other firms** that deal with only institutional clients, bou-
    tiques, and those that would in some way fall into areas
    between the major categories. Clearly, firms do come in
    all shapes and sizes.

Together, these firms make for an extremely competitive
market in Nasdaq securities. At the end of 1990, only 380 of the
4,706 securities in Nasdaq had fewer than three market makers,
and 136 securities had 26 or more. Those 136 securities accounted
for the vast majority of the market value in Nasdaq as of December 31, 1990. (See Exhibit 14–2.)

Capital Commitment

Capital committed to market making is another
important ingredient in the effectiveness of the process. The over-

Exhibit 14–2   Market Value Distribution* According to Number of Market Makers

	Nasdaq/NMS		Total Nasdaq	
Market Makers	Number of Issues	Average Market Value (000s)	Number of Issues	Average Market Value (000s)
Less than 3	106	$ 19,356	380	$ 9,599
3-5	546	36,967	1,223	19,709
6-10	790	51,502	1,467	31,273
11-15	572	103,059	913	68,150
16-20	304	145,647	427	114,802
21-25	134	296,551	160	252,291
26 or more	119	800,622	136	716,173

* Data are as of December 31, 1990.

all capital of a firm is not necessarily the prime measure of the strength of a market-making firm. Rather, the amount of capital allocated per security would give a better indication of the depth or strength of the market. The amount of capital committed to a department for market making can range from thousands of dollars to millions of dollars.

Firms have not generally found a lack of capital to be a concern recently. The strong trading markets of the 1980s have added funds to their coffers, as did the raising of capital by the underwriting departments of the firms during the same time. Many firms also sold their own stock to the public during this time, thereby increasing their capital.

A regional firm can be as effective as a much larger firm, even if it has less overall capital, if it limits available capital to a smaller number of local securities. Such a firm would not always be able to compete in trading a large number of securities or may not be able to commit to a very large block of stock, but it may be very effective in the distribution of a stock it knows well.

Broad Spectrum of Firms

Market-making firms come in all varieties. They are local, regional, and national, and they are located in all parts of the United States and abroad. As of the end of 1990, market-making firms were registered with the NASD and located in 38 states, the District of Columbia, and the United Kingdom. The number of securities in which market makers were making markets grew from 2,969 in 1971 to 4,706 in 1990; in 1987 this number had reached a high of 5,537 (see Exhibit 14–3). The number of active market makers as of December 31, 1990, was 421, up from a low of 365 in 1976. Moreover, the number of market-making positions in 1990 was 44,243, compared with a low of 12,715 in 1974. The high of 49,670 was hit in 1989.

The capital commitment of all the market-making firms in Nasdaq at the end of 1990 was about $1 billion, and the market value of the securities that the market makers were trading on Nasdaq/NMS and Nasdaq was $322.7 billion.

Exhibit 14-3   Nasdaq Securities and Market Makers: 1980-1990

Year	Number of Securities	Active Market Makers	Market-Making Positions	Average Market Makers Per Security
1990	4,706	421	44,243	9.4
1989	4,963	458	49,670	10.0
1988	5,144	570	48,370	9.4
1987	5,537	545	41,397	7.5
1986	5,189	526	41,312	8.0
1985	4,784	500	40,093	8.4
1984	4,728	473	38,820	8.2
1983	4,467	441	32,923	7.4
1982	3,664	407	27,734	7.6
1981	3,687	420	26,935	7.4
1980	3,050	394	22,360	7.3

Benefits of Competition

Competition among market makers in Nasdaq is strong. The average stock on Nasdaq has almost 10 market makers, and very active stocks have several times as many competing for order flow. Furthermore, each market maker's price quotations can be retrieved on the 2,600 Nasdaq Workstation terminals located in member firms across the U.S. and in the United Kingdom, as well as on 400 similar terminals used by financial institutions to monitor their portfolios of Nasdaq securities.

The Nasdaq Workstation screen displays the "inside quote," the most favorable price available to investors — the highest bid (price at which a market maker is willing to buy a particular stock) and the lowest ask (price at which a market maker will sell a stock). A sampling on four days in September 1990 found that about half of the average number of market makers in Nasdaq National Market securities were at the inside quote and that 11 market makers were at the inside in the most actively traded stocks. (See Exhibit 14–4.)

The Nasdaq computer system and market data vendor organizations transmit these inside quotes to 200,000 terminals of securities professionals and investors worldwide.

That means when a customer wishes to buy or sell a Nasdaq security, his or her brokerage firm will direct the order to a mar-

---

Exhibit 14–4   Average Number of Market Makers at Inside Market in Nasdaq National Market Stocks December 1990 (4 Sample Days)

Average Daily Share Volume	Number of Stocks	Average Number of Market Makers at Inside	Average Number of Market Makers
10,000 or less	1,219	4.6	7.0
10,001 to 50,000	712	6.0	12.6
50,001 to 200,000	355	8.3	19.8
200,001 or more	83	11.2	30.6
All	2,431	5.8	11.4

ket maker with the best price available at the time the order is entered, as required by the best-execution rule.

Moreover, at least one-quarter of the trading volume in Nasdaq stocks is executed at prices more favorable to customers than are the best bid or ask prices displayed on the Nasdaq screen. These prices result from negotiation between market participants competing for the order.

Major Industry Force

The past 20 years dramatically illustrate that the Nasdaq market maker has become a major force in the securities industry. The electronic, negotiated market has made its place in world equity trading and will continue to meet the challenges of the future.

Chapter
Fifteen

Bernard L. Madoff founded Bernard L. Madoff Investment Securities in 1960 and its London affiliate in the early 1980s. He has served as chairman of the board of the National Securities Clearing Corporation and on the NASD Board of Governors. He is currently chairman of the board of directors of Nasdaq, Inc., an NASD subsidiary, and is a member of the strategic planning committee.

Screen-Based Trading and the Globalization of Markets

by Bernard L. Madoff
Principal
Bernard L. Madoff Investment Securities

Most markets, like most products, develop in response to a particular need. Typically, they are shaped by the technology available at the time they are launched. The concept of an exchange floor grew out of the need to bring buyers and sellers together in an era before the invention of telephones.

The traditional exchange uses a specialist system, which normally gives a single specialist an exclusive franchise to make a market in a particular security. The basic function of a specialist is to maintain an orderly market while allowing public agency orders to interact with each other. His or her compensation is based on the commissions paid by the broker executing these agency orders. This all takes place in a single location called a "floor," where orders are routed for execution in a "crowd" environment.

The Nasdaq market, on the other hand, employs a system of multiple market makers that are linked together via a screen-based trading system. As many as 50 market makers openly compete with one another in many actively traded securities. Market-maker compensation is derived from successful spread and position trading, as well as commissions when acting as agent on behalf of clients.

A market-making firm's main responsibility is to service its clients. It is a misconception that, because market makers are often trading for their proprietary account, they are competing with public orders. The great majority of market makers' trading is done to facilitate public orders. Even when a market maker is trading for its own account, it is usually to provide immediate liquidity to a customer-related transaction.

Market-maker and specialist systems are driven primarily by orders, whether those orders are sent to exchanges or market makers. The most important difference between the two markets is the multiple market-maker competition in Nasdaq versus the single specialist system of an exchange.

Nasdaq was developed to add visibility to a marketplace that previously had none. The development of computers made it possible to broadcast the quotations of market makers that were geographically dispersed across the nation onto Nasdaq screens. Not only could brokers and investors view the quotations of competing market makers with a few keystrokes, those same market makers could see their competitors' markets and tighten their own quotes to attract business.

Nasdaq has the flexibility to meet almost everyone's needs. The ability of Nasdaq's screen-based, competitive dealer system to interface with other domestic and world securities markets has proven to be the most efficient and cost-effective marketplace in the world.

While an exchange is limited to the confines of its floor, Nasdaq literally knows no boundaries. It is mainly for that reason that Nasdaq has been chosen as the model for most European and Asian securities markets trying to define and develop new marketplaces or upgrade and change existing ones.

Significant Steps Toward a More Global Market

Governments worldwide appear to be serious about creating a more global market. In the U.S., the combination of SEC Rule 144A and Regulation S is giving greater liquidity and openness to the private placement market. As a result of the Free Trade Treaty approved by the U.S. and Canadian governments, a tremendous barrier-breaking trade agreement, U.S. securities firms can do business in Canada much more easily. The development of the "single passport" system in Europe in 1992 will go a long way toward breaking down many trade barriers and creating both a need for capital and a scrambling to provide financial services to this vast economic entity.

A major force in globalization has been the growth in screen-based trading systems. In 1971, Nasdaq's electronic, screen-based system demonstrated that it was technologically feasible to lift trading away from the physical confines of the exchange floor. Once the technological barrier was broken, screen-based systems multiplied.

The London Stock Exchange (LSE) switched to screen-based trading in 1986. But even before that so-called "Big Bang," London introduced a screen-based system called SEAQ, which linked with Nasdaq in April 1986. The Stock Exchange of Singapore also has modeled an automated system after Nasdaq. The Singaporean system is called SESDAQ. In Japan, Nasdaq's system has served as the prototype for a new automated information network now being built for the exciting Japanese over-the-counter market. To be called JASDAQ, it is scheduled to come on line late in 1991.

These systems are dealer-quote driven. There are also many order-driven screen-based markets. Toronto's CATS system is the prototype of the latter category. CATS stands for Computer Assisted Trading System. CATS technology has gained considerable acceptance in Europe. Paris, Brussels, and Madrid are other examples of CATS screen-based technology.

We are now beginning to see a new development. Markets have begun to take the most advantageous features of dealer quote-driven systems and order-driven systems and meld them together into a hybrid screen-based system. As the merging of systems continues to occur, the ability to link markets, regardless of whether they are quote driven or order driven, will increase.

Global integration is proliferating. Nasdaq has implemented a linkage with the LSE, which shows quotations for about 300 Nasdaq securities, and the NASD quotes a similar number of LSE securities.

A trans-Pacific link between Nasdaq and SESDAQ, the automated quotations system of the Singapore Stock Exchange, became fully operational in March 1988, with a daily exchange of quotations on 35 Nasdaq securities traded in both markets.

There is also the Shared Information Distribution System, agreed on in September 1989 by the European Community's (EC) Federation of Stock Exchanges. It is a pan-European electronic information network that will carry not only regulated price information but also company and key market information throughout the EC on a consolidated basis.

The same reasons that have made screen-based trading popular in the past decade will contribute to their popularity in the years ahead. Those advantages include such things as high visibility where stock prices and orders are seen, not shouted, and easy interface with other electronic markets. Screen-based systems are "quick-change" artists. They are able to evolve and improve without regard to geography or physical space requirements.

We are ushering in a computer-literate generation of securities professionals — people who no longer fear computers. Tomorrow's traders, investors, and financial managers will be more screen-friendly than ever. The question markets such as the New York Stock Exchange and those in Germany are asking now is: Can we afford NOT to use either a CATS-type or Nasdaq-type, or hybrid screen-based system? By developing the electronic trading systems to compete with the veteran screen-based markets, they are answering the question: No, they can't. Electronic trading is the way to go.

Information Flow

The most important tool traders or investors can have at their disposal is information. The faster that information is provided, the better. In today's investment environment, traders and investors are evaluating endless streams of information that emanate from different locations around the world.

The days of just watching one domestic marketplace to make your investment decisions are over. Today's traders base their decisions on global events. They are viewing and interacting in a series of markets both domestic and foreign. The only way to do this effectively is from an "upstairs," screen-based environment.

To better understand this, it might prove valuable to use my own firm's daily activity as an example. We are market makers in some 1,000 issues. These issues trade in the U.S. Nasdaq market, the U.S. over-the-counter market, the seven domestic exchange markets, and numerous foreign markets. Many of these issues have derivative instruments such as options, futures, convertible bonds, and preferred stocks. They also are the components of stock and index futures in which we are active trading participants.

In this kind of environment, a market maker is at a distinct advantage if it has access to as many of these diverse markets as possible. Our firm must consider all related derivative instruments to hedge our market-making positions. In today's volatile markets, the ability to hedge adds liquidity to the marketplace.

Each of our market makers continually views more than 20 information screens such as Nasdaq, Reuters, Dow Jones, and Bridge. They trade actively in more than 16 different markets around the world.

By linking The Nasdaq Stock Market with other screen-based systems and our own fully automated proprietary trading system, any of our market makers in New York and London can trade around the globe in a matter of seconds. Our broker-dealer and institutional clients can route orders to us for immediate execution in seconds worldwide. All of these trades are instantly executed, reported, and locked into clearing for settlement by computer without human intervention.

At the same time, these executions are incorporated into our firm's inventory positions on our trader's workstations, which can then be monitored and evaluated so trading decisions and strategies can be carried out. Ninety-five percent of our trades are fully automated. It is because of this automation that our firm can handle 20,000 to 25,000 transactions on an average day with only 40 traders.

Technology Gives Flexibility

Nasdaq's technology provides unlimited flexibility. Each market-maker firm has the flexibility to design new proprietary systems that can be comparable to and interactive with Nasdaq. If one firm wants to be innovative in its own design, it has that ability. Our own firm wanted to build an expanded limit-order execution capability for our broker-dealer clients that was competitive with the exchange markets and was somewhat different from that of the Nasdaq market's limit-order system.

By integrating our own system with Nasdaq's technology, we have achieved what we believe to be a limit-order system that is superior to those of exchange markets. One example of its benefits is that it is not necessary to query individual floor locations and specialists to keep track of each limit-order status or execution as you do on exchanges. Our clients only have to access a single data-base screen display for immediate information on all orders residing within our system.

The technology of screen-based systems allows our limit-order file to be fully automated, which is impossible to accomplish on an exchange floor due to the "crowd" concept of exchanges. Furthermore, all executions that occur within our limit-order file are effected by a computer system that monitors not only our activity but all markets where activity in these securities is taking place. This ensures our clients the fastest and most efficient execution possible.

Issuers Want Worldwide Visibility

Most issuers want to be allowed to tap world markets for capital. Recent experience has shown that the ability to raise capital in different parts of the world is a major advantage. Because of the varying levels of interest rates in different economies, companies want to be able to reach into these markets to raise capital. This is possible only if their shares are traded by and familiar to foreign investors. The easiest way to accomplish this is to allow foreign investors and brokers to have access to U.S. market makers through electronic linkages between world markets.

Because the Nasdaq design is compatible with that of so many other market centers, companies can easily gain exposure by encouraging their primary markets to interface with Nasdaq and other screen-based systems, thereby eliminating the costly process of listing in foreign markets to get exposure.

While Nasdaq has brought many advantages to market makers such as ourselves, these advantages have been translated into benefits to investors and issuers as well by providing immediate information and liquidity.

Our firm has been a part of the development of Nasdaq from its inception. As one of the pilot firms, we had first-hand experience with the evolution, design, and application of the system. It was because Nasdaq was conceived, designed, and implemented with the users as part of the process that it has met with such success.

Chapter
Sixteen

John T. Wall is executive vice president of marketing and market operations for the National Association of Securities Dealers, Inc. He is responsible for the operation, promotion, and strategic planning of The Nasdaq Stock Market. Since assuming his position in 1982, Mr. Wall has spearheaded many major initiatives, including automation of all Nasdaq trading systems and development of the OTC Bulletin Board. He joined the NASD in 1965.

Nasdaq Technologies and Services: Innovative, Growing, and Global

by John T. Wall
Executive Vice President
Marketing and Market Operations
National Association of Securities Dealers, Inc.

From yesterday's rudimentary stone tools to tomorrow's space stations, our technology defines us. It drives our progress. Modern innovations have telescoped us beyond mere existence to ever-expanding prosperity as they remake our world into one where individuals flourish and communities thrive.

In 1798, Thomas Malthus, relying on the prevailing wisdom of his age, postulated that humanity was doomed to deprivation and desolation. He reasoned logically that food production would fail to keep pace with a soaring population and therefore mass starvation would become the order of the day. But he was wrong.

The population not only soared — it prospered. Individual life span increased, and the quality of life grew enormously. Why was Malthus so abysmally wrong? He failed to factor in technology. Or, more precisely, technological innovations applied to agriculture . . . transportation . . . industry . . . in short, to the myriad institutions that form civilization itself.

All of modern life reflects the effects of innovation, but no innovation has shaped modern life more than the computer technology of the last half of this century. It makes space travel possible. It spreads knowledge at nearly the speed of light. It lowers the cost of vital goods and services. It adds to the world's store of wealth.

Application of this new technology has revolutionized all sectors of our economy. And none more so than the financial services sector. It transformed, virtually overnight, the financial services industry from green-eyeshade bookkeepers mulling over ledger books in dimly lit back offices to multiscreened computer terminals that electronically connect to worldwide market centers.

The Nasdaq Stock Market

All the markets comprising the financial services industry rely, to a greater or lesser extent, on today's computer and telecommunications technology to meet the needs of customers and participants. But only one market, The Nasdaq Stock Market, owes its existence and leadership to this very technology.

Because of that direct relationship, The Nasdaq Stock Market has always been an innovator in technology. It was the first market to introduce screen-based trading as an efficient and practical alternative to the single-location trading floor. Nasdaq has improved that concept until it now offers multifunction workstations that put entire markets at traders' fingertips.

Nasdaq's success has made it the model of overseas markets. The London Stock Exchange (LSE), with its multiple marketmaker system, and the Stock Exchange of Singapore (SES) now operate screen-based, floorless trading facilities, and Nasdaq-type markets are being developed in Japan and elsewhere in Europe.

Why is Nasdaq being emulated? Because it provides participants with a full-service stock market that uses information technologies to network with other participants worldwide. Participants can establish and connect these electronic markets to others very quickly, thus improving existing market structures or adding new ones where none existed before.

Technology Advances the Market

The computer and communications facility for The Nasdaq Stock Market can process daily trading volume of more than 300 million shares. Planned enhancements will allow Nasdaq to support 450-million-share days. Through its network and computer complex, Nasdaq regularly processes more than two million transactions (quote and price queries, quote updates, trade and volume reports, and supervisory activities) each day, with an average response time of less than two seconds.

The central computer complex is located in Trumbull, Connecticut. A second facility in Rockville, Maryland provides back-up computer systems and telecommunications circuits to continue Nasdaq service in the event of an outage at the primary location. Nasdaq is the world's first equity market to establish a full and complete disaster-recovery facility as a safety resource.

Connecting Trumbull and Rockville are more than 100,000 miles of leased telephone lines over which the quotations of competing dealers in each Nasdaq security are sent to trading terminals in securities firms and financial institutions. Also connected to Trumbull and Rockville are computers of market data vendors. They distribute best bid and ask prices and volume information on all Nasdaq securities to stockbrokers and others on desktop terminals in almost 50 countries.

Nasdaq Offers Three Levels of Service

These securities industry participants can choose among three levels of Nasdaq service.

- **Level 1 Service** is distributed through more than 189,000 terminals leased by organizational and individual subscribers from market-data vendors, such as Quotron, Reuters, Telekurs, ADP, and others. Of these terminals, more than three-quarters are located in the U.S. The rest are in 51 other countries. This service distributes the best bid and asked prices in all Nasdaq securities to salespersons and dealers, giving these securities broad visibility. In addition, it broadcasts periodic information about several market indexes.

  Nasdaq computers are likewise connected to the computers of research bureaus, such as Datastream and Telerate, and to the computers of Associated Press, United Press International, and other wire services, which provide Nasdaq stock tables to about 220 newspapers, including four in Europe and one in the Far East.

  The service also broadcasts last-sale price and volume information on issues listed on The Nasdaq Stock Market to market-data vendors. This information, representing trade details reported by dealers within 90 seconds of execution, also is displayed on most of the same terminals that provide Nasdaq quote information.

- **Levels 2 and 3 Service** are provided through subscriber-owned personal computers. On inquiry, Level 2 service supplies subscribers with a composite display with individual current quotes submitted by the market makers in each issue; the inside-market quotation (the highest bid and lowest ask prices among all of the competing market makers in an issue); and indexes, volume, and market-summary information. Mainly financial institutions use Level 2 service to monitor their portfolios of Nasdaq securities and to make trading decisions. Nasdaq also makes individual market-maker quotes available through a broadcast feed to market-data vendors.

  Level 3 service allows the more than 400 registered, authorized market makers to interact with Nasdaq — that is, to update their quotations and report trades and daily volume to the system as well as receive Level 2 information. This service also provides market makers with access, through their desktop terminals, to Nasdaq's enhanced automated execution and order-routing services.

Nasdaq Workstation Terminals

The NASD has developed software that makes it possible for subscribers to use their PCs to access the Nasdaq data base. By installing this software, subscribers can turn their ordinary stand-alone machines into powerful multiscreen, multifunction Nasdaq Workstation terminals.

This third-generation Nasdaq terminal relies on a dynamically distributed data base that Nasdaq continuously updates throughout the trading day. Use of this technology boosts productivity by offering instantaneous access to most of the information needed for trading. Along with the traditional Level 2 and 3 services, the Nasdaq Workstation terminal includes these features:

- Market minding provides automatic price updates on up to 30 securities.

- Limit alerts warn of last-sale price or bid/ask quote parameter breaks for specified securities.

- Personal tickers track changes in the inside market (best bid and offer), trade executions, individual market-maker quotes, or trade-volume parameters for up to 100 securities each.

- Unsolicited messages record the day's automated trade executions.

Updated information flashes on the screen and is color highlighted to attract the user's attention. Customized pages tailor Nasdaq's services to the subscriber's individual needs. A multifunction menu line facilitates the selection of a service.

The NASD has also introduced the Digital Interface Server, which allows subscribers to have a single Nasdaq data line routed into their local area networks. That line has the capability to support up to 16 separate terminal devices simultaneously.

The primary advantage of the Digital Interface Server is that members can receive information comparable to that obtained via the Nasdaq Workstation service. They then can use their own internally developed programming to display the Nasdaq data in a customized PC format on their terminals. The Digital Interface Server provides real-time Level 3 information and services.

Advanced Market Services

Through its advanced, electronic network, Nasdaq provides innovative, market-related services to the industry. They include:

- **The Small Order Execution System (SOES)** can automatically execute customer agency orders for up to 1,000 shares in Nasdaq National Market issues and up to 500 shares in other Nasdaq issues. SOES, a system that provides an efficient means of handling small orders, guarantees the customer's order will be executed at the best price in the market at the time the order was entered.

    SOES also automatically reports the trades to Nasdaq and sends transaction details to the clearing corporation for comparison and settlement, saving securities firms considerable time and paperwork. A limit-order service, which operates as part of SOES, accepts and holds in a separate file a customer's day and good-till-canceled orders for 1,000 shares or less. When a market maker's quote in an issue equals or betters a limit-order price, the service executes the order.

    This limit-order service also provides for automatic matching of customer orders that enter the file. These include any orders priced between the inside bid and ask. If they match on both sides, the orders are executed at that price. If they don't match on both sides but are crossed between the inside, they are executed at the midpoint of the best buy and sell prices.

    The file holds all such orders for five minutes before automatically executing them to give market makers an opportunity to execute the orders first. If none step in to take out the orders, then the automatic execution occurs.

- **SelectNet** is an on-line screen negotiation and execution service that permits firms to send orders of any size and for any account to a specific market maker or to all market makers over a Nasdaq terminal without using the telephone.

  Firms that subscribe to Nasdaq can use this service to obtain fast, low-cost, efficient execution of orders that exceed SOES tier sizes. This enhances the opportunity for finding the best price and effecting the best execution.

  The service allows broker-dealer firms to effect transactions in Nasdaq securities in several ways. For example, firms can preference an active market maker in an issue, send an unpreferenced order to all market makers in an issue, or preference an order with an option to broadcast any unfilled quantity to all market makers. A firm that is a market maker in a particular security and acts in an order-entry capacity also may broadcast orders to all Nasdaq subscribers.

  The market-making firm may respond electronically to the trade information in three ways: by accepting, rejecting, or countering the order with new terms.

  With a counter offer, negotiations are considered in progress. All remaining counters enter a queue and are sent to the order-entry firm on a first-in/first-out basis after negotiations with the first party are completed. The two parties then exchange counters until they reach agreement or decide to drop the transaction.

  These negotiations may produce a full, partial, or no execution. In each case, market makers that have viewed the original order will be notified on the computer screen of any updated status. If no execution or a partial execution results, other parties can continue to respond.

- **The Advanced Computerized Execution System (ACES)** is a flexible, easy-to-use proprietary order-routing and execution system that gives NASD broker-dealers with Nasdaq service the ability to participate in an automated execution system. ACES provides users with a tailored, functional system without the huge startup costs incurred when building a stand-alone system. Using ACES, market makers execute orders automatically in certain securities up to specified amounts at the best price available in Nasdaq at the time such orders are entered into ACES.

The customizing features of ACES let a broker-dealer set up a file of the firms it deals with regularly and then determine the minimum order size it will accept for each security and for each firm. The broker-dealer can instruct ACES to suspend or restore the ability of one, a few, or all of its trading partners to route orders into the system for automatic execution.

- **The Automated Confirmation Transaction (ACT)** service is the most technologically advanced system for comparison offered by any market. ACT enables parties on either side of a telephone-negotiated trade to use the same locked-in trade features of the Nasdaq automated market execution services. ACT accomplishes same-day comparison within 20 minutes of the trade for about 90 percent of the Nasdaq trades and next-day comparison for substantially all Nasdaq trades. To maximize the efficiency of the system, ACT is mandatory for executions in Nasdaq securities. All automated executions in Nasdaq issues are reported through ACT to generate locked-in trades.

- **The Trade Acceptance and Reconciliation Service (TARS)** is an on-line data base of trade information that assists broker-dealers in resolving uncompared trades processed through participating clearing corporations. Subscribers can view on their terminal screens all the information contained on their daily contract reports, which are provided by the clearing corporation to reconcile the items that are outstanding.

TARS also can handle the original entry of trading information for transmission to clearing houses. As linkages with clearing organizations worldwide are developed, this feature will greatly enhance the processing of international trades.

Taking Advantage of Technology

As new generations of technology come on the scene, The Nasdaq Stock Market takes full advantage of them. Now, Nasdaq is reconfiguring its hardware, software, and communication facilities to support the electronic global marketplace of the future.

Over a five-year development period, Nasdaq is reorganizing and modernizing the basic architecture that comprises its technical platform to take advantage of emerging new technologies. The actions go beyond hardware and communications changes to include changes to system software, network management, and applications structure and development. Designed to support The Nasdaq Stock Market into the 21st century, this redesigned technical platform will make it easier to add new services and expand existing ones.

The new architecture will ensure access to Nasdaq data by members, issuers, regulatory bodies, other exchanges, and all those who rely on Nasdaq information to fulfill their role in the market. All the components (hardware, software, and applications development tools) of this new platform are geared to provide responsive and innovative support for market-driven efforts to implement trading, comparison and clearing systems, and other corporate information services.

The ultimate goal of this program is to develop a planned systems environment capable of interacting with a variety of hardware and software configurations to:

- Reduce the "time to market" for new automated products and services and their cost of implementation.

- Minimize the cost of operating and maintaining the technical infrastructure supporting all automated products and services.

- Create innovative business opportunities through the cost-effective application of new technologies.

Systems for the Global Marketplace

Just as modern technology enables high-volume markets to operate in their own national environments, it also opens up the prospect of internationally linked markets.

International standardization of communications interfaces and protocols, the extremely low error rates of satellite links, and the processing capacity of even the smallest computers will permit practically any market, regardless of its size or location, to link with practically any other. The low cost of computer and communications technology enables securities markets and brokerage houses of all types and sizes to automate and markets all over the world to link together.

A parallel development of vital importance in the evolution of international trading markets is the new link between the International Securities Clearing Corporation (ISCC) in the U.S. and LSE's settlement system. In the U.S. securities industry, the cornerstones of the high-volume marketplaces are continuous net settlement of trades and the option to take book entry rather than actual delivery of shares. The NASD played a pioneering role in both developments.

Refining and modernizing the international clearance and settlement process is not nearly as glamorous and exciting as building international trading links, but marketplace development will not reach its optimum benefits without it.

Nasdaq's Initial Foreign Forays

Nasdaq's first major actions in the globalization arena involved linkages in the international marketplace to strengthen its international communications capability. These included the first international market-to-market linkage, a communications link for exchanging quotations with the London Stock Exchange, and the trans-Pacific link between Nasdaq and the Stock Exchange of Singapore.

As important as they are, these quotation exchanges are but the first stage of a more comprehensive, automated market linkage. For Nasdaq, the next step in this process was Nasdaq International, an innovative service developed to provide securities firms, investors, and world-class companies with the opportunity to participate in a new transatlantic securities market — one that features an international quotation network, and efficient, computerized trade reporting. Clearance and settlement of inter-dealer transactions is through National Securities Clearing Corporation and other U.S. clearing organizations, assuring participants of compared transactions and five-day rolling clearance and settlement.

Equity securities eligible for listing on the new international service include The Nasdaq Stock Market domestic securities and all domestic securities listed on U.S. exchanges, including the New York Stock Exchange (NYSE) and the American Stock Exchange (Amex). In addition, all American Depositary Receipts (ADRs) and foreign equities (except Canadian stocks) listed on The Nasdaq Stock Market, NYSE, and Amex are also eligible.

Next Step: The World

Facilitated by advances in telecommunications technology, cross-border equity trading has almost doubled in the last three years and increased 16-fold since 1979. By the year 2000, it is expected to reach nearly $5 trillion annually. As investors, issuers, and securities firms each expand their horizons in search of the best return, low-cost capital, and international business opportunities, the globalization of world capital markets will accelerate.

The NASD and Nasdaq continue to work for the benefit of investors, public companies, and members by launching new markets. The Nasdaq Stock Market's technology has turned the U.S. into a 3,000-mile-long trading floor and enabled it to become one of the largest markets in the world.

Tomorrow, the technology that Nasdaq has pioneered has the potential to turn the world into a 25,000-mile-long trading floor — a vast, international confederation of automated dealer markets.

PART V

Nasdaq as a National Economic Institution

Chapter
Seventeen

Hans R. Stoll is the Anne Marie and Thomas B. Walker, Jr., professor of finance at Vanderbilt University's Owen Graduate School of Management in Nashville, Tennessee. Mr. Stoll has taught management and finance courses for 25 years and has written extensively about domestic and international markets. He also has been a consultant to governmental and private agencies.

The Economics of Market Making

by Hans R. Stoll
Professor of Finance
Vanderbilt University

A market maker facilitates trading. The particular services provided by a market maker depend on the market structure in which he operates and range from purely clerical services to active involvement as a principal.[1] In auction markets, such as some of the European markets, a market maker may simply facilitate trading by others, rarely taking positions for his own account. In The Nasdaq Stock Market, market makers play a much more central role by trading as principals and making two-sided markets.

In this chapter, the term "dealer" is used instead of the more general term "market maker" when trading as a principal is to be emphasized. It is important to recognize that a market maker does not set the fundamental price of a security; price is determined by much more powerful forces. Instead, he sets a price for the services he provides. In Nasdaq and other U.S. dealer markets, dealers stand ready at any time to buy at the bid price or sell at the ask price. They are therefore said to provide the service of immediacy.[2] The economics of market making, therefore, deals with the demand for and the supply of this service, not with the demand for and supply of securities.

Partly by coincidence and partly by cause, the transformation of the over-the-counter stock market from a sleepy, paper-oriented market in the late 1960s to a modern, computerized system coincided with the growth of academic research on the economics of market makers.[3] G.J. Stigler, in 1964, reacting to the SEC's *Special Study of the Securities Markets*,[4] and H. Demsetz, in 1968, provided the first look at the economics of the market maker.

Stimulated by S. Smidt's work in the SEC's *Institutional Investor Study*,[5] in 1972 Seha Tinic[6] developed a model of the New York Stock Exchange (NYSE) specialist and carried out empirical tests of the effect of competition on the bid/ask spread. In 1978, Hans R. Stoll[7] provided an explicit theoretical framework for the dealer based on the inventory risk facing the dealer and a variety of other factors.

Empirical tests of the factors affecting bid/ask spreads both on exchange markets and The Nasdaq Stock Market — volume, risk, stock[8] price, competition — appeared in the mid-1970s.[9] More recently, theoretical models have been developed[10] of the spread as a means to protect the dealer against adverse information possessed by other traders. Suffice it to say that academic study of market making is nearly as hot a topic as The Nasdaq Stock Market itself.

Demand for and Supply of Dealer Services

The demand for dealer services arises from imbalances between public buyers and public sellers in a particular security. Suppose that fundamental information justifies a price of P^* for a security. An imbalance arises if buyers at that price exceed sellers at that price, as shown in Exhibit 17–1 (the amount A-B). Such imbalances are almost inevitable since one cannot ex-

Exhibit 17–1   Demand for and Supply of Dealer Services

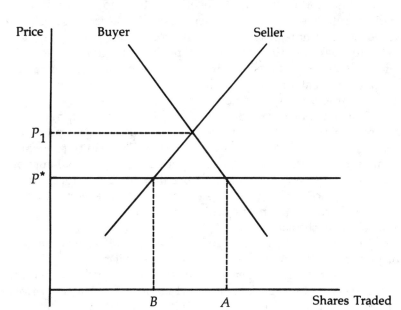

pect public sellers to match public buyers during any particular interval of time.

In the absence of intervention by a dealer, certain buyers would not trade and other buyers would trade only at a high price, P_1, in excess of the true price, P^*. A dealer would be willing to intervene by selling shares below P_1 and above P^*, thereby limiting unjustified deviations of transaction prices from the true underlying prices.

In every type of market, including most call-auction markets that have no dealers, a mechanism exists for responding to the type of imbalances pictured in Exhibit 17–1. Sometimes other investors or floor traders are able to respond to imbalances (for example, scalpers in futures markets). Sometimes trading is carried out periodically so that many orders may be batched and imbalances publicized before transactions occur.

Call-auction markets operate in this manner. But call-auction markets have the disadvantage of investors not being able to trade at all times. That is, the service of immediacy is not provided. Furthermore, a call-auction market does not eliminate the need for participation by market professionals. In most call-auction markets, professional traders intervene on one side or the other to prevent the transaction price from deviating too much from the true underlying price.

Organized dealer markets, such as Nasdaq, are distinguished by the fact that professional traders — dealers — are prepared continuously to quote a two-sided market. They do not respond to an imbalance after the fact, as might be the case in call-auction markets. They limit imbalances before they have the opportunity to arise. Market-making services are supplied in response to economic rewards — the profit realized from buying at the bid price and selling at the ask price.

In competitive markets, the bid/ask spread reflects the cost of providing dealer services — for dealers will not stay in business unless they are compensated for their costs, and new dealers will enter if profits are too great. Fluctuations of transaction prices around the true price, as in Exhibit 17–1, are limited by the bid/ask spread established by dealers. The higher the cost of providing dealer services, the larger the bid/ask spread and the wider the possible fluctuations of the transaction price around the true price.

A desirable characteristic of a market is, therefore, to provide dealer services at a cost that is as low as possible. This cost depends on the economics of the individual dealer and the degree of competition among dealers.

The Economics of the Individual Dealer

There are three types of costs facing an individual dealer: order-processing costs, risk-bearing costs, and adverse-information costs. The profits earned from buying at the bid price and selling at the ask price must cover these costs if a dealer is to stay in business.

1. **Order-Processing Costs.** Order-processing costs include fixed-and variable-cost components. Some costs are fixed over a particular planning horizon, such as a month or year. These include the cost of space, the cost of communications equipment, most labor costs, and the cost of the dealer's time. Certain transaction costs are fixed in that they do not vary depending on the size of the transaction. These might include fixed minimum costs for communications and clearing.

   Certain costs may vary with the size of a transaction. For example, larger transactions incur larger clearing costs and may require more attention from the dealer. However, because of the fixed-cost component, economies of scale exist in trading. In other words, the per-dollar cost of handling a transaction is lower for larger transactions than it is for smaller transactions because the fixed costs of a large transaction can be spread over more dollars.

2. **Risk-Bearing Costs.** By buying at the bid price or selling at the ask price, the dealer takes on an inventory position (either "long" or "short") that imposes inventory risk.[11] The risk arises from unpredictable changes in the stock price after the dealer takes on inventory. The larger the variance of the rate of return of the stock and the larger the transaction size, the larger the risk. The lower the capitalization of the dealer and the more risk averse the dealer, the greater the effect of risk on the dealer.

   The dealer changes his bid and ask prices after taking on inventory to create incentives for public traders to even out the dealer's inventory position. For example, after a dealer buys stock, he lowers his bid price to discourage further sales to his own inventory, and he lowers the ask price to encourage purchases of the inventory from him. Thus, while the spread between the bid and the ask prices need not change, the parallel shifting of the bid and the ask prices encourages public transactions that even out the dealer's inventory position.

3. **Adverse-Information Costs.** Because the dealer quotes prices at which he will trade a stated amount, he can be

victimized by traders who possess superior information. Thus, a trader with information that justifies a price below the dealer's bid price will sell to the dealer at the bid price, and the dealer will tend to lose to this information trader.

Papers by T.C. Copeland and D. Galai[12] and by Lawrence R. Glosten and Paul R. Milgrom[13] show that the spread must be widened to offset the adverse effects of information trading. In principle, the spread is established so that the dealer's losses to information traders are offset by the dealer's gains from traders without information.

The Quoted Bid/Ask Spread

The quoted bid/ask spread that appears in the newspapers or is available from computer quotation services reflects two underlying economic forces:

1. **The Reservation Spread.** The "reservation spread" is the spread at which the dealer just covers the marginal costs of carrying out the next transaction. That spread reflects the marginal order-processing, risk-bearing, and adverse-information costs. From time to time, the reservation bid or ask price can be quite favorable to public investors.

    For example, suppose a dealer has a long position in a particular stock. In this circumstance, the dealer may be willing to sell at a low price simply to dispose of his inventory. Alternatively, a dealer with a heavy fixed investment in personnel and computer equipment may be willing to execute a transaction at a bid or ask price that fails to make a contribution to these fixed costs. However, as in any business, market-demand conditions must allow the dealer to price sufficiently above the reservation spread so as to make a contribution to overhead that over the long term covers the fixed costs of being in the dealer business.

2. **The Role of Competition.** Competition determines the extent to which dealers can quote bid and ask prices that exceed their reservation prices. In a market without competition, in which a dealer has a monopoly, quoted bid and ask prices can be set in excess of the reservation spread to yield a monopoly profit that exceeds the fixed costs of being in business. In other words, in a market without competition, the dealer has the opportunity to consistently set the bid price below the reservation bid price and to set the ask price above the reservation ask price.

Nasdaq's requirement that each Nasdaq security have at least two market makers limits the monopoly pricing power of any dealer. Exhibit 17–2 shows that 96 percent of the securities in the Nasdaq National Market System (Nasdaq/NMS) have more than two dealers and 87 percent of non-Nasdaq/NMS securities have more than two dealers. Nasdaq/NMS securities are the more actively traded securities for which last-sale information (transaction price and volume) and the current bid/ask spread are reported. In non-Nasdaq/NMS securities, only current bid/ask spreads and aggregate volumes for the day are reported.

Aside from competition from other dealers, competition can arise from limit orders placed by investors. On the New York Stock Exchange (NYSE), where specialists have monopoly franchises in stocks, individual investors who find the spread too large can place limit orders inside the spread. This competition from limit orders has the effect of narrowing the spread on the NYSE relative to the spread that would exist in the absence of limit orders.[14]

Recent changes in Nasdaq now also allow customers to trade inside the quoted spread. The SelectNet service permits customer limit orders to be broadcast to Nasdaq subscribers who can execute automatically against the customer limit order. The Small Order Execution System (SOES) exposes (small) limit orders to incoming market orders.[15]

Exhibit 17–2   Distribution of Nasdaq Securities by Number of Market Makers (As of December 31, 1990)

Number of Market Makers	Number of Securities	
	Nasdaq/NMS	Non-Nasdaq/NMS
Less than 3	106	274
3 to 5	546	677
6 to 10	790	677
11 to 15	572	341
16 to 20	304	123
21 to 25	134	26
26 or more	119	17
Totals	**2,571**	**2,135**

When several dealers are in a stock, bid and ask prices can vary across dealers. The "inside quote" is the highest bid price of any dealer and the lowest ask price of any dealer. Competition and the tendency of order flow to go to the best dealer keep the bid and ask prices of different dealers from deviating from each other very much. However, inventory differences and other factors may cause different dealers to quote different prices. As a result, the inside quote frequently involves two different dealers.

Determinants of the Quoted Bid/Ask Spread

A casual examination of inside quotes in Nasdaq stocks or in stocks in other markets indicates that spreads differ substantially across stocks. The economics of market making should explain these variations of spreads across different stocks — for if it could not, one would be compelled to argue that spreads are due to haphazard factors.

That spreads vary across stocks is shown in Exhibit 17–3. Because proportional spreads are known to increase for low-priced stocks, stocks are classified into three major price groups. As expected, proportional spreads are much higher for low-priced stocks than for high-priced stocks. Within the high-priced category ($10 or more) for Nasdaq/NMS stocks, spreads still vary considerably — the lowest 10 percent of stocks have spreads of less than 1.37 percent, and the highest 10 percent have spreads greater than 8.76 percent.

Economists have attempted to explain the cross-sectional variation in spreads as a function of observable variables that represent the theoretical constructs discussed previously. While it is not always possible to find observable variables that adequately represent all the theoretical factors, a number of variables consistently seem to be related to differences in spreads. Some of these include:

1. The greater the volume of trading in a stock, the smaller the spreads tend to be. This is, in part, because a stock with high volume shortens the dealer's holding period, therefore lowering his inventory risk. Also, high-volume stocks may enable a dealer to achieve certain economies of scale in order processing.

2. More volatile stocks tend to have wider spreads. For a given holding period, a stock with a large variance in rate of return imposes greater risk on a dealer than does a stock with a low variance in rate of return.

3. High-priced stocks tend to have smaller proportional spreads than low-priced stocks. The price of the stock per se should have little effect on the proportional bid/ask spread. The fact that it does is ascribed to the possibility that the price of the stock may proxy for certain other factors, such as the risk of the stock or the size of the issuing company. In addition, dollar transaction sizes in low-priced stocks tend to be small and require a larger proportional spread to cover the fixed costs of the trade.

4. The more dealers in a stock, the lower the spread. The greater the number of dealers, the greater the competi-

Exhibit 17-3 Decile Values of the Proportional Spread* by Type of Nasdaq Common Stock

Decile	Nasdaq/NMS Stocks			Non-Nasdaq/NMS Stocks		
	$10 or More	$3 to $10	Less Than $3	$10 or More	$3 to $10	Less Than $3
Lowest	.0034	.0097	.0348	.0082	.0172	.0231
1	.0137	.0355	.0708	.0225	.0370	.0881
2	.0189	.0455	.0939	.0319	.0509	.1204
3	.0234	.0535	.1099	.0389	.0721	.1579
4	.0286	.0613	.1291	.0509	.0899	.1888
5	.0336	.0713	.1557	.0645	.1132	.2246
6	.0401	.0845	.1802	.0819	.1295	.2754
7	.0470	.0991	.2153	.0975	.1760	.3467
8	.0606	.1241	.2691	.1304	.2070	.4444
9	.0876	.1678	.3628	.1905	.2579	.6439
Highest	.3091	.5185	.9333	.2412	.4844	1.2000
Observations	906	965	590	101	213	1,083

* Data are from January 1991; the spread for each stock is the average proportional closing inside quote from January, and deciles are determined from this number.

tion, which tends to limit any deviations of the spread from the reservation spread of any dealer. In addition, stocks with a large number of dealers tend to be high-activity stocks in which the risks to the dealer are small.

The importance of these four factors on the spread is reflected in the following cross-sectional regression using data for January 1991:

$$s = .0163 + .1673\sigma - .3043P - .1259V - .4931MM$$
$$\quad (80.8) \quad (17.8) \quad (-36.3) \quad (-23.3) \quad (-33.7)$$

observations = 3640
R-squared = .8777

where

s = ln [average $(P_a - P_b)$ / P_m], where the average is taken over all trading days in January 1991, where P_m = $(P_a + P_b)$ / 2, and where ln indicates that the natural logarithm is taken.

P_a = lowest closing ask price of any dealer.

P_b = highest closing bid price of any dealer.

P = ln [$(P_a + P_b)$ / 2].

σ = ln [standard deviation of daily return in January 1991]. Return is defined as $(P_t - P_{t-1})$ / P_{t-1} and is adjusted for dividends and splits.

V = ln [average daily dollar volume of trading in January 1991].

MM = ln [average number of market makers in January 1991].

This regression result is consistent with the results of previous investigators: a positive sign on the risk variable and negative signs on volume, price, and the number of market makers. The coefficients in the regression are interpreted as elasticities since the variables are expressed in logarithms. For example, the coefficient on the variability measure means that a 1 percent increase in the variability of the stock causes the spread to go up by .1673 percent. The variables in the regression explain 88 percent of the cross-sectional variation of spreads. This substantial explanatory power indicates that underlying economic factors determine observed differences in spreads.

Dealer Structure

Other than the requirement for at least two market makers in each Nasdaq security, entry and exit from dealing in a particular stock are relatively free. Therefore, it is instructive to observe how the dealers align themselves, for it explains how dealers, left to themselves, would choose the securities in which to make a market.

It could be possible, for example, that each security would have only the minimum number of dealers — two. Such a result would suggest the existence of substantial economies of scale from concentrating all trading activity in a stock in a particular dealer. Exhibit 17–2 shows that this is not the case, however. Most securities have more than two dealers, and many have in excess of 20 dealers. This implies that market making is not a natural monopoly with unlimited economies of scale.

Thomas Ho[16] examines the factors that determine the number of dealers in a particular stock. The basic argument is as follows: A dealer makes a market in a stock if he believes he has sufficient opportunity to price above his reservation spread so he can cover the fixed costs of entering that market. The opportunity to earn more than his reservation spread depends on the volume of trading in the stock and the number of other dealers in the stock. If volume is high, he has correspondingly more opportunities to earn above the reservation fee. If the number of dealers is high, it limits a dealer's opportunity to quote above his reservation spread. These two factors balance each other in such a way that the number of dealers increases with the volume of trading in the stock, but it increases at a decreasing rate.

Another factor influencing the distribution of dealers among stocks is the number of stocks in which a dealer decides to make a market. A dealer who concentrates on one or relatively few stocks may acquire a larger market share of those stocks, but he is subject to unexpected imbalances in relatively few stocks and is

Exhibit 17–4   Distribution of the Number of Markets Made in Nasdaq Stocks by Nasdaq Market Makers (As of December 31, 1990)

Number of Markets Made	Number of Market Makers
1 to 5	70
6 to 10	49
11 to 20	65
21 to 30	49
31 to 40	24
41 to 50	23
51 to 100	52
101 to 200	41
201 to 300	25
301 to 500	6
501 to 1,000	10
More than 1,000	7
Total	**421**

dependent on activity in those few stocks. On the other hand, the dealer that makes a market in a large number of stocks has greater flexibility to move resources from stocks that are currently inactive to stocks that are currently more active.

Dealers may view these tradeoffs in different ways. As a result, one sees not only differences across stocks in a number of dealers. One observes, as well, differences across dealers in the number of stocks. Exhibit 17–4 illustrates that some dealers make markets in relatively few stocks while other dealers make markets in a large number of stocks. In December 1990, of the 421 Nasdaq market makers, 70 made markets in one to five common or preferred stocks; 7 dealers made markets in more than 1,000 common and preferred stocks.

In recent years, the number of dealers in Nasdaq has declined absolutely and in relation to the number of securities. This is illustrated in Exhibit 17–5. Absolutely, the number of dealers reached its peak of 570 in 1988. Relative to the number of securities, the peak of 10.9 dealers per security was reached in 1989. The number of dealers dropped from 458 in 1989 to 421 in 1990.

These trends seem to reflect reduced profitability of dealers. Reduced profitability, in turn, may be attributed to increased obligations imposed on dealers by the NASD (such as the obligation to trade a minimum of 1,000 shares in the major stocks) and to general economic conditions.

Dynamics of the Dealer and the Realized Bid/Ask Spread

The profits earned by a dealer depend on the dynamics of the price over time. A dealer who buys at the bid price hopes to sell later at an ask price that is above that bid price. If there is no systematic tendency for the ask price to fall after a dealer's purchase, the dealer will, on average, realize a spread that is equal to the spread he quotes.

Exhibit 17–5   Nasdaq Securities and Market Makers: 1980–1990

Year	Number of Securities	Active Market Makers	Market-Making Positions	Average Market Makers Per Security
1990	4,706	421	44,243	9.4
1989	4,963	458	49,670	10.0
1988	5,144	570	48,370	9.4
1987	5,537	545	41,397	7.5
1986	5,189	526	41,312	8.0
1985	4,784	500	40,093	8.4
1984	4,728	473	38,820	8.2
1983	4,467	441	32,923	7.4
1982	3,664	407	27,734	7.6
1981	3,687	420	26,935	7.4
1980	3,050	394	22,360	7.3

On the other hand, if there is a systematic tendency for the ask price to fall after a dealer's purchase and for the bid price to rise after a dealer's sale, the dealer's realized spread will be less than the quoted spread. If it is assumed that prices have a systematic tendency to move against the dealer and that transactions are reversed in one period, the relation between the dealer's realized spread and his quoted spread can be expressed as follows:

1. Dealer purchase followed by dealer sale:

$$P^q_{t+1} - P^b_t < P^q_t - P^b_t$$

2. Dealer sale followed by dealer purchase:

$$P^q_t - P^b_{t+1} < P^q_t - P^b_t$$

where, $P^q_t - P^b_t$ is the quoted spread at time t, and the left side of the inequality spread realized between t and $t + 1$.

Two factors lead one to believe that realized spreads will tend to be less than quoted spreads, as indicated in the above inequalities. First, in managing his inventory, the dealer will tend to lower both the bid and ask prices after a dealer purchase because he is less eager to buy additional shares and more eager to sell the shares he has just acquired. Similarly, after a dealer sells, he will tend to raise both the bid and ask prices because he is more anxious to buy shares and less anxious to sell additional shares.

Second, the presence of adverse-information costs associated with the existence of public traders who may have superior information causes similar adjustments in prices. If someone sells stock to a dealer at the dealer's bid price, the dealer reasons that there is a greater probability of adverse information about the stock than positive information about the stock. Thus, he will tend to lower both his bid and ask prices to reflect the information conveyed by a public sale transaction.

Similarly, if an investor purchases stock from a dealer at the dealer's ask price, the dealer infers that there is a greater probability of good news than bad news about the stock; as a result, the dealer increases both his bid and ask prices. The dealer's attempts to limit his inventory exposure and to adjust for adverse information cause bid and ask prices to move systematically in a way that reduces the realized spread relative to the quoted spread.

Empirical evidence supports the view that the realized spread falls short of the quoted spread. Stoll[17] shows that there is a systematic tendency for prices to fall after a dealer purchase and to rise after a dealer sale. The data in Stoll[18] and Richard Roll[19] suggest that the realized spread on the NYSE is about one half the quoted spread on that exchange. A similar relation appears to hold for Nasdaq stocks.[20]

The realized spread measures the amount the market maker earns. The difference between the quoted spread and realized spread measures the amount he loses to informed traders and the price concession he makes to induce the public to take unwanted inventory off his hands. Traders who possess superior information can, in effect, cut the quoted spread by making trading gains from their knowledge. Traders who do not possess superior information pay the full, quoted spread.

On average, the dealer's losses to informed traders are offset by his earnings on the full, quoted spread from traders who do not possess superior information. This point was first made by Walter Bagehot.[21]

The Future of Dealer Markets

Two forces have been instrumental in the past growth of dealer markets and are likely to be important in the future growth of such markets. The first of these forces is the institutionalization of savings in the hands of pension funds, mutual funds, and similar institutions.

Institutional investors have, for a long time, dominated the debt markets and, with the development of the telephone, most trading in debt instruments moved off exchange floors to competing-dealer markets. In the 1960s and 1970s, as the role of institutions in equity markets increased dramatically, the locus of institutional trading in equity instruments also moved off-floor to the dispersed trading desks of major dealers — although much of this trading continues to be brought to or reported to the floor of stock exchanges when executed.

The second of these forces is the technological change in communication and order execution. Technological developments have also made possible dispersed dealer markets in noninstitutional-sized orders. Automation has extended the range of transaction sizes for which such markets are feasible. A major characteristic of The Nasdaq Stock Market is its ability to accommodate inactively traded securities as well as actively traded securities.

Modern communications technologies make face-to-face trading on the floor of a stock exchange increasingly obsolete, and these technologies have resulted in the transfer of trading activity to systems connecting dispersed trading rooms.[22] Even in floor-type exchange markets, many transactions are executed more or less automatically. The improvements in technology and the enhancement of existing execution systems — to accommodate automatic execution and to incorporate a consolidated limit-order book, for example — hold the prospect of even further growth in off-floor dealer markets.

The future of dealer markets in general and The Nasdaq Stock Market in particular is much rosier today than in the 1960s when price quotations were provided by the pink sheets. The Nasdaq Stock Market provides a flexible framework in which the demand for and supply of market-making services can be equilibrated. Market makers are free to enter in response to a demand for additional market-making services, or they may exit if trading activity no longer warrants their participation.

Nasdaq provides a communications network within which competition among market makers can take place. This competition helps to assure that the bid/ask spread reflects the economic costs of providing market-making services in each security traded on The Nasdaq Stock Market.

Endnotes

[1] For a description of alternative roles of market makers, see Hans R. Stoll, *Market Making and the Changing Structure of the*

Securities Industry, "Alternative Views of Market Making," in Amihud, Ho, and Schwartz (eds.), Lexington Books, 1985.

2 H. Demsetz, *Quarterly Journal of Economics,* "The Cost of Transacting," February 1968.

3 G.J. Stigler, *Journal of Business,* "Public Regulation of the Securities Markets," April 1964.

4 U.S. Securities and Exchange Commission (SEC), Report of the Special Study of Securities Markets, 88th Congress, 1st Session, U.S. Government Printing Office, Washington, D.C., 1963, Chap. 5.

5 U.S. Securities and Exchange Commission (SEC), *Institutional Investor Study Report,* 92nd Congress, 1st Session, U.S. Government Printing Office, Washington, D.C., 1971.

S. Smidt, *Financial Analysts Journal,* "Which Road to an Efficient Stock Market? Implications of the SEC Institutional Investor Study," September-October 1971, Vol. 27.

6 Seha Tinic, *Quarterly Journal of Economics,* "The Economics of Liquidity Services," February 1972, Vol. 86, pp. 79–93.

7 Hans R. Stoll, *Journal of Finance,* "The Supply of Dealer Services in Securities Markets," September 1978.

8 The term "stock" is generally used because most analyses have been made using common-stock data. In nearly all instances, the statements are also true for securities generally. The term "security" is used in certain instances because the narrower term "stock" might be misleading.

9 Seha Tinic, and R. West, *Journal of Financial and Quantitative Analysis,* "Competition and the Pricing of Dealer Services in the Over-the-Counter Market," June 1972, Vol. 7, pp. 1701–1728.

Ben Branch, and W. Freed, *Journal of Finance,* "Bid/Asked Spreads on the AMEX and the Big Board," 1977, Vol. 32.

Hans R. Stoll, *Journal of Finance*, "The Pricing of Securities Dealer Services: An Empirical Study of NASDAQ Stocks," September 1978.

J. Hamilton, *Journal of Financial and Quantitative Analysis*, "Competition, Scale Economics and Transaction Cost in the Stock Market," December 1976, Vol. 11, pp. 779–802.

[10] T.C. Copeland, and D. Galai, *Journal of Finance*, "Information Effects on the Bid/Ask Spread," December 1983, Vol. 38, pp. 1457–1469.

Lawrence R. Glosten, and Paul R. Milgrom, *Journal of Financial Economics*, "Bid, Ask and Transaction Prices in a Specialist Market with Heterogeneously Informed Traders," 1985, Vol. 14.

More complete reviews of the burgeoning literature on market making are contained in K. Cohen, S. Maier, R. Schwartz, and D. Whitcomb, *Journal of Financial and Quantitative Analysis*, "Market Makers and the Market Spread: A Review of Recent Literature," November 1979, Vol. 14; and Stoll, 1985.

[11] For models of how inventory risk affects the bid/ask spread, see Hans R. Stoll, *Journal of Finance*, "The Supply of Dealer Services in Securities Markets," September 1978; Thomas Ho and Hans R. Stoll, *Journal of Financial Economics*, "Optimal Dealer Pricing Under Transactions and Return Uncertainty," March 1981, Vol. 9.

[12] T.C. Copeland and D. Galai, *Journal of Finance*, "Information Effects on the Bid/Ask Spread," December 1983, Vol. 38, pp. 1457–1469.

[13] Lawrence R. Glosten and Paul R. Milgrom, *Journal of Financial Economics*, "Bid, Ask and Transaction Prices in a Specialist Market with Heterogeneously Informed Traders," March 1985, Vol. 14.

[14] The economics of the specialists and the role of the limit-order book in narrowing the spread are discussed in Hans R.

Stoll's *Monograph Series in Finance and Economics*, "The New York Stock Exchange Specialist System," 1985, p. 1985–92.

15 In both SelectNet and SOES, market makers receive some priority. In SelectNet, only market makers can broadcast limit orders to nonmarket maker subscribers (much in the same way that the specialist on the NYSE handles limit orders). In SOES, market makers have priority in "taking out" a public limit order before other public investors have the opportunity to trade against the limit order.

16 Thomas Ho, *Market Making and the Changing Structure of the Securities Industry*, "Dealer Market Structure and Performance," In Amihud, Ho, and Schwartz (eds.), Lexington Books, 1985. *See also* Bruno Biais, "Price Formation and the Supply of Liquidity in Fragmented and Centralized Markets," Working Paper, October 1990, HEC, Jouy en Josas, France; and Paul Laux, "Securities Markets with Competing Dealers: Theory and Evidence," Working Paper, University of Texas, October 1989.

17 Hans R. Stoll, *Journal of Financial and Quantitative Analysis*, "Dealer Inventory Behavior: An Empirical Investigation of NASDAQ Stocks," September 1976, pp. 359–380.

18 Hans R. Stoll, *Market Making and the Changing Structure of the Securities Industry*, "Alternative Views of Market Making," in Amihud, Ho, and Schwartz (eds.), Lexington Books, 1985.

19 Richard Roll, *The Journal of Finance*, "A Simple Implicit Measure of the Effective Bid/Ask Spread in an Efficient Market," September 1984, Vol. 39, No. 4, pp. 1127–1139.

20 Hans R. Stoll, *Journal of Finance*, "Inferring the Components of the Bid/Ask Spread," March 1989, Vol. 44, pp. 115–134.

21 Walter Bagehot (pseud.), *Financial Analysts Journal*, "The Only Game in Town," March-April 1971, Vol. 27.

22 This process was dramatically illustrated by the shift of the bulk of trading in London from the floor to the Nasdaq-like Stock Exchange Automated Quotations (SEAQ) system over

a period of weeks after the October 27, 1986, introduction of SEAQ, unfixing of commissions, and removal of the trading rules. See "'Big Bang' Killing a Tradition," *The New York Times*, November 28, 1986.

Chapter
Eighteen

J. Ernest Tanner is professor of economics at Tulane University in New Orleans, Louisiana. He has written extensively on macroeconomic policy, forecasting, consumer behavior, and financial markets. Mr. Tanner previously served as an economist at the Securities and Exchange Commission.

Jonathan B. Pritchett is assistant professor of economics at Tulane University. He received a Ph.D. from the University of Chicago. Mr. Pritchett's interests include the economics of education and the history of the American economy.

The Pricing of Market-Maker Services Under Siege: Nasdaq vs. NYSE on Black Monday[1]

by J. Ernest Tanner
Professor of Economics
Tulane University

Jonathan B. Pritchett
Assistant Professor of Economics
Tulane University

An efficient securities market requires that market makers stand willing and able to trade for their own accounts and thereby provide the public the opportunity to trade almost immediately. Efficient financial intermediation performed by mar-

ket makers is important in providing liquidity for the capital markets needed for the growth of the American economy.

For 100 years, the New York Stock Exchange (NYSE) performed the role of market maker for America's leading corporations, and only in the last 20 years has significant competition
arisen in the form of The Nasdaq Stock Market. Complaints about
the lack of liquidity in the securities markets on Monday, October
19, 1987, when share prices lost 22 percent from the previous
Friday's close, warrant further examination of the market-maker
services of Nasdaq and the NYSE.

Data from that "Black Monday" will be used in this chapter
to analyze the efficiency of the NYSE and Nasdaq markets in performing their primary services. The fundamental question we address is, "Should the market of the future look more like the
traditional NYSE system, where market makers are specialists
with significant monopoly elements, or more like The Nasdaq
Stock Market, where market makers have significant competition
in the provision of the service?"

On this score, many newspaper business editors believe that
the NYSE system will perform better than The Nasdaq Stock
Market during periods of severe stress.[2] The evidence from the
scientific literature is divided. On the one hand, some argue that
market makers are natural monopolists[3] and the NYSE specialist
system is the best possible method to make a ready market in the
stock of a corporation.

On the other hand, other economists studying the problem
find that market makers' services are no different from most other
forms of economic activity and that competition would lead to
market making at the lowest cost.[4] This fateful Monday was chosen for study because it is the one day when the benefits of cen-
tralization would appear to be greatest and competition would be
least effective.[5]

The October 1987 Crash

The market fell on Monday, October 19, 1987, with
the Dow Jones Industrial Average plunging 508 points, resulting
in a near collapse of the NYSE by noon on Tuesday. This unprece-

dented price volatility, mostly down but occasionally sharply up, was accompanied by record-breaking volume. The record volume kept the exchanges so busy that information about the market often lagged considerably. Many market orders were transacted at prices bearing little relationship to the prices thought to prevail at the time of the order.

On the Nasdaq market, the trading was so heavy that many market makers were unable (or unwilling) to answer their phones, effectively closing the markets for many small companies. Because of this behavior, Nasdaq authorities have now instituted reforms that allow computer trades to occur for small transactions of up to 1,000 shares without a telephone confirmation.[6] In contrast to the criticisms leveled at Nasdaq, the general feeling was that, under the circumstances, the specialists on the NYSE did a commendable job when shares changed hands.[7]

Yet, *The Wall Street Journal* (November 20, 1987, p. 16) reported "two-thirds of the specialists'" total $3 billion of buying power had been wiped out on Monday. Some specialists refused to open trading in stocks on Tuesday until they had enough buy orders to enable the shares to trade at higher prices. Many stocks took more than an hour to open. When they did, they were markedly up from Monday's close. The Dow opened about 200 points higher, an extraordinary gain according to the *Journal's* story. But the euphoria was short-lived. Specialists and major firms quickly unloaded their huge inventories.

It is against this background, when the strains on the system were greatest due to heavy volume and large price moves, that we wish to examine the efficiency of the NYSE specialist system in providing liquidity for the equity market. For it is precisely under these conditions that the system most desperately needs to provide an efficient, fair, and orderly market.

By examining transactions costs when the market maker is under siege with sell orders and trying to cope with record heavy volume causing information delays, we hope to provide evidence on the relative merits of the specialist system compared with those of the relatively open Nasdaq market system. Our evaluation relies heavily on the empirical literature developed to explain transaction costs on the major exchanges and Nasdaq market and applies those results to evaluating the exchanges that Monday in

October when equities lost about 22 percent of their value on al-most double the previous peak volume.

Cost of Market-Maker Services

The primary feature of the services provided by the market maker is immediacy. This results from the market maker for an individual security trading from his own portfolio, thereby providing the public the opportunity to transact immedi-ately.[8] The market maker is compensated for this service by sell-ing at the ask price and buying at the bid price. The expenses of the market maker involve costs of holding inventory, transaction costs involved with handling the orders, and costs due to unfore-seen adverse price moves often resulting from informed traders (or arbitrageurs) in the securities in which he makes a market.

Demsetz argues that the costs of providing the public imme-diacy by the NYSE market makers is a function of price, the vol-ume of transactions, and the amount of competition from regional and foreign markets on which a particular issue is traded. Others[9] find that the degree of competition from other markets has a sig-nificant effect on the NYSE bid-ask spread.

Studies of The Nasdaq Stock Market show similar results. Benston and Hagerman find that the market maker's costs de-crease with the volume of transactions and the amount of compe-tition as measured by the number of market makers but increase with the risk of dealing with insiders who have superior informa-tion.[10] Stoll[11] also found that greater market-maker wealth would have a positive effect on risk taking and, therefore, would lower the costs of transacting for the public.[12]

The literature on transaction costs suggests that the follow-ing variables have an impact on the costs of trading:

- **Volume of trading in a stock**. The higher the volume, the lower the costs since economies of scale are realized.

- **Price of the stock**. The higher the price of the stock, the greater the costs of transacting.

- **Inventory risk of market makers.** The higher the risk market makers incur due to price change, the greater the costs of trading.

- **Insider losses to market makers.** The larger the number of insiders trading on information that market makers do not have, the higher the trading costs.

- **Adverse information.** The larger the dealings of market makers with informed traders, the higher the trading costs.

- **Number of market makers.** The greater the number of market makers in the stock, the lower the transaction costs.

- **Capital commitment of market makers.** The larger the amount of wealth of market makers, the lower the trading costs.

The Data Set

To evaluate the merits of the NYSE versus the Nasdaq market when volume is heavy and prices are volatile, our data set consists of actively traded NYSE and Nasdaq stocks on Monday, October 19, 1987. For the Nasdaq sample, firms with the largest value of shares traded on Monday, October 19, were chosen. We used firms trading more than 100,000 shares and selling above $50 per share, more than 200,000 shares and prices above $40, more than 300,000 shares and prices above $30, more than 400,000 shares and prices above $20, and more than 500,000 shares with prices above $5 per share. The sliding scale of decreasing price and increasing volume guaranteed actively traded companies with value of trading similar to the NYSE issues.[13]

For the NYSE sample, we used the most actively traded list from *The Wall Street Journal* for that Monday and the previous two Mondays. In addition, a random sample of firms with less than one million shares traded was included in the NYSE sample to make the average volume in the two samples of comparable size. The sampling of firms included 22.7 percent of the total volume in the Nasdaq market and 22.8 percent of the total volume in the NYSE. In summary, our sample included 121 firms, with 50 issues trading on Nasdaq and 71 firms trading on the NYSE.

As a measure of the cost of transacting on October 19, 1987, we used the difference between the closing price and the low of the day. As the market fell all day and was under severe selling pressure at the close, a stock closing off the low could be an indication of unusual costs to the investing public. In this regard, at "3:00 a.m., the Dow was down nearly 300 points" (*The Wall Street Journal*, December 16, 1987, p. 16) and ended the day down 508 points with December futures selling at a 10 percent discount to the cash price at the close. Because the futures would normally sell at a premium to the cash price, the discount of futures to cash and the market falling 100 points in the last half hour of trading indicate that most stocks should have ended the day on or very near their lows.

Given that the usual measure of the cost of transacting in the literature is the bid/ask spread, our measure not only incorporates this spread but also is more appropriate on Black Monday because of the factors noted in the above paragraph. Price volatility would be the primary cost of transacting during periods of fast market conditions, as characterized the market late in the day on the 19th. The lack of current information and rapidly changing prices resulted in frequent "blind" trading by investors. With the market under severe selling pressure late in the day with the Dow Jones falling more than 200 points in the final hour, any close off the low must represent a market buy order. As a result of a lack of current price information, the gap between this market buy order and the more typical market sell order accurately reflects the cost of transacting under the conditions of that Monday. Because of the volatile market and the late tape, the bid/ask spread is only a component of the true cost that is better reflected in our "close-low" variable.

The assumption that the difference between closing price and the daily low price is the cost of transacting implies that all stocks at the close were priced to systematic risk and prices were trading continually lower. However, because firm-specific volatility would raise some prices off their lows, all the firm-specific information found to be important in the literature for explaining market-making costs is included plus the exchange on which the security is traded.

To explain the trading costs, the volume of shares traded (V) on that Monday in the individual stocks is used. For the price of stock (P) data, we used the final closing prices for Monday as reported in the New Orleans *Times-Picayune*, which said the data arrived several hours later than usual. *The Wall Street Journal*, at least in the edition available in the eastern region, contained only mid-afternoon prices. The two risk variables were measured by the conventional "beta" parameter and by Value Line's "safety rank." The Value Line safety rank ranges from 1 (safest) to 5 (least safe). The rank is based on the individual stock's price stability and the company's current financial strength.

The number of competitors (N), market-maker wealth (W), and the proxy for inventory risk (R) are all captured by the exchange on which the security is traded. Because of limited capital availability, specialists on the NYSE are market makers in fewer securities than are market makers in Nasdaq stocks. Not only are the listed stocks larger, but the specialist companies are limited in their ability to raise capital.

While the NYSE specialists are prohibited from being publicly held, no such capital limitation is placed on the Nasdaq market makers that are often publicly traded corporations. Because of the greater access to capital by the Nasdaq market makers and because of the relatively small size of many Nasdaq firms in comparison to NYSE-listed firms, Nasdaq market makers frequently deal in more than 100 companies and can diversify away some unsystematic risk in market making and should be willing to take more market risk. In the same vein, most heavily traded Nasdaq companies have 15 or more market makers, further increasing the capital available for market making in any particular stock. However, because of barriers to entry, the NYSE specialists do not have this degree of competition nor are they capable of diversifying away risk as they make a market in comparatively few companies.

In addition to these standard variables, a number of others were used to better capture the unique features of the crash day. We used volume of shares traded as a percentage of shares outstanding as an indication of pressure on the market maker's ability to provide liquidity. The percentage of shares controlled by insiders and the percentage of shares owned by institutions were taken from Value Line and measure I and A, respectively. Because mutual fund redemptions were more than double the normal rate over the weekend and Monday (*The Wall Street Journal*, December 16, 1987, p. 16), heavy institutional ownership would be expected to have a detrimental effect on the market maker's ability to maintain a liquid market.

Empirical Results

Exhibit 18–1 presents some of the summary statistics. Nasdaq stocks traded 2.37 percent off their lows on average, while NYSE stocks closed 3.65 percent off their lows. Thus, the cost of transacting in NYSE stocks, relative to Nasdaq stocks, appears to be 54 percent higher or about 1.3 percent (3.65% − 2.37%) of the share price. It should be noted, however, that most securities on both markets closed near or on their low of the day. The average for the NYSE exceeded the average on Nasdaq because many more firms traded on the NYSE closed significantly above their lows than did firms traded on Nasdaq. Nine of the 10 firms in our sample that closed at least 10 percent above their low were traded on the NYSE.

Other statistics in the table point to only slight differences between the Nasdaq and NYSE samples. For example, systematic risk, the beta coefficient, in the Nasdaq sample is only marginally higher than for stocks in the NYSE sample. Similarly, total risk, as measured by Value Line's safety rank, shows slightly higher risk in the Nasdaq sample. Insider ownership, institutional ownership, percentage of stocks with listed put and call options, and percentage price decline were fairly equal across the NYSE and Nasdaq samples. But our NYSE sample had a higher absolute trading volume than did the Nasdaq sample despite the higher percentage of the outstanding shares traded in the Nasdaq sample.

The results of using a fairly broad spectrum of variables to explain costs on Black Monday are contained in Exhibit 18–2. The results are generally as expected based on previous results.

As in the studies of Tinic for a sample of NYSE stocks and Tinic and West[14] for Nasdaq stocks with short sample periods,

Exhibit 18–1   Summary Statistics of Variables Used in Study

Variable	Mean	Standard Deviation	Standard Error of Mean	Median
Total Sample: _N_ = 121				
Close As % Off Low	3.12	5.11	0.46	1.22
Closing Price Per Share	$26.85	$17.56	$1.60	$23.00
Volume*	1,557.88	2,312.71	210.25	561.20
% Price Change	17.74	9.28	0.84	17.93
Safety	2.94	0.93	0.08	3
% of Outstanding Shares Traded	1.98	3.07	0.28	1.26
Beta	1.12	0.29	0.03	1.10
% Held by Insiders	13.88	16.74	1.52	7.0
% Held by Institutions	42.91	17.52	1.59	44.24
% With Option	58.68	N.M.	N.M.	1
Nasdaq: _N_ = 50				
Close As % Off Low	2.37	2.47	0.35	1.72
Closing Price Per Share	$22.30	$11.84	$1.67	$20.50
Volume*	1,013.45	1,081.43	152.94	599.40
% Price Change	17.1	7.9	1.1	17.30
Safety	3.12	0.80	0.11	3
% of Outstanding Shares Traded	2.26	2.02	0.29	1.67
Beta	1.20	0.24	0.03	1.20
% Held by Insiders	15.40	16.83	2.38	9.0
% Held by Institutions	44.83	16.80	2.38	44.91

(*continued*)

Variable	Mean	Standard Deviation	Standard Error of Mean	Median
Nasdaq: N = 50 (continued)				
% With Option	62.00	N.M.	N.M.	1
New York Stock Exchange: N = 71				
Close As % Off Low	3.65	6.31	0.75	1.09
Closing Price Per Share	$30.06	$20.13	$2.39	$24.25
Volume*	1,941.28	2,826.59	335.45	561.20
% Price Change	18.2	10.2	1.2	18.17
Safety	2.82	0.99	0.28	3
% of Outstanding Shares Traded	1.78	3.64	0.43	0.93
Beta	1.07	0.31	0.04	1.05
% Held by Insiders	12.81	16.71	1.98	3.0
% Held by Institutions	41.56	18.00	2.14	42.85
% With Option	56.34	N.M.	N.M.	1

* Thousands of shares traded.

N.M. = Not Meaningful

Exhibit 18–2   Regression Results Using Percent Off Low as Dependent Value

Independent Variable	Coefficient	Significance Level (%)
Constant	–0.113	7.85
Nasdaq Dummy	–0.024	1.38
Closing Price	–0.014	12.10
Volume	0.016	0.02
% Price Change	–0.137	0.96
Safety	–0.003	67.63
% of Outstanding Shares Traded	–0.322	6.97
Beta	0.009	61.73
% Held by Insiders	0.043	15.96
% Held by Institutions	0.016	58.68
Option Dummy	0.001	91.56

our risk variables (beta and Value Line's safety rank) are statistically insignificant. Our results, however, differ from those of Benston and Hagerman,[15] and Stoll,[16] who find significant effects for risk. The significant risk effects are probably due to a longer time-series data set. (*See* Stoll.)

The lack of significance in the percentage of shares-held-by-institutions variable is surprising given the popular press conclusion regarding Black Monday that a "few institutional traders" caused the market to collapse in their scramble to get out. Our initial assumption was that greater institutional ownership would increase market-making costs because of the additional risk to the market maker of having to provide liquidity for those large, informed traders. This would have been especially true if many institutions were to reach the same "sell" conclusion at approximately the same time as on that Monday. However, only three mutual fund groups accounted for the selling. According to the Brady Commission's report,[17] excluding the three funds, the mutual fund industry was a net buyer of stocks on Black Monday, and this probably accounts for the insignificance of the institutional ownership variable.

We also found surprising the lack of significance in the dummy variable for stocks with listed options. Our hypothesis was that because the market was under downward pressure all day, stocks with options would have arbitrage behavior pushing their prices lower. As a consequence, we anticipated a significant negative coefficient for the option dummy variable. But again, because of the breakdown in the market, the Brady Commission noted that arbitrage activity almost disappeared late in the day.[18] Probably because of this, the option dummy variable was statistically insignificant.

Deleting these four insignificant variables produced the results found in Exhibit 18–3. The coefficients on the remaining variables changed very little and, as a group, are significant at a very high level of confidence. The negative coefficient for the Nasdaq dummy is consistent with the increased competition in market-maker services found in that market. The negative coefficient on closing prices indicates that higher share prices have lower proportional dealer spreads and result in reductions in transaction costs.[19] Adverse information cost[20] to market makers, as represented by insider holdings, has the expected sign and is marginally significant (at about the 14 percent level).

**Exhibit 18–3   Dependent Variable: Percent Off Low
Lowest Standard Error of the Regression Experiment**

Independent Variable	Coefficient	Significance Level (%)
Constant	–0.120	0.53
Nasdaq Dummy	–0.022	1.69
Closing Price	–0.010	13.10
Volume	0.016	0.01
% Price Change	–0.133	0.97
% of Outstanding Shares Traded	–0.358	2.17
% Held by Insiders	0.040	13.51

While we cannot find in the literature a significant effect of the day's price change on a market maker's costs, the percentage change in price from the close on Friday, October 16 to the close on Monday, October 19 is consistent with our initial assumptions on the behavior of a random variable. The data show that the greater the price change on the 19th, the more apt it was to close at or near the low of the day.

Not consistent with the literature are the coefficients on volume and percentage of shares outstanding traded. This may, however, be due to collinearity between these two variables themselves and each of the exchange dummy variables. Clearly, higher volume relative to shares outstanding, other things being equal, is correlated with higher absolute volume. The simple correlation coefficient between these two variables was 0.40, which is significant at the 0.01 percent level of confidence. Also, as noted above, the NYSE had higher absolute volume, but the Nasdaq sample had a higher volume in terms of shares outstanding. By contrast to our results, the literature (e.g., Stoll) generally finds that increased volume lowers transaction costs while increases in the percentage of outstanding shares traded raises market-making costs.

Because our sample of firms included many that closed at the low of the day, our estimates of the true costs of transacting may be understated. Due to the heavy selling pressure near the close of trading, it seems reasonable to assume that shares trading off the low on the close were executed at the asked price — indicating that it was initiated by a market buy order. Because the low price was initiated by a sell order, the close-low would measure the bid/ask spread. While such reasoning misses much of what we consider the true costs of transacting that day (i.e., the volatility of the market and having to trade without current information, often resulting in executions substantially different from the expected), using only stocks closing off their lows would be an alternative measure of the costs of transacting. The results of this experiment are given in Exhibit 18–4.

Using only those shares that finished off their lows (40 NYSE issues and 37 Nasdaq issues), Exhibit 18–4 shows only marginal differences from Exhibit 18–3, which is based on the larger sample of stocks. However, the coefficient on the Nasdaq dummy variable has increased in magnitude to –3.4 percent and remains

Exhibit 18–4   Dependent Variable: Percent Off Low
Sample Constrained to Those Stocks Closing Off
Their Lows

Independent Variable	Coefficient	Significance Level (%)
Constant	−0.082	19.81
Nasdaq Dummy	−0.034	0.56
Closing Price	−0.009	36.15
Volume	0.016	0.18
% Price Change	−0.175	1.07
% of Outstanding Shares Traded	−0.417	2.51
% Held by Insiders	0.039	26.79

highly significant. The higher spread to 3.4 percent of the share's average price clearly demonstrates the relative failure of the NYSE specialist system in providing market-maker services on Black Monday. While providing no direct evidence on the NYSE versus Nasdaq markets, the existing literature suggests a number of explanations for this extremely high cost.

First, numerous studies find that increased competition, as measured by the number of dealers that compete in making a market for a stock, reduces the bid-ask spread. Clearly, the typical Nasdaq stock has significantly more market makers than a NYSE stock of comparable price and trading volume.

Second, increased competition in the form of lower concentration among the major market makers lowers transaction costs. For example, in the Nasdaq market, a larger concentration ratio — such as the proportion of total volume transacted by the largest dealers — increases transaction costs. Clearly, for most stocks of comparable market value and trading volume, the concentration ratio is higher for NYSE stocks than for Nasdaq stocks.

Third, the literature shows that greater capital availability to the market makers relative to market risk lowers the cost of transacting. While many Nasdaq market makers are publicly owned, such is not the case for NYSE specialists, which are privately owned. Because the NYSE specialist risks a higher percentage of its capital when trading for its own portfolio than does the typical Nasdaq market maker, the cost of transacting would be expected to be smaller in Nasdaq stocks.

Related to this last point is the greater opportunity of Nasdaq market makers, compared with the typical NYSE specialist, to diversify their portfolios. For example, Shearson Lehman Brothers makes a market in scores of companies, effectively diversifying away unsystematic risk. Because the literature shows that risk increases the cost of transacting, the greater ability of Nasdaq market makers to diversify their portfolios compared with that of NYSE specialists would lower the cost associated with trading stocks on The Nasdaq Stock Market.

Summary and Conclusions

While several studies have estimated the costs of providing liquidity in our financial markets, few have provided evidence on the costs of the competitive Nasdaq system relative to those of the monopolistic NYSE specialist system, and none has provided estimates of the costs when the systems were under heavy stress. Nevertheless, conventional wisdom suggests that the NYSE specialist system is preferable to the Nasdaq alternative.

The present study, which in most respects supports earlier conclusions on providing market liquidity for Nasdaq stocks, is at odds with conventional wisdom on the efficacy of the NYSE when compared with the more competitive Nasdaq market. Using data for Monday, October 19, 1987, when the market suffered the largest percentage one-day decline in history on record volume, the evidence suggests that the costs of transacting in the heavily traded stocks of the Nasdaq market were significantly less than for using the NYSE specialist system.

Why? First, the competition among market makers in the Nasdaq market lowers the cost to the customers of buying their services. The NYSE specialist has competition from a few floor traders and other exchanges that typically trade only selected issues. By contrast, the requirement of making a market in Nasdaq stocks is substantially less, often resulting in a score or more market makers in stocks of sufficient size (and volume) to be eligible for NYSE listing.

Second, market makers in Nasdaq stocks can themselves be publicly traded. By contrast, NYSE specialists are privately owned and frequently do not have the necessary capital to take the financial risks required to provide liquidity in the larger stocks such as IBM, GM, or Dow Chemical.

Third, because Nasdaq stocks typically have several market makers, the financial risks on Black Monday were less severe for an individual market maker. For example, Apple Computer currently has 51 market makers, while the typical NYSE stock, trading an equal dollar volume, would have only 1 to 3 specialists. Because of this, the market makers have a significantly smaller percentage of their capital exposed to the risks of an individual issue and can diversify away much of the unsystematic risk.

Endnotes

[1] An earlier version of this chapter was published in *Investing* (Summer 1989).

[2] The Business News Editor, Manny Alesandra, of the New Orleans *Times-Picayune*, maintains that, at least with NYSE-listed securities, you could sell on October 19, while many Nasdaq market makers would not answer their phones. This is not quite true, especially on Tuesday, October 20, when many NYSE stocks did not trade for extended periods of time because of "order imbalances." We know of no similar examples in actively traded — similar in volume to trading halts on many of the large NYSE issues — securities in the OTC market on this day.

[3] William F. Baxter, "NYSE Commission Rates: A Private Cartel Goes Public," *Stanford Law Review* (April 1970), pp. 675–712.

[4] See Thomas Ho and Hans Stoll, "The Dynamics of Dealer Markets Under Competition," *Journal of Finance* 38 (1983), pp. 1053–1074; Seha M. Tinic and Richard R. West, "Competition

and the Pricing of Dealer Services in the Over-The-Counter Stock Market," *Journal of Financial and Quantitative Analysis* (1972), pp. 1701–1728; George J. Benston and Robert L. Hagerman, "Determinants of Bid-Ask Spreads in the Over-The-Counter Market," *Journal of Financial Economics* (1974), pp. 353–364; and Paul A. Laux, "The Operation of Dealer Markets Under Competition," (Ph.D. dissertation, Vanderbilt University, January 1988); among others.

[5] The NYSE market makers have an obligation to provide a "fair and orderly market" in their stock by trading for their own accounts, while no such explicit obligation exists for the OTC market maker. (See Nicholas F. Brady, *Report of the Presidential Task Force on Market Mechanisms*, (Washington, D.C., GPO, 1988) pp. 50 and VI–7.

[6] Proposed solutions include penalties for the unexcused withdrawal of market makers, mandatory participation of market makers in SOES (the automated execution system), and provision for SOES executions when market quotes are locked or crossed. (See Brady, pp. VI–63.)

[7] See, for example, Brady, pp. VI–40.

[8] See Harold Demsetz, "The Cost of Transacting," *Quarterly Journal of Economics* (February 1968), pp. 33–53, for the development of this notion.

[9] Seha M. Tinic, "The Economics of Liquidity Services," *Quarterly Journal of Economics* (February 1972), pp. 79–83.

[10] More recent adverse information theories of spread include Thomas E. Copeland and Dan Galai, "Information Effects on the Bid-Ask Spread," *Journal of Finance* (December 1983), pp. 1457–1469; Lawrence R. Glosten and Paul R. Milgrom, "Bid, Ask, and Transaction Prices in a Specialist Market with Heterogeneously Informed Traders," *Journal of Financial Economics* (March 1985), pp. 71–100; and D. Easley and M. O'Hara, "Price, Quantity, and Information in Securities' Markets," *Journal of Financial Economics* (March 1987), pp. 69–90.

[11] Hans R. Stoll, "The Pricing of Security Dealer Services: An Empirical Study of NASDAQ Stocks," *Journal of Finance* (September 1978), pp. 1153–1172.

[12] Others using spread to approximate the cost of transacting include Ho and Stoll; and Richard R. West and Seha M. Tinic, *The Economics of The Stock Market*, (New York, Praeger, 1971). More recently, within the context of variable investment time horizon, see Yakov Amihud and Haim Mendelson, "Asset Pricing and the Bid-Ask Spread," *Journal of Financial Economics* (1986), pp. 223–249. In the context of government bonds, see J. Ernest Tanner and Levis A. Kochin, "The Determinants of the Difference Between Bid and Ask Prices on Government Bonds," *Journal of Business* (October 1971), pp. 375–379, and, in the context of options, see Susan M. Phillips and Clifford W. Smith, "Trading Costs For Listed Options: The Implications For Market Efficiency," *Journal of Financial Economics* (1980), pp. 179–201.

[13] Such large volume guaranteed that our Nasdaq sample did not have issues that did not trade because market makers did not answer their phones — a common complaint about the Nasdaq market at the time. Reforms instituted by Nasdaq since October 19, 1987, have largely mitigated this problem for the average investor trading less than 1,000-share blocks. However, the high-volume Nasdaq companies did ensure that the overload problems of the NYSE most likely would also fall on our Nasdaq sample.

[14] Tinic and West, *op. cit.*

[15] Benston and Hagerman, *op. cit.*

[16] Stoll, *op. cit.*

[17] Brady, pp. IV–1.

[18] *Ibid*, p. 34.

[19] See Benston and Hagerman, and Stoll.

[20] See P.C. Venkatesh and R. Chiang, "Information Asymmetry and the Dealer's Bid-Ask Spread: A Case Study of Earnings and Dividend Announcements," *Journal of Finance* (December 1986), pp. 1089–1102; Glosten and Milgrom; and Stoll.

Chapter Nineteen

H. Kent Baker is professor of finance at the Kogod College of Business Administration at The American University in Washington, D.C. Mr. Baker, a chartered financial analyst, has written more than 100 articles appearing in such publications as the *Harvard Business Review, Journal of Finance, Journal of Accountancy,* and *Financial Management.*

The Cost of Capital to Nasdaq and Exchange-Listed Companies

by H. Kent Baker
Professor of Finance
The American University

Each year, the American (Amex) and New York (NYSE) stock exchanges approach many Nasdaq companies for listing. Most remain in The Nasdaq Stock Market even though they meet the financial requirements for initial listing. For example, in 1990 at least 600 Nasdaq National Market System (Nasdaq/NMS) stocks met the financial requirements for NYSE listing, and more than 1,100 additional stocks met the requirements for Amex listing.

The intense competition for listings among these marketplaces underscores the difference in views about them. Some people believe that exchange listing benefits the company and its stockholders; others do not. Before the arrival of Nasdaq, market observers commonly held that listing improved liquidity, provided more efficient pricing, reduced transaction costs, and lowered the cost of capital to the company.[1] Many economic studies tried to confirm these beliefs.

While clear confirmation of these beliefs was difficult even before Nasdaq, the development of Nasdaq increased the efficiency of the over-the-counter (OTC) market and altered the equation sharply. There is no longer undisputed evidence to support a decision to list. In fact, the presumption favoring listing has clearly changed, and most companies now reject listing after careful analysis of the relative merits of The Nasdaq Stock Market and the exchanges.

Researchers must continually update listing studies because of the rapid and continuing relative improvement in The Nasdaq Stock Market. Each year brings changes that lessen the validity of some previous studies.[2] Yet, past studies shed some light on the motives for exchange listing. For example, Baker and Johnson[3] used three groups to get managers' opinions about exchange listing: companies that were newly listed on the NYSE from 1985 to mid-1987, those that listed on the Amex between 1982 and mid-1987, and Nasdaq/NMS companies eligible for listing on the Amex or NYSE.

Based on their analysis of 284 responses, Baker and Johnson drew four conclusions:

- Managers have both economic and noneconomic motives for listing. The two most frequently cited reasons for listing were visibility and prestige.

- The importance of motives for exchange listing had changed since 1981 among Amex but not among NYSE companies. For example, both visibility and prestige declined as motives for listing among Amex companies.

- Managers perceived that exchange listing had declined in prestige during the 1980s. They cited the prominence gained by Nasdaq/NMS as one explanation for this change.

- The major reasons companies remained in the Nasdaq market had changed little since 1981. Managers perceived that the benefits of listing on an exchange did not outweigh the costs. The respondents also preferred Nasdaq's multiple market-maker system to the specialist system on exchanges.

Reduced-Cost-of-Capital Hypothesis

This chapter examines one potential motive for exchange listing: Does exchange listing reduce a company's cost of equity capital? For convenience, this issue is labeled the reduced-cost of-capital hypothesis. The topic interests members of the academic community, representatives of different markets, and corporate managers. For example, representatives of the exchanges and the NASD perennially debate the impact of exchange listing on the cost of capital.

Corporate managers, especially of growing firms, also are concerned about whether listing lowers their firm's cost of capital. The term *cost of capital* means the rate that the company must pay for its funds. There is a positive relation between the cost of equity capital and the market's perception of the risk associated with a firm's common stock. Because a firm's total cost of capital includes the costs of both debt and equity, reducing the cost of equity capital would affect its total cost of capital. In theory, management tries to find some optimal balance of debt and equity that simultaneously maximizes the firm's total market value and stock price while minimizing its average cost of capital. Thus, if listing in a particular market reduces a company's cost of equity capital, a firm would receive something of value by listing on that market.

Managers want to lower their firm's cost of capital because it affects corporate decision making. For example, corporate managers use the company's cost of capital for making capital budgeting decisions and capital structure decisions. The cost of capital provides a hurdle rate to determine acceptable projects using discounted cash-flow techniques. The cost of capital also measures the effectiveness of the firm's capital structure. That is, the company can approach its optimal capital structure by lowering its cost of capital.

Underlying Theory

In its simplest form, the theoretical underpinning for the reduced-cost-of-capital hypothesis centers on the risk/return tradeoff. The risk/return tradeoff states that investors expect to receive higher returns for taking higher levels of risk. If listing reduces the market's perception of a stock's risk, then it also should reduce the investors' required return and the firm's cost of equity capital.

Some contend that a stock's risk (total, systematic, and unsystematic) may temporarily change when it qualifies for listing.[4] Reduced risk could stem from an increase in trading liquidity or a decline in the perceived inherent risk of the security due to its new status. Lower risk also may result from information factors around the news of listing. Attention here focuses on the relationship between perceived risk and information. There are two controversies on this issue. One centers on whether a listing action contains information content, and the other focuses on whether exchange listing increases information availability.

Information-Content View

According to the information-content view, the listing action has information content that affects the risk and return of the securities. Ying, Lewellen, Schlarbaum, and Lease[5] contend that eligible candidates for listing are companies that are experiencing significant growth in assets and earnings. Market participants may view the listing application as a signal expressing managerial confidence in the company's business prospects.

There also is a similarity between the independent evaluation and approval by an exchange and the certification function of an investment banker.[6] As applied to exchange listing, the certification hypothesis suggests a firm may use an exchange to "certify" that it meets certain quantitative and qualitative standards. By approving an application for listing, an exchange risks its reputational capital. Exchange evaluation and approval may signal management's confidence in the firm and thus may have a positive influence on the public's expectations about the firm's prospects. The allegedly positive information content of the listing action may result in less perceived risk and may lower the firm's cost of equity capital.

Opponents of this information-content view contend that while a change in trading location may result from a change in a company's character, the company's stock price should already reflect this change. Any shift in stock returns, risk, or cost of capital should occur over time and should not result from listing unless listing reflects new information. If listing does convey new information, then, in an efficient market, prices of individual securities should adjust very rapidly to a new equilibrium. A securities market is efficient if the price instantaneously and fully reflects all relevant available information.

One way to determine whether listing has information content is to examine stock price behavior around the listing action. If listing has information content, it is reasonable to hypothesize the possible existence of abnormal positive investment returns around the listing action. Capital-market theory is pessimistic about the possible existence in the market of locales of persistent opportunities for realizing superior investment results (i.e., abnormal risk-adjusted returns).

Information-Availability View

According to the information-availability view, exchange listing increases information availability, which reduces perceived risk about the company's current and future affairs.[7] Some argue that this reduction of perceived risk makes listed securities more attractive to investors, and it thus lowers the cost of capital to firms. Proponents of this view contend that unlisted firms may suffer from an information deficiency compared with listed firms. Yet, there is much debate on how to measure this information deficiency. The lower riskiness of listed shares also may lead to lower flotation costs, which would reduce the cost of raising external equity.

Several authors contend that increased availability of financial information is likely to reduce the cost of equity capital.[8] For example, Dhaliwal[9] states that:

. . . exchange-listing is likely to reduce the cost of equity capital to the firm because the investment community is likely to gather and disseminate more financial information on a firm once it becomes listed. This increased availability of information reduces the uncertainty about the present and future affairs of the company, and the company is perceived to be less risky. So, investors are willing to accept a lower rate of return on their investment, which implies a lower cost of equity capital to the firm.

Opponents of the information-availability view, such as Philips and Zecher,[10] argue that having more information available or distributed more broadly does not guarantee that investors will lower their perception of a firm's risk, causing a change in the cost of capital. Opponents also contend that if this lack of information is a source of risk, such risk is diversifiable. Thus, investors should not expect compensation for the risk that results from the lack of information about firms and the securities they issue.

According to the capital-asset-pricing theory, investors receive rewards only for accepting systematic risk, as measured by beta. In an efficient capital market, the decision to list on an exchange would not change the level of systematic risk. If both exchange and nonexchange markets are efficient, each market would offer an equal opportunity for issuers to minimize their cost of equity capital. Thus, trading location would neither affect a company's systematic risk level nor its cost of equity capital.

More recent research[11] suggests that, even in an efficient market, investors should expect a higher return on shares of firms for which little information is available. If risk is measured by traditional methods such as beta, without adjusting for the relative information of the securities, then securities for which there is less information would appear to earn excess returns.[12] Yet, the results would not be excessive if the risk measure contained information factors.

Observers also note that several developments resulting in the upgrading of the OTC market now make any information gap between marketplaces less likely to exist. These developments include the SEC amendment of 1964, which expanded the periodic information disclosure requirement to OTC firms, the introduction of Nasdaq and tighter internal regulation of OTC dealers, the interlinkage of the various markets, the increased number and activity of institutional investors, and the growth in newspaper coverage of The Nasdaq Stock Market.[13]

Other factors leading to a narrower information gap between exchange and nonexchange stocks include increased computerization and electronic communication and the development of Nasdaq/NMS. As noted earlier, the rapidly changing Nasdaq environment requires continuous evaluation.

Does Listing Lower a Stock's Risk?

Listing on an exchange may change the risk characteristics of a firm's common stock and affect a firm's cost of capital. Early exchange listing studies[14] did not consider explicitly possible risk-level changes. The failure to do so could imply a bias in the empirical results in these studies.

Reints and Vandenberg[15] tried to correct this deficiency by testing whether listing on an exchange affects a stock's systematic risk (beta). Their sample included 32 companies that listed on NYSE from May to August 1968. They found no significant changes in systematic risk associated with listing on the exchange.

Ying, Lewellen, Schlarbaum, and Lease[16] examined the prelisting and postlisting betas for a sample of 248 companies that listed their common shares on NYSE or Amex during the period 1966-1968. Only 13 of the 248 betas changed significantly after listing and, of these, 9 increased. Their evidence confirmed the findings of Reints and Vandenberg.

Fabozzi and Hershkoff[17] also studied if there was a change in a stock's systematic risk after listing. Their sample contained stocks transferring from Nasdaq to the Amex between 1972 and 1975. Their results showed that a change in trading location did not influence a stock's systematic risk.

McConnell and Sanger[18] and Sanger and McConnell[19] examined whether listing on NYSE changed the riskiness of a company's stock. Using a sample of 153 pre-Nasdaq and 166 post-Nasdaq stocks, they measured the total risk (standard deviation of return) and systematic risk (beta) before and after the firms listed on NYSE. On average, neither risk measure changed significantly around the time of listing. McConnell and Sanger concluded that "for purposes of portfolio risk management or cost of capital estimation, listing on the NYSE appears to be a nonevent."

Temporary Risk Change

None of these studies considered the chance of a temporary risk change immediately after exchange listing. Bhandari, Grammatikos, Makhija, and Papaioannou[20] found that the riskiness of new exchange-listed stocks undergoes a seasoning process. Instead of lower risk after listing, riskiness was greater than in later periods.

Managers have an interest in any relationship between listing and risk because of the direct link between a change in risk and the firm's cost of capital. When deciding to list their firm's stock on a major exchange, managers consider many variables including the potential for lowering their firm's cost of equity capital.

Fabozzi[21] examined the price behavior of 83 firms switching to Amex between 1972 and 1975. He hypothesized that listing on Amex was valuable because it lowers the cost of equity before flotation costs to the newly listed company. Fabozzi found that the market reacted favorably to news of listing, but the postlisting declines offset the positive prelisting gains. Thus, the market clearly overreacted to news of listing because it did not uphold the prelisting increase. Finding no change in systematic risk after listing, Fabozzi (pp. 49–50) concluded "management must anticipate benefits other than reduced equity costs before flotation expenses to justify listing."

Another Study's Conclusion

Dhaliwal[22] reached a different conclusion. He postulated that exchange listing reduces a firm's cost of capital because of greater information flows and less risk. Dhaliwal reasoned that if greater information accessibility reduces uncertainty, then investors should accept a lower rate of return, which in turn should reduce a firm's cost of capital. Using matched pairs based on asset size and industry of 35 exchange-listed and OTC companies, Dhaliwal tested for statistically significant differences between the average number of news items appearing in *The Wall Street Journal* during 1972 for the two groups of stocks. The evidence showed that the average number of news items for the exchange-listed firms exceeded that for similar OTC firms.[23]

Dhaliwal also tested for differences in the cost of capital between the exchange-listed and OTC companies using systematic risk and total risk.[24] He used cross-sectional and time-series analysis of 29 of the original 35 matched pairs used to test for information availability. Dhaliwal concluded that the cost of equity capital of exchange-listed firms was significantly lower than the cost for similar OTC firms.

Philips and Zecher[25] replicated Dhaliwal's statistical tests using more recent data. They also extended the analysis by using market-adjusted portfolio returns around the exchange listing date. Their study used two risk measures, beta and standard deviation of returns, for 26 matched pairs of OTC and listed companies for 1978 and 11 pairs for 1972. The results revealed no clear tendency for either the OTC or listed stocks to have consistently higher risk. They did a second set of tests on a random sample of companies that listed on Amex and NYSE during 1977 and 1978. The findings showed no differences in risk associated with listing on either exchange. "In sum, listing status does not affect risk or the cost of capital for companies of similar asset size, industry group, and trading volume," Philips and Zecher (p. 20) concluded. "Further, the decision to list does not appear to have any predictable effect on risk or the cost of capital for the listing company."

Study Uses Three Measurements

Baker and Spitzfaden[26] studied the impact of exchange listing on the cost of equity capital in three ways. First, they matched 15 Nasdaq-Amex and 14 Nasdaq-NYSE firms on asset size, industry, and debt ratio to determine media visibility, as measured by news items in *The Wall Street Journal* from 1978 to 1980. They found that Amex — but not NYSE — listed stocks received more news coverage than similar Nasdaq stocks.

Second, they used a cross-sectional analysis to figure out whether the cost of equity capital, using beta and standard deviation as risk proxies, was lower for exchange-listed firms than for comparable Nasdaq firms. They found no significant differences in the cost of equity capital between members of matched pairs.

Finally, Baker and Spitzfaden used a time-series analysis of the prelisting and postlisting performances of 15 former Nasdaq companies that listed on the Amex and 23 former Nasdaq companies that listed on the NYSE to decide whether exchange listing lowered the cost of a firm's equity capital. Again, their findings showed no significant differences in either risk measure.

"Although some differential amounts of news coverage appear to exist between comparable listed and Nasdaq stocks, these differences did not appear significant enough to reduce the perceived riskiness of listed stocks, to lower investors' rate of return, or to reduce the cost of equity capital," they concluded.

Surveying Financial Executives

Baker and Pettit[27] took a different approach to investigating listing issues. Instead of examining market data, they surveyed a sample of financial executives of newly listed NYSE and Amex companies during 1975 to 1980 and Nasdaq companies that met the minimum requirements for listing on the Amex. The evidence showed that the respondents did not perceive listing as having substantial price effects. Also, the managers, on average, disagreed with statements such as "investors are willing to accept a lower rate of return on listed securities than they otherwise would require if the same securities were unlisted" and "listing reduces the cost of equity capital." Baker and Pettit concluded "the managers surveyed did not feel that listing led to either stock price enhancement or to reduced equity costs."

Baker and Johnson[28] updated and expanded the previous survey by surveying managers of Amex, NYSE, and

Nasdaq/NMS companies to get opinions about exchange listing. Based on their analysis of 284 responses, Baker and Johnson found that these managers generally disagreed with the statement that "listing reduces a firm's cost of equity capital."

In summary, all studies except Dhaliwal showed that the risk characteristics of common stock did not change for new exchange-listed stocks, except temporarily right after listing. Therefore, exchange listing lacked a significant effect on a firm's cost of capital. The evidence suggests that management should consider other motives for listing besides reducing risk and the firm's cost of equity capital.

Conclusions and Future Research

Because markets are improving, continuing research is needed to provide current evidence about the reduced-cost-of-capital hypothesis. Yet, the existing evidence does not support this hypothesis. Except for the Dhaliwal study, research shows that listing status has not altered the risk attributes and the cost of equity capital of the companies studied. This finding implies that Nasdaq offers a market equal to the major exchanges for companies trying to minimize their costs of equity capital. Corporate managers cannot expect reduced equity costs from listing.

Finally, the evidence is limited and mixed on whether listing improves the availability of financial information. Studies by Dhaliwal and Baker and Spitzfaden, which use the number of news items reported in *The Wall Street Journal* as a proxy for information availability, provide a starting point for investigation. Further research should use other measures of information availability and should examine whether information availability depends on factors other than listing.

Endnotes

[1] F. J. Fabozzi, *Financial Management*, "Does Listing on the Amex Increase the Value of Equity?" Spring 1982, pp. 43–50; and T.

Grammatikos and G. Papaioannou, *Journal of Financial Research*, "Market Reaction to NYSE Listings: Tests of the Marketability Gains Hypothesis," Fall 1986, pp. 215–227.

[2] For a discussion of research on exchange listings and delistings, see H.K. Baker and S.E. Meeks, *Financial Practice and Education*, "Research on Listings and Delistings: A Review and Synthesis," Spring 1991, pp. 57–71.

[3] H.K. Baker and M. Johnson, *Quarterly Journal of Business and Economics*, "A Survey of Management's Views of Exchange Listing," Autumn 1990, pp. 3–20.

[4] L.K.W. Ying, W.G. Lewellen, G.G. Schlarbaum and R.C. Lease, *Journal of Financial and Quantitative Analysis*, "Stock Exchange Listing and Securities Returns," September 1977, pp. 415–432; and A. Bhandari, T. Grammatikos, A.K. Makhija, and G. Papaioannou, *Journal of Financial Research*, "Risk and Return on Newly Listed Stocks: The Post-Listing Experience," Summer 1989, pp. 93–102.

[5] *Ibid.*

[6] J.R. Booth and R.L. Smith, II, *Journal of Financial Economics*, "Capital Raising, Underwriting and the Certification Hypothesis," January/February 1986, pp. 261–281.

[7] D.S. Dhaliwal, *Journal of Business Research*, "Exchange-Listing Effects on a Firm's Cost of Equity Capital," Spring 1983, pp. 139–151. Dhaliwal presents several arguments that an increase in financial information should reduce the dispersion of security prices and reduce the cost of equity capital.

[8] W.W. Alberts and S.H. Archer, *Journal of Financial and Quantitative Analysis*, "Some Evidence on the Effect of Company Size on the Cost of Equity Capital," March 1973, pp. 229–245; F.D.S. Choi, *Accounting and Business Research*, "Financial Disclosure in Relation to a Firm's Costs," Autumn 1973, pp. 149–175; and Dhaliwal, pp. 139–151.

[9] Dhaliwal, p. 140.

[10] S.M. Philips and J.R. Zecher, *Capital Market Working Paper*, "Exchange Listing and the Cost of Equity Capital," Securities and Exchange Commission, Washington, D.C., March 1982.

[11] A. Arbel, *Journal of Portfolio Management*, "Generic Stocks: An Old Product in a New Package," Winter 1985, pp. 4–13; and C.B. Barry and S.J. Brown, *Journal of Portfolio Management*, "Limited Information as a Source of Risk," Winter 1986, pp. 66–72.

[12] The quantity of information (information deficiency) related to a particular security is difficult to measure. Barry and Brown (pp. 66–72) suggest several measures such as the period of listing, extent of analyst agreement or disagreement about the prospects of a security, firm size, and the number of citations of news items about a security in key financial publications.

[13] Grammatikos and Papaioannou, pp. 215–227.

[14] R.W. Furst, *Journal of Business*, "Does Listing Increase the Market Price of Common Stocks?" April 1970, pp. 174–180; J.C. Van Horne, *Journal of Finance*, "New Listings and Their Price Behavior," September 1970, pp. 783–894; and W.M. Goulet, *Financial Management*, "Price Changes, Managerial Actions and Insider Trading at the Time of Listing," Spring 1974, pp. 30–36.

[15] W.W. Reints and P.A. Vandenberg, *Journal of Financial and Quantitative Analysis*, "The Impact of Changes in Trading Location on a Security's Systematic Risk," December 1975, pp. 881–890.

[16] Ying, Lewellen, Schlarbaum, and Lease, pp. 415–432.

[17] F.J. Fabozzi and R.A. Hershkoff, *Review of Business and Economic Research*, "The Effect of the Decision to List on a Stock's Systematic Risk," Spring 1979, pp. 77–82.

[18] J.J. McConnell and G.C. Sanger, *Financial Analysts Journal*, "A Trading Strategy for New Listing on the NYSE," January/February 1984, pp. 34–38.

[19] G.C. Sanger and J.J. McConnell, *Journal of Financial and Quantitative Analysis*, "Stock Exchange Listings, Firm Value, and Security Market Efficiency: The Impact of Nasdaq," March 1986, pp. 1–25.

[20] Bhandari, Grammatikos, Makhija, Papaioannou, pp. 93–102.

[21] F.J. Fabozzi, *Financial Management*, "Does Listing on the Amex Increase the Value of Equity?" Spring 1981, pp. 43–50.

[22] Dhaliwal, pp. 139–151.

[23] E.B. Grant, *Journal of Accounting Research*, "Market Implications of Differential Amounts of Interim Information," Spring 1980, pp. 255–268. Grant shows that more information is released to the public through *The Wall Street Journal* on NYSE companies than on OTC companies. Yet, he ignores that NYSE firms are normally larger than firms traded on the OTC market. Dhaliwal overcomes this problem by matching listed and OTC companies based on asset size.

[24] Beta may be a less-than-satisfactory surrogate for the cost of equity capital. For example, W.W. Alberts and S.H. Archer in the *Journal of Financial and Quantitative Analysis*, "Some Evidence on the Effect of Company Sizes on the Cost of Equity Capital," March 1973, pp. 220–245, argue that where the major conditions of the capital-asset-pricing model are violated, the strongest substitute for beta is the total risk (standard deviation) of the rate of return. R. Roll, *Journal of Financial Economics*, "A Critique of Asset Pricing Theory's Tests," October 1977, pp. 129–176; and H. Levy, *American Economic Review*, "Equilibrium in an Imperfect Market: A Constraint on the Number of Securities in the Portfolio," September 1978, pp. 643–658, provide additional support for using the standard deviation as a reasonable surrogate for the cost of equity capital.

[25] S.M. Phillips and J.R. Zecher, *Exchange Listing and the Cost of Equity Capital*, Capital Market Working Papers, Washington, D.C., U.S. Securities and Exchange Commission, March 1982.

[26] H.K. Baker and J. Spitzfaden, *Financial Review*, "The Impact of Exchange Listing on the Cost of Equity Capital," September 1982, pp. 128–138.

[27] H.K. Baker and G. Pettit, *Akron Business and Economic Review*, "Management's View of Stock Exchange Listing," Winter 1982, pp. 12–17.

[28] H.K. Baker and M.C. Johnson, *Quarterly Journal of Business and Economics Review*, "A Survey of Management Views on Exchange Listing," Autumn 1990, pp. 3–20.

Chapter Twenty

John C. Groth is professor of finance in the College of Business Administration at Texas A&M University. Mr. Groth serves as a consultant and expert witness in the areas of corporate finance, investments, and management education. His research has focused primarily on the efficiency and functioning of the securities markets, and results have appeared in *The Journal of Finance and Quantitative Analysis*, *Journal of Portfolio Management*, and numerous other journals.

David A. Dubofsky is an associate professor in the College of Business Administration at Texas A&M University. Mr. Dubofsky's articles on corporate finance and investments have appeared in such publications as the *Southern Economic Journal*, *Journal of Financial Research*, and *Financial Review*.

The Liquidity Factor

by John C. Groth
Professor of Finance
Texas A&M University

David A. Dubofsky
Associate Professor
Texas A&M University

For financial assets, a relationship exists among liquidity, risk, and the value of the security. As expected liquidity increases, risk decreases, and asset values increase.[1]

This chapter defines relevant liquidity from the perspective of the investor. Many argue that holders of a security expect a liquidity premium to compensate them for the risk of not being able to sell the security immediately and at the posted price. Thus, there is a trade-off between the time and price dimensions. Specialists on exchanges and market makers stand ready to provide liquidity for a normal volume of securities. However, they logically extract a tariff for this service.

Two Liquidity Premium Components

A liquidity premium can be broken down into two components: the pure liquidity price-time component and a liquidity-induced price risk component.

- **Pure Component**. Suppose all factors that affect a security's value are held constant. You want to sell 1,000 shares, but no buyer is present at the current market price for *all* the shares you wish to sell at this price. A buyer exists only for 600 shares at the current and desired price. However, to sell *at the same price* the remaining 400 shares, you expect to have to wait 12 minutes. The personal circumstances of the seller affect the cost of waiting. In addition, higher transaction costs may affect the seller because of the split sale. The absence of pure liquidity from this seller's perspective was the inability to sell the full 1,000 shares at the initial time of sale. Such "pure liquidity" factors induce a liquidity premium and therefore affect the price of a stock.

- **Volatility Component or Price Risk Liquidity Premium**. Needless to say, factors that affect a stock's price are not expected to remain constant as one waits to sell the remaining 400 shares in the example. It is unrealistic to expect a risky asset to trade at a constant price. Market or security-specific factors, unpredictable in an efficient market, might cause price to change. The risk exists of not being able to realize the desired price on the sale of the remaining 400 shares. Logically, investors incorporate this risk in the valuation scheme that determines the market price of a stock.

Therefore, the absence of "pure liquidity" (buyer-seller time-price matching alone) also results in a second component of the liquidity premium tied to the risk of price change of the stock as one waits to transact at a future and uncertain price. The greater the risk of price change of a security during the waiting period, the greater the induced price-volatility liquidity premium. The alternative is to avoid the price risk and accept a lower immediate selling price to complete the sale of the 1,000 shares at the initial time of execution. The premise we offer is that the more volatile a security's price, the greater the risk-induced liquidity premium.

The greater the perceived risk of price concession for an immediate transaction and the greater the volatility and, in turn, the risk of waiting for price realization, the greater the total liquidity premium. One can think of security and market-induced liquidity premiums as the price for waiting and the risk that waiting will not yield the price that would be available at the desired execution time if greater liquidity existed.

Numerous factors affect an asset's actual liquidity as measured in terms of price realization and time to realization. Some are directly linked to the security. Others are tied to the nature of the market(s) in which it trades. The induced-liquidity premium that results for a given level of liquidity varies for a host of reasons. The factors and their relative weighting probably vary across time, causing time variation of liquidity. For example, there are times when investors feel uncertain and seemingly favor a more liquid position. Under these circumstances, the premium for a given level of liquidity for a security differs from that demanded during a more robust market.

In addition, the actual liquidity of the security also probably varies as factors exogenous to the market mechanism affect the reception of the security in the marketplace. For example, a shift from the "popular" to the "unpopular" status — for whatever reason — undoubtedly affects the liquidity of an issue independent of the actual exchange or market-maker mechanisms.

To summarize: (1) security and market or systematic liquidity are traceable to time immediacy and volatility-price risk; (2) the liquidity of a security varies over time; and (3) the premium demanded for a given liquidity varies over time because of other factors related to security and market mechanism characteristics.

Because the prospective buyer or seller of an illiquid asset faces uncertainty as to the value ultimately realized, until the point at which the buy or sell occurs, one may cast these relationships in an expectations framework. This issue takes on importance in how one views the appropriateness of certain measures and tests of liquidity.

Factors Affecting Liquidity

Liquidity is a function of a number of factors, including the characteristics of the asset, the nature and availability of other assets, the nature of the market(s) in which it is traded, the characteristics of market participants, economic circumstances and trends, the psychology of the times, and possibly other influences. In addition, the importance of liquidity in terms of its effect on an asset's value undoubtedly varies according to changes in economic conditions, personal circumstances of any clientele that may exist for a particular asset, and changes in the "price" of bearing risk. There also probably is an asymmetric relationship between changes in liquidity, risk measures such as beta, security returns, and the market value of an asset. These dimensions of liquidity are often overlooked. They will warrant increased attention in the future.

The nature of trading markets for securities varies. For example, on The Nasdaq Stock Market, competing dealers or market makers quote two-sided bid and offer markets for securities. On the New York Stock Exchange (NYSE), a single specialist maintains a book of limit orders and bids and offers for his or her own account when the book bid and offer, set by investors' limit orders, are too far apart. When there are many shares outstanding, many shareholders, and a large float, the chances are greater that public orders will intersect from the buy and sell sides as market orders are executed against limit orders on the book. The existence of market makers — the distinguishing characteristic of the Nasdaq market — ensures a buy and sell price even in the absence, at the desired trading times, of matches between buyers and sellers. Thus, market makers contribute significantly to the liquidity of equity securities.

Liquidity differs considerably for the shares of large companies, such as General Motors and MCI Communications, versus the shares of small companies. Less actively traded shares and those of firms with fewer shareholders, fewer outstanding shares, and smaller float may not enjoy high levels of liquidity.

Market Differences and Liquidity

Some of the differences that exist between The Nasdaq Stock Market and the exchanges appear to affect prices and the filling of buy and sell orders.

1. **Competition.** The Nasdaq market consists of competing dealers. Each market maker quotes a price at which it will buy (the bid) and a price at which it will sell (the asked) a company's stock. In 1990, Nasdaq had 421 market makers, with the average security having 9.9 market makers.

   By contrast, a stock traded on the NYSE has a specialist charged with "maintaining fair and orderly markets." A specialist often acts as a "broker's broker," executing orders for a commission, or as a dealer, trading for his or her own account.

   Some argue that specialists have an inherent conflict of interest. They are required to maintain an orderly market for their assigned stocks, yet they wish to earn profits by trading for their own accounts. At times, stabilization activities could lead to actions that result in zero profits or even losses. In these instances, it would seem that the task of maintaining an orderly market would be at variance with the specialist's goal of earning profits.

   The specialist was once regarded as a monopolist in providing "liquidity services" for investors. While today's specialists still possess monopolistic information by knowing limit orders, they compete with floor traders, investors' limit orders, regional exchanges, and Nasdaq dealers that make markets in exchange-listed stocks in the "third market." More recently, new "systems" away from the exchange floors afford sophisticated investors other avenues for trading securities.

   To be sure, Nasdaq market makers also promote their economic interests. But for securities traded on Nasdaq, market makers face existing competition as well as the threat of immediate additional competition from potential new market makers. The competition among multiple market makers vying for business enforces a competitive discipline on the market.

This competitive-dealer mechanism, versus the single-specialist market-making mechanism, is a primary difference between the Nasdaq market and the exchanges. Because of the unrestricted entry into Nasdaq market making, firms with sufficient capital and the willingness to bear risk can become market makers without much difficulty.

Relatively free entry is an important issue. If economic profits become "excessive," added competition will arise and increase the level of liquidity (in part reflected by a reduced bid/ask spread) to competitive or zero economic profit levels. In Nasdaq, new market makers in a stock can enter the market in 24 hours or less. On the other hand, restricted entry could keep prices of liquidity services unduly high on the organized exchanges.

As noted earlier, there is some competition for the specialist. Floor traders at the exchanges allow for trades between the specialists' bid and ask quotes, but this is tantamount to one dealer maintaining his or her bid/ask quotes and occasionally transacting at a price between those quotes.

2. **Distribution of Risk.** Liquidity offered by market makers is likely to be sensitive to the capital available and the willingness to expose that capital to risk. Multiple market makers may be superior to the specialist system for several reasons. First, the total amount of aggregate capital available to several Nasdaq dealers for making a market in a given stock may exceed the amount available to a single exchange specialist.

The second advantage is the risk-willingness "portfolio effect." The risk associated with a given amount of capital is spread or diversified over several market makers. Each market maker bears only a portion of the total risk. If only one individual market maker is willing to

bear a level of risk slightly greater than his or her proportional share, that capital along with the capital from
the remaining market makers would yield increased liquidity.

Moreover, a given market maker's capital may be better diversified to the extent the market maker is diversified across more securities than is a specialist. This could
add liquidity in the event of security-specific shock effects that might place a specialist in a financially precari-
ous position or prompt the specialist to interrupt
liquidity to avoid getting into such a position.

3. **Depth of Market.** The readiness to trade a minimum
   transaction volume affects liquidity. Thus, the minimum
   number of shares available at the quoted prices is relevant to liquidity. Each specialist's bid/ask quote holds
   for at least 100 shares. By contrast, market makers are
   required to execute an order at posted prices for a minimum number of shares that varies according to activity
   in a security. The minimum number of shares for *each*
   market maker quoting prices is 200, 500, or 1,000 in the
   case of Nasdaq National Market stocks, and 500 shares
   for regular Nasdaq stocks.

   For example, in the Small Order Execution System, as
   of December 31, 1990, the number of Nasdaq National
   Market issues for the different minimum execution levels
   were: minimum 1,000 (1,772 of 2,573 issues); minimum
   500 (508 of 2,573); and minimum 200 (293 of 2,573). Thus,
   if several dealers all quote the same or nearly the same
   bid/ask prices and then jointly they are compared with
   the specialist, the dealers publicly and effectively are
   "good" for a relatively large number of shares at posted
   prices.

4. **Competition for Information.** Just as multiple market
   makers compete for business, it is logical they compete
   for information. To be sure, the specialist also is constantly trying to glean information from the environment
   that might affect security prices. Both specialists and
   market makers are likely to contribute to the efficiency of
   the market for information. However, multiple market

makers, each of them motivated by economic interests, may more effectively unearth information and capture it in share price.

5. **Inventory Adjustment.** Assume a specialist and a Nasdaq market maker desire to adjust their inventory positions in a stock. The specialist must make inventory adjustments against the market (i.e., by adjusting prices against the external market). Those price adjustments have their origin in the personal circumstances of the specialist rather than in economic factors related to the firm's stock.

In the case of multiple market makers, the worst-case inventory adjustment is the same as with the specialist. *But the presence of several market makers allows for something better than the worst case. Suppose one or more market makers desires to alter inventory in a particular stock.* The prospect exists of making such adjustments internally, against other market makers that desire to alter their inventories in a counter way. Thus, there is the chance of internal, cross market-maker inventory adjustment. In fact, systems exist to allow market makers to adjust inventory by broadcasting or targeting other market makers or potential market makers. The result is that it may not be necessary to effectively charge the external market for the cost of market-maker inventory adjustments.

Measuring Liquidity

There is no single, unambiguous, theoretically correct measure of liquidity. Some use the bid/ask spread as a measure of "immediacy"[2] because an investor can execute some shares at the ask (or bid) price quoted by the specialist or Nasdaq market maker. In the Nasdaq market, the investor would preferably trade at the highest bid or lowest asked prices. These are called "inside" quotes and may originate from two or more different dealers.

The bid/asked spread also is called the "price" that market makers charge for liquidity services. To establish a true cost of trading on either exchanges or Nasdaq, brokerage commissions must be added because they are effectively part of the price concession one makes to execute a trade quickly. Lawrence Harris offers unique perspectives on the cost and measurement of liquidity.[3]

However, the spread is only one dimension of liquidity. The bid/ask spread fails as a liquidity measure for three reasons — it does not account for the number of shares that can be traded at the quoted price, it does not reflect the price change that is necessary for a large block of shares to trade, and it doesn't consider that trades can and do take place within the quoted spread.

Liquidity measures should account for both trading volume and concurrent price changes. A liquid market absorbs large volume with little price change. An illiquid market yields price concessions on low trading volume.

The Amivest Liquidity Ratio is one indicator of liquidity, measuring the dollar volume of trading per percentage of price change as follows:

$$L_{it} = \frac{\text{Total dollar volume of a stock traded during the previous four weeks}}{\text{The sum of the absolute value of daily price changes during the previous four weeks}}$$

A high value of L_{it} means that many shares trade with little change in price — a property possessed by a liquid stock. The four-week (20-trading-day) period is the time period often used by practitioners.

There are other variants of the Amivest Liquidity Ratio. For example, some suggest that a better liquidity measure would use intraday high and low prices because a stock could experience wide fluctuations in price on one day, yet close unchanged in price from the previous day.

The list of possible liquidity measures could be extended; nevertheless, there remains a debate about what is "best." We will indicate the measure used in studies we discuss. Generally, the Amivest ratio has desirable properties because it reflects the practical ability to trade significant amounts of stock at close to posted prices.

Trading Location and Liquidity

In the February 1985 *Journal of Economics and Business*, "Liquidity, Exchange Listing, and Common Stock Performance," Cooper, Groth, and Avera compared the liquidity of similarly sized firms that trade in different markets. The authors sorted NYSE, American Stock Exchange (Amex), and 1,015 Nasdaq common stocks by their market capitalization and then placed the stocks into one of 10 market-capitalization deciles. Use of the Amivest Liquidity Ratios as of April 30, 1981, yielded the summary statistics presented in Exhibit 20–1.

The results support the notion that greater market value tends to accompany greater liquidity. *However, size does not always lead to higher liquidity.* As evidenced by the liquidity ratio range, at least one large firm on the NYSE, Amex, and Nasdaq had very low liquidity. Liquidity ratios of zero exist in the Amex and Nasdaq markets because some stocks had zero volume in the 20-day period.

Of greater interest is the comparison of average liquidity ratios for similarly sized companies that trade on the NYSE, Amex, and Nasdaq. The average liquidity ratios for Nasdaq-traded stocks exceeded those of Amex-listed stocks in every decile. In addition, in comparing the NYSE with the Amex, liquidity for the NYSE exceeded that of the Amex except for the third decile.

With the exception of the very smallest companies (decile 1) and the very largest companies (decile 10), the average liquidity ratio of Nasdaq-traded stocks also exceeded those of NYSE-listed stocks. In deciles 2 through 9, the liquidity of Nasdaq stocks exceeded the liquidity of both NYSE-listed and Amex-listed stocks. The researchers conclude that Nasdaq "appears to offer liquidity that is very competitive with that offered by the New York and American stock exchanges."

In a subsequent study, Dubofsky and Groth used a different approach to examine trading location and liquidity. The results are summarized in "Exchange Listing and Liquidity," published in the Winter 1984 *Journal of Financial Research*.

Several previous studies concluded that trading location has no consistent impact, one way or the other, on stockholders' returns or firms' cost of capital. Other unpublished studies mea-

Exhibit 20-1   Liquidity Ratio of Common Stocks Sorted by Aggregate Market Value

	NYSE			Amex			Nasdaq		
Decile	Number of Stocks	Average Liquidity Ratio*	Liquidity Ratio Range	Number of Stocks	Average Liquidity Ratio*	Liquidity Ratio Range	Number of Stocks	Average Liquidity Ratio*	Liquidity Ratio Range
1	10	7.900	(1-38)	206	3.369	(0-34)	157	7.420	(0-58)
2	44	15.545	(1-65)	154	12.636	(0-60)	163	30.135	(1-417)
3	58	26.069	(2-151)	101	35.148	(2-1099)	115	49.009	(4-328)
4	51	41.510	(12-164)	65	36.508	(5-135)	85	57.671	(4-280)
5	59	57.407	(8-212)	47	46.149	(5-325)	68	120.029	(9-1923)
6	50	58.580	(10-207)	28	54.429	(8-257)	52	116.885	(5-328)
7	103	94.524	(17-275)	51	82.392	(5-290)	63	142.555	(1-589)
8	73	124.685	(27-430)	23	81.435	(14-186)	47	158.191	(29-517)
9	228	223.364	(34-1491)	57	135.948	(0-510)	118	293.873	(16-936)
10	839	1699.181	(34-35579)	69	530.623	(1-5557)	96	668.885	(9-3579)

* Defined as thousands of dollars required to effect a 1 percent change in market price.

sured liquidity differently and reported different results. Despite these findings, some corporations change their trading locations, citing higher stock returns and lower capital costs as one consideration prompting a switch. Other reasons often mentioned include what they consider the greater prestige of listing on an exchange such as the NYSE.

To test the belief that an exchange listing improves liquidity, Dubofsky and Groth examined liquidity changes for three groups: 112 stocks switching from Nasdaq to Amex, 128 switching from Nasdaq to NYSE, and 104 switching from Amex to NYSE. These represent virtually all of the switches that occurred during 1975 through 1981. While the first study compared the liquidity of stocks of similar size, this one focused on changes in liquidity of stocks that actually made the switch.

Using the Media General Daily Price History Tapes for price and volume data, Dubofsky and Groth performed for each switching stock a time-series analysis of liquidity ratios after each calendar switch date, which they call the "event day." Exhibits 20–2, 20–3, and 20–4 summarize the results. In each group, different calendar days for the individual stocks are all grouped and examined relative to the switch day. Thus, although the switches occurred on different calendar days, for each switch, liquidity is examined for the same number of previous and subsequent days around the event day.

The findings depicted in Exhibit 20–2 indicate a sharp and apparently permanent decline in average liquidity for securities switching from Nasdaq to NYSE.[4] Liquidity declined 24 percent from the switch day (day 46) to day 66 and declined an additional 13 percent thereafter. These results should not be extended beyond the range of the sample or time period or be interpreted to mean that all securities moving from Nasdaq to NYSE will suffer a decline in liquidity.

Exhibit 20–3 illustrates average liquidity of the 112 stocks that switched from Nasdaq to Amex. These stocks were in general less liquid than those switching to NYSE from Nasdaq. (Note that the values on the vertical axis of the graphs differ in Exhibits 20–2, 20–3, and 20–4.) Average liquidity increases as the switch date nears, from 50 on day 1 to 58 on day 46. Once a stock is listed on Amex, however, average liquidity declines by 26 percent. The pre-listing improvement might be attributed to the increased publicity

**Exhibit 20–2   Liquidity of Stocks Switching From Nasdaq to NYSE
Number of Stocks = 128**

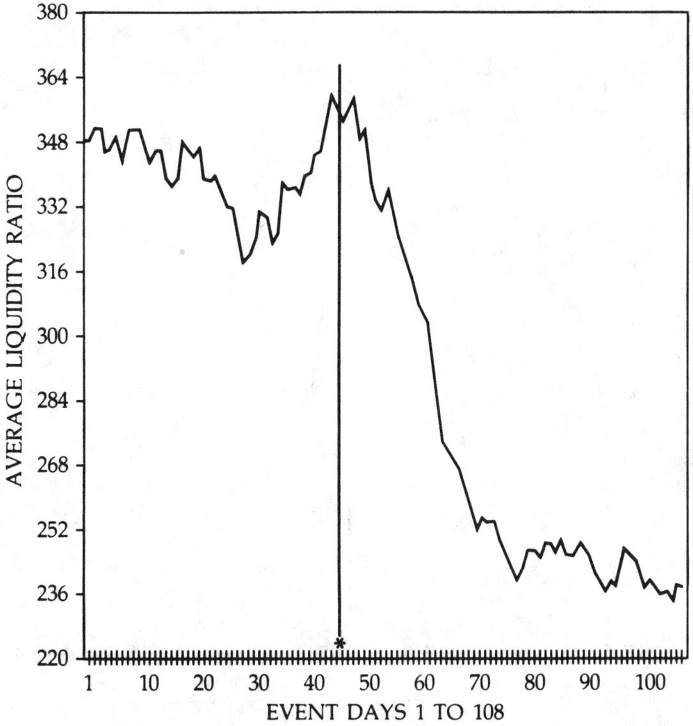

* = Date of switch.

and market attention surrounding the stock, or a "using up" of latent liquidity, which is followed by a decline after listing.

Exhibit 20–4 summarizes the findings for stocks switching from Amex to NYSE. These stocks realize an increase in liquidity just after the switch date, followed by a gradual decline to near preswitch levels.

Dubofsky and Groth used another liquidity measure developed by Peter Martin[5] and drew conclusions identical to those

---

Exhibit 20–3   Liquidity of Stocks Switching From Nasdaq to Amex
Number of Stocks = 112

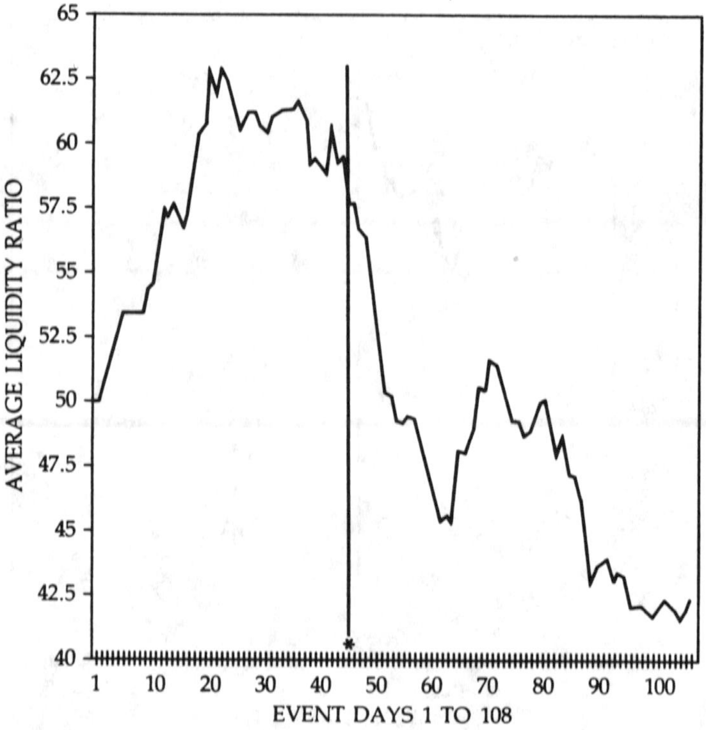

EVENT DAYS 1 TO 108

---

* = Date of switch.

---

above: securities moving from The Nasdaq Stock Market to either of the organized exchanges decline markedly in liquidity.

Historically, bank stocks have tended to trade on Nasdaq. This observation led to a third study by Fraser and Groth that examined the liquidity of bank stocks. "Listing and the Liquidity of Bank Stocks," published in the Autumn 1985 issue of the *Journal of Bank Research*, presents their findings. The authors regress liquidity ratios on a set of explanatory variables, one of which is trading location (exchange listed vs. Nasdaq; the variable was a

**Exhibit 20–4   Liquidity of Stocks Switching From Amex to NYSE
Number of Stocks = 104**

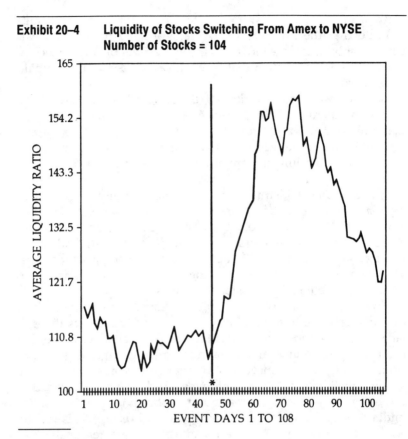

* = Date of switch.

"dummy variable" that took on a value of one if the bank stock was listed). This approach takes into account the differences in average characteristics of the firms traded on the exchanges and Nasdaq, such as in size.

The regression yielded a coefficient of −148.8 for the trading location variable, a value statistically different from zero at the 5 percent level of confidence. This means that all else being equal, $148,800 more in dollar volume of trades would be required to move the price of bank stocks one percent if the stock traded on

Nasdaq rather than on an exchange. In other words, the results indicate that the liquidity of a Nasdaq-traded bank stock was considerably greater, after removing the effects of different company characteristics, than that of bank stocks listed on an organized exchange.

Fraser and Groth attributed their results to aspects of the trading mechanism: "The presence of several . . . market makers may offer a depth and breadth of 'inventory' and greater capital committed (or at the ready) to support a buy/sell willingness that far surpasses the limited capital and/or commitment of the specialist."

The studies, which use one particular liquidity ratio applied over an extended period, warrant thought and consideration. The Amex and NYSE have commissioned liquidity studies that use different measures of liquidity and/or different statistical methodologies and report results that vary from those presented here. The Amex- and NYSE-commissioned studies have not yet been published in refereed professional journals.

We view the use of a conventional liquidity measure such as the Amivest Liquidity Ratio to be important. It measures the dollar volume of trades per percentage of price change. Because it captures both volume and concurrent price change, it is an appealing and practical measure. Alternative measures of liquidity should take into account the volume of stock that can be traded at posted prices — not just spreads and the behavior of spreads. For findings to be valid, tests of liquidity should use controls for the size of the company and reflect trading during a reasonable period of time. Sanford J. Grossman and Merton H. Miller[6] criticize the Amivest Liquidity Ratio because it does not measure the price effect of an unusually large order and because the source of the stock's volatility (the denominator of the ratio) is unknown. Are historical price changes caused by illiquidity or by new information?

All three of the papers discussed above cover approximately the same period. The Cooper, Groth, and Avera study and the Fraser and Groth study use liquidity ratios measured during the 20-day period ending April 30, 1981. However, the Dubofsky and Groth study covers switches in trading location during an extended seven-year period ending in 1981. Although relative liquidity could differ for other periods, the nature of the Nasdaq dealer market vis-à-vis the exchange specialist system appears to create different degrees of liquidity for similar stocks when size and time factors are adequately considered.

In "Risk and Return on Newly Listed Stocks: The Post-Listing Experience" appearing in *The Journal of Financial Research*, Summer 1989, Bhandari *et al.* examined the performance of stocks during the post-listing period. In addition to other interesting findings, the authors concluded that "instead of lower risk, riskiness is found to be greater immediately after listing than in later periods." They provide insightful comments that may explain their observations.

We add the following point for consideration. Any changes in liquidity that may occur with exchange listing will likely map through to measures of risk-return and may account for a portion of the observed increase in risk. The authors also suggested that any post-listing decline in liquidity may be attributable to market makers that close their equity positions after exchange listing. This in turn suggests that market makers create liquidity that is not supplied by exchange specialists.

In another *Journal of Financial Research* (Winter 1990) paper, Baker and Edelman scrutinized stocks switching to the Nasdaq National Market System (Nasdaq/NMS) and the resultant effects on liquidity and returns. Their results suggest "average percent spreads narrow, Amivest liquidity ratios increase, and volume increases after NMS inclusion. These changes suggest that liquidity improves after NMS inclusion."

Grammatikos and Papaioannou propose the "marketability gains hypothesis" in their Fall 1986 *Journal of Financial Research* paper, "Market Reaction to NYSE Listings: Tests of the Marketability Gains Hypothesis." According to the authors, investors expect that Nasdaq stocks with low liquidity will experience greater liquidity on listing on an exchange. Therefore, less liquid Nasdaq stocks react positively to an exchange-listing announcement. Highly liquid Nasdaq stocks have little or no potential to increase their liquidity on an exchange, so their stock prices do not react to an announcement that they will list on an exchange.

The marketability gains hypothesis is supported by the empirical work performed by Grammatikos and Papaioannou, and by Edelman and Baker in their paper titled "Liquidity and Stock Exchange Listing" in the May 1990 *Financial Review*.

Sanger and McConnell find evidence that indicates "that the introduction of Nasdaq in the OTC market has reduced the liquidity advantage provided by the NYSE." Their findings are in "Stock Exchange Listings, Firm Value, and Security Market Efficiency: The Impact of NASDAQ," published in the March 1986 issue of the *Journal of Financial and Quantitative Analysis*.

Conclusion

Still, there remain issues related to the measurement of liquidity. Unanswered questions include:

- How and why does liquidity change over time for individual assets?
- How and why do different market-making mechanisms affect liquidity?
- How and why does a change in liquidity affect risk?
- Can liquidity be decomposed into more elementary forces?

Though we know of no perfect definition of liquidity, it is still an important determinant of equity value. Greater liquidity probably lowers risk and increases value. We urge that any definition that is used take the viewpoint of the investor. Namely, it should capture the ability of an investor to trade his or her desired volumes without a significant effect on the price paid or received.

We conclude that trading location and liquidity are linked.

Endnotes

[1] See Yakov Amihud and Haim Mendelson, "Asset Pricing and the Bid-Ask Spread," *Journal of Financial Economics*, December 1986, Vol. 17, pp. 223–249.

[2] Harold Demsetz, "The Costs of Transacting," *Quarterly Journal of Economics*, January 1968, Vol. 82, pp. 33–53.

3 Lawrence Harris, "Liquidity, Trading Rules, and Electronic Trading Systems," Draft I.D., November 1990, University of Southern California.

4 These daily liquidity ratios are averaged in event time. For example, day 46 is the switch date, and the liquidity ratio of a stock on day 46 utilizes price and volume data during the previous 20 days relative to its switch date. Each stock has its own given switch date in calendar time, and there is a liquidity ratio for each on day 46 — its switch date. To get the average liquidity ratio for all switched on day 46 for the 128 (or 112 or 104) observations, day-46 liquidity ratios were averaged. The same was done on each of 108 days.

5 Peter Martin, *Analysis of the Impact of Competitive Rates on the Liquidity of NYSE Stocks*, Economic Staff Paper 75–3, Securities and Exchange Commission, July 1975.

6 Sanford J. Grossman and Merton H. Miller, "Liquidity and Market Structure," *Journal of Finance*, Vol. 43, July 1988, pp. 617–634.

Chapter
Twenty One

James H. Lorie is the Eli B. and Harriet B. Williams professor of business administration at the Graduate School of Business at the University of Chicago. Mr. Lorie has written extensively on marketing, consumer spending, and business finance and served as a consultant to many governmental and private agencies.

How Nasdaq Contributes to Economic Efficiency

by James H. Lorie
Professor of Business Administration
University of Chicago

We are now deluged with news of movements in stock prices. Newspapers, radios, television sets, and even re-corded phone messages tell us almost continuously what is happening to "the market." It would be understandable if the nearly 50 million people who own stocks in this country became so pre-occupied with short-term fluctuations in their wealth that they lost sight of the purpose of organized markets.

Their primary purpose is to reduce the cost of transacting. Reducing this cost is obviously important to investors; less obvious, perhaps, is its importance to the economy as a whole. This general importance stems from the fact that a reduction in the cost of buying and selling securities makes them more liquid and hence more valuable and thereby reduces the cost of capital for the corporations (or governments) that issue them. And this reduction in the cost of capital makes it possible to build more plants, roads, and other durable facilities and to buy more equipment, or to do these things more cheaply. Everyone benefits.

A second important function of organized markets is to determine the prices of securities. These prices determine the cost of capital for issuers of securities and channel investors' funds to various enterprises in accordance with their risk and promise of gain.

By any international standard of comparison, our principal securities markets are very efficient in performing their functions of reducing transaction costs. Thus, they decrease our cost of capital below that which would exist with the relatively inefficient markets of many countries and appear to achieve an economic allocation of resources. The cost of capital in the United States is almost certainly significantly higher than in Japan, but this American disadvantage is primarily attributable to our tax on capital gains.

The United States has many organized markets for securities. The two largest are the New York Stock Exchange (NYSE) and The Nasdaq Stock Market. The NYSE is larger and older; Nasdaq is more technologically advanced and rapidly growing. They are organized in different ways and operate according to different principles.

The central problem of any market is to bring buyers and sellers together so that a seller has a chance to deal with the buyer making the highest bid, and a buyer has a chance to deal with the seller making the lowest offer. The NYSE solves this problem by having all bids and offers come together at specialist posts. "Specialists" are persons or firms who are given franchises, which in practice have amounted to monopolies, to match orders to buy and sell specified stocks. Brokers with orders from customers converge at the posts of specialists and either deal with each other or with the specialist, who can act as a dealer and buy or sell for his own account or act as a broker on behalf of a customer.

In exchange for their monopoly, specialists take on affirmative and negative obligations designed to protect the public investor. Perhaps the most important of these obligations is to provide instant liquidity by buying or selling for their own accounts when the flow of public orders to buy and sell is imbalanced. Other obligations are to preserve an "orderly" market, maintain reasonable spreads between bids and offers, and to execute public orders ahead of their own.

The Nasdaq Stock Market solves the problem of bringing buyers and sellers together in a totally different way. Instead of relying on monopolists with obligations designed to protect the public, Nasdaq relies on competition. The competition is between dealers, called market makers, who buy for and sell from their own inventories.

In discussing the way in which Nasdaq contributes to economic efficiency, it will be useful to compare the different ways in which it and the NYSE solve the basic problem of organized markets — bringing buyers and sellers together. Before doing that, however, a benchmark for both modes of organization can be provided by describing an ideal market.

Four Characteristics of an Ideal Market

Unconstrained by reality, it is easy to describe an ideal market. It would deal with the component problems of organizing a market as follows:

1. **Information.** Investors would be quickly, cheaply, completely, and accurately informed about all the factors pertinent to making an investment decision. This information would deal with facts about the issuers of securities as well as facts about the market. Among the former would be data on earnings, dividends, orders, shipments, product development, and the myriad other details that affect a company's future prosperity; among the latter would be data on prices, bids and offers, and trading volume. The optimum frequency and substance of the flow of information may vary for different securities, and the ideal market will accommodate such differences.

2. **Equity.** Notions of equity are necessarily subjective, but there is a strong consensus on what constitutes equity in a financial transaction: the consummation of a transaction should depend exclusively on its terms rather than

on the characteristics of the persons doing the transacting. As a matter of law, we do not discriminate with respect to color, creed, sex, or age. Perfect equity in financial transactions requires that we go further and renounce discrimination based on factors such as location, the size of the transaction, or the historical business or personal relationships that often do not have an economic significance. The only things that should matter are the price at which the investor is willing to transact and the time at which he makes his commitment.

For convenience, this principle is called "price-time priority." A higher bidder gets stock before someone making a lower bid, and a lower offeror makes the sale before a higher offeror. If two bidders or offerors are willing to transact at the same price, the one who made the commitment first takes precedence, whether the bid/offer is that of "Aunt Jane," a large institution, or a professional dealer.

3. **Efficiency.** "Efficiency" is used in two senses. In the first, the word refers to the cost and speed of the various tasks necessary to the completion of a transaction. These include communicating between the investor and the broker, communicating between the broker and brokers representing other investors, making the deal, notifying the clearing corporation and the transfer agent, notifying the investors who completed the transaction, possibly delivering the stock, etc. An ideal market would perform these tasks quickly, at minimal cost, and without error.

    In its second sense, "efficiency" refers to the speed with which prices in the market adjust to changed perceptions of value (i.e., pricing efficiency). In an ideal market, prices adjust instantaneously. Any impairment of the adjustment process would be unfair to either buyers or sellers. If prices did not rise in response to perceptions of increased value, sellers would be disadvantaged; if prices did not fall in response to perceptions of decreased value, buyers would be harmed. Ideally, the price adjustment mechanism should favor neither buyer nor seller.

4. **Integrity.** Everyone is for integrity. Integrity of financial markets means a number of things. Investors must have absolute confidence that contracts will be honored. Buyers must know that they will receive the stock for which they have contracted, and sellers must know that they will receive their money. Investors must feel that the playing field is level. They must feel that other players do not have an advantage in the information that is available to them or the priority given their orders. Investors must be protected against fraud and manipulation by a strong surveillance system and vigorous enforcement of laws and regulations.

Ideal System Tested

The elements of a system that is very close to ideal have been conceived, designed, and tested on a small scale. About 15 years ago, Peake, Mendelson, and Williams, on the one hand, and Merrill Lynch on the other made public proposals which, in theory, seemed radical but very promising.[1] Their market would be organized around a system of computers and telephone lines, which would solve most of the problems discussed above. Orders could be entered by any qualified broker-dealer (without limit as to number), either for its own account or for the account of public customers. These orders would be stored in a central computer where automatic execution would take place whenever bids and offers matched. Execution would be in accordance with price-time priority.

Obviously, all orders to buy or sell would interact, thus ensuring that sellers would hit the highest bid and that buyers would cross with the lowest offer. All information on bids, offers, and transaction prices would be available to everyone, unlike the system on the NYSE where information on bids and offers "away from the market" is restricted to specialists.

Efficiency, in the first sense, would be achieved because almost all communication would be instantaneous and electronic. The only remaining voice communication would be between the investor and the broker when the public order was placed; other communication, between broker-dealers and with the clearing corporation and the transfer agent, would be automatic. Efficiency, in the second sense, would be achieved because there would be no impediments to the instantaneous adjustment of prices to market forces as reflected by the flow of orders.

Surveillance would be effective and relatively cheap because the computer would keep an almost permanent record of the parties responsible for all bids, offers, and transactions. Because of price-time priority, complete disclosure of bids, offers, and prices, and the easy possibility of effective surveillance, investors would have almost all the elements necessary for high confidence in the integrity of the system. The missing element is information about the issuers of securities, and this is not an integral part of the trading mechanism, although it is important for the market.

These conceptions of an automated market have been tested on a small scale at the Cincinnati Stock Exchange and on a system called Instinet. Although neither market has achieved a very large trading volume, nothing in their experiences suggests that there are technological obstacles in the way of developing an automated system for the scale of trading on the NYSE or Nasdaq.

Both the NYSE and Nasdaq have been evolving in ways that bring them closer to the ideal system, but, for reasons discussed later, Nasdaq is more likely to reach that goal.

Some Comments on Nasdaq and the NYSE

Nasdaq and the NYSE rely on the same information systems to inform investors. All firms listed on Nasdaq or on the NYSE are required to make annual reports, quarterly reports, and other more detailed reports to the Securities and Exchange Commission (SEC). The definitions and procedures underlying the data in these reports are prescribed by the SEC. Further, both the Nasdaq National Market System (Nasdaq/NMS) and the NYSE continuously provide during trading hours the same information on transaction prices with approximately the same speed.

The two markets differ with respect to information on bids and offers. Nasdaq displays on desktop terminals throughout the world the bids and offers of registered market makers in each stock, together with an indication of the number of shares that would be bought or sold in response to a public order. The NYSE discloses only the specialists' bids and offers through the same terminals.

The surveillance systems of the two markets differ. The Nasdaq Stock Market has the more precise audit trail, permitting the reconstruction of all transactions, but the NYSE is also sensitive to fraud and manipulation.

Nasdaq's competing market makers have more capital for market making than do the specialists, but the NYSE has adapted to the need to trade large blocks of stock by arranging for them to be traded through upstairs traders who work away from the exchange. As a result, the liquidity of the two markets probably does not differ much. A 1985 comparative study shows that the distribution of trades by size of trade is similar for the two markets.[2]

Other comparative studies of the two markets have been conducted.[3] They differ in details and in some conclusions because of differences in concept and econometric techniques, but it is reasonable to conclude that in today's environment there are not important differences in the efficiency with which the two markets perform their basic economic function. If that were not true, we would observe the hundreds of firms on Nasdaq/NMS that qualify for listing on the NYSE moving to that exchange. Or, we would see a reverse movement.[4]

Globalization of Securities Trading

In the market environment of the future — probably the near future — the trading mechanism of Nasdaq is likely to prove decisively superior. The important change that is taking place is the globalization of securities trading.

Recently, United States firms were allowed to join the Tokyo Stock Exchange, and several did. And the number of U.S. companies listing on the Tokyo Stock Exchange is increasing.

On October 27, 1986, the London Stock Exchange had its "Big Bang." The rules changed in London to require competitive commissions and to permit individual firms to act as both brokers and market makers. The result was an influx of financial firms into the London market and a decision by many firms to act as both brokers and market makers.

Now there are three great international financial centers: New York, London, and Tokyo. One or more of these markets is open through 20 hours of every business day. The volume of international capital flows is enormous and increasing. The U.S. in the past 10 years has, to a significant degree, gotten over its long-standing provincialism and is increasingly turning to foreign securities. The trend toward international diversification is based on sound reasons and is going to increase.

Issuers of securities are acting more and more on the realization that there is a global market for securities. Firms in the U.S. and other developed countries are raising capital in the national markets that seem most favorable and are denominating securities in the currencies best suited to their individual circumstances.

In this global market, the kind of trading mechanism used by Nasdaq is likely to be superior to the mechanism of the NYSE. The Nasdaq mechanism has the ability to evolve easily until it is like the ideal system described earlier. That system differs from Nasdaq in important respects, but none of the differences is hard to overcome.

The most important difference is that Nasdaq does not have a consolidated book. That is, the bids and offers of the individual market makers are listed separately rather than being consolidated. As a consequence, orders must be transmitted to individual market markers. In the event that an order, because of its size, requires the participation of more than one market maker, more than one order must be transmitted. In an era of many large blocks and volatile markets, the need to communicate with more than one market maker to consummate an order is a significant shortcoming. A consolidated book in which all bids and offers at the same price are consolidated eliminates this problem.

If Nasdaq consolidates its book, the system must decide how to choose the market maker to whom to direct an order among the several having a common bid or offer. As discussed above, the equitable way is to allocate the order to market makers in accordance with the times at which they made their commitments — the price-time priority principle. There is no technological obstacle to doing this.

At present, Nasdaq's Small Order Execution System (SOES) is limited to orders of not more than 1,000 shares for companies on Nasdaq/NMS and 500 shares or less for other Nasdaq stocks. There is no technological or economic reason for this upper limit. Dealers' bids and offers must be good for orders up to these limits. This requirement prevents the entry of improved bids or offers on behalf of public customers.

In 1990, Nasdaq significantly increased its capacity for automatic negotiation and execution of orders by launching the SelectNet service. Transactions eligible for SelectNet include both customer and principal orders that are in amounts larger than those qualifying for SOES.

SelectNet adds to efficiency by allowing participants, without the need for verbal communication, to preference an order to an active market maker in the security or send an unpreferenced order to all market makers in the issue, among other options. Participating firms may "shop" an order and counter the offers of other firms to get the best execution for the customer. And orders executed through SelectNet are automatically confirmed and sent to the clearing corporation as "locked in" trades.

Evolution of Nasdaq

The superiority of the ideal system for purely domestic trading is substantial in comparison to the NYSE. For global trading, the superiority is overwhelming. It is easy to see the efficiency and general attractiveness of a global system that simultaneously informs all broker-dealers of the information in the consolidated book and permits the automatic execution of orders from any broker-dealer, wherever he may be on the face of the planet.

The Nasdaq Stock Market can easily evolve into such a global trading system. The evolution of the trading mechanism of the NYSE into such a system is probably impossible as long as all orders must be channeled to the specialist for his participation. Thus, The Nasdaq Stock Market can evolve into an ideal global trading system while the NYSE cannot.

Endnotes

[1] J.W. Peake, M. Mendelson, and J. Williams, "The National Book System," April 30, 1976, and Merrill Lynch, Pierce, Fenner and Smith Incorporated, "Proposal for a National Market System," October 16, 1975.

[2] Laszlo Birinyi, Jr., and Julie M. Morrison, *The Over-the-Counter Market, Analysis, Groups, and Flows*, Salomon Brothers Inc., July 1985.

[3] See, for example, H.K. Baker and J. Spitzfaden, "The Impact of Exchange Listing on the Cost of Equity Capital," *Financial Review*, September 1982, pp. 128–138; K. Cooper, J.C. Groth, and W.E. Avera, unpublished working paper, 1983; David A. Dubofsky and John C. Groth, "Exchange Listing and Stock Liquidity," *The Journal of Financial Research*, Winter 1984, pp. 291–302; F.K. Reilly and W. Wong, "The Effect of a Stock Exchange Listing on Trading Volume, Market Liquidity, and Stock Price Volatility," unpublished paper, 1982; W.W. Reints and P.A. Vandenberg, "The Impact of Changes in Trading Location on a Security's Systematic Risk," *Journal of Financial and Quantitative Analysis*, December 1975, pp. 881–890.

[4] A reverse movement (i.e., from the NYSE to Nasdaq) is seriously impeded by the contract that firms sign with the NYSE when they list. This contract prohibits delisting unless approved by owners of a super-majority of the shares entitled to vote.

Glossary

Glossary

American Depositary Receipt (ADR) A receipt or certificate issued by a U.S. bank, representing title to a specified number of shares of a foreign security. The actual foreign shares are held in a depository in the issuing company's country of domicile.

bear market A market in which the overall trend in prices is declining. (See bull market.)

best efforts An underwriting agreement under which a securities firm promises an issuer that it will do its best to sell an offering but does not guarantee to sell the entire issue at the offering price.

beta coefficient A measure of the movement of a security's price in relation to the overall stock market. The larger the security's beta measure, the greater the security's volatility.

bid/ask spread The difference between the highest price that any buyer is willing to pay for a security and the lowest price that any seller is willing to receive for the security.

block trade The purchase or sale of stock in a large quantity, generally 10,000 shares or more.

block volume The aggregate volume of trades of 10,000 shares or more.

blue chips Securities of strong, well-established companies.

blue-sky laws State laws that require issuers of securities to register their offerings with the state before they can be sold there.

broker-dealer A firm that both buys and sells securities as an agent for public customers (broker) and also buys and sells securities for its own account and risk (dealer).

bull market A market in which the prevailing price trend is upward. (See bear market.)

Central Registration Depository (CRD) A computerized system in which the NASD maintains the employment, qualification, and disciplinary histories of more than 400,000 securities industry professionals who deal with the public.

Computer-to-Computer Interface (CTCI) A link between Nasdaq and a securities firm's in-house computer. The link permits a firm to report its trades simultaneously to its internal copier for recordkeeping purposes and to Nasdaq for trade-reporting purposes by a single set of entries on a single terminal.

Consolidated Quotation Service (CQS) A service available on Nasdaq Level 2 and 3 terminals, providing quotations of all participating exchange specialists and market makers on all stocks, rights, and warrants listed on the New York Stock Exchange (NYSE) and the American Stock Exchange (Amex), and in selected securities listed on regional stock exchanges.

continuous net settlement An ongoing accounting system used by a clearing corporation that settles transactions in each security between securities firms and the clearing corporation on a daily net basis. The system generates net tallies of firms' accounts in each security and overall with the clearing corporation on a daily basis and substantially reduces the need for certificate deliveries and cash payments for the settlement of individual transactions.

direct participation program (DPP) An investment program that provides flow-through tax consequences to investors. Such programs include ones related to real estate, oil and gas, and agriculture; they do not include real estate investment trusts.

Financial and Operational Combined Uniform Single (FOCUS) Report A financial report filed by a broker-dealer with its self-regulatory organization on a monthly (Part I) and quarterly (Part II) basis.

firm commitment An agreement by which an underwriter guarantees to sell the entire issue of a company's securities and assumes the risk of being unable to sell all the securities at the offering price.

firm quotation A bid or offer quotation on a security that is good for at least the specified quantity.

float The portion of a company's outstanding shares that is held by the investing public, not by insiders.

flotation cost The expenses that a company incurs in connection with offering securities to the public, including underwriter's compensation, legal and accounting fees, printing costs, and others.

index (stock) A measurement of market price changes based on the prices of a fixed selection of securities indexed to a base year (i.e., 1971=100).

initial public offering (IPO) The first offering of a company's equity securities to the public.

inside quote The highest bid and the lowest ask in a security from any market maker.

last-sale reporting Notification to The Nasdaq Stock Market by a securities firm of the price and number of shares involved in a transaction in a Nasdaq security within 90 seconds of the execution of the transaction. Transactions in listed securities are similarly reported to the exchanges.

Level 1 service A Nasdaq information service provided through market data vendor organizations to more than 200,000 terminals around the world, mostly used by brokers and other securities professionals. The service includes the inside quotations on all Nasdaq securities, last-sale information on Nasdaq/NMS securities, and market summary data.

Level 2 service A Nasdaq service provided through subscriber-owned terminals in the trading rooms of broker-dealers and financial institutions. In addition to Level 1 information, Level 2 service provides all the quotations of all the market makers in all Nasdaq securities.

Level 3 service A Nasdaq service provided through subscriber-owned terminals and authorized "foreign" terminals used by market makers. In addition to providing Level 2 information, it enables market makers to enter and update quotations, execute orders, and make last-sale reports, as well as provides market makers with access to Nasdaq's enhanced services.

limit order An order to buy or sell a stated amount of a security for a specified price when it reaches that price or better.

liquidity The resilience of the price of a security to buying and selling pressures. The greater the liquidity, the larger the dollar volume of shares bought or sold needed to change the price per share.

locked-in trade A transaction in which all of the terms and conditions agreed on or accepted by the parties are captured or recorded at the same time that it occurs.

making a market Standing ready to buy and sell a security at specified prices. Firms and individuals engaged in this activity are referred to as market makers.

managing underwriter In a public offering of securities, the firm that manages both the offering and the syndicate involved in its distribution.

margin The amount of money deposited by a buyer in connection with the purchase of securities on credit.

markdown The difference between the current wholesale bid and the price a retail customer receives when selling a security to a firm acting as a dealer (i.e., as principal) for its own account and risk.

market maker A securities firm that buys and sells securities for its own account and risk at stated bid and offer prices.

market order An order to immediately buy or sell a stated amount of a security at the best price available at the time the order is executed.

markup The difference between the current wholesale offer and the price a retail customer pays when purchasing a security from a firm acting as a dealer (i.e., as principal) for its own account and risk.

Municipal Securities Rulemaking Board (MSRB) An independent, self-regulatory board established by the Securities Acts Amendments of 1975 and charged with primary rulemaking authority for the municipal securities industry.

Nasdaq Composite Index A measure of the aggregate performance of all Nasdaq/NMS stocks (except warrants) and all other Nasdaq domestic common stocks. It is a market-value-weighted index — the influence of each stock on the index is proportionate to its price times the number of shares outstanding.

Nasdaq National Market System (Nasdaq/NMS) The segment of The Nasdaq Stock Market in which securities are subject to real-time trade reporting. It encompasses approximately half of all Nasdaq securities, and accounts for more than two-thirds of Nasdaq share volume and in excess of 90 percent of aggregate Nasdaq market value.

Nasdaq Workstation A computerized trading tool, comprised of a personal computer and NASD-developed and NASD-supplied software that together form a dynamically updated workstation through which Nasdaq subscribers may access Nasdaq services.

National Association of Securities Dealers, Inc. (NASD) The self-regulatory organization of the securities industry responsible for operating and regulating the Nasdaq and over-the-counter securities markets.

National Securities Clearing Corporation (NSCC) A securities clearing corporation formed in 1977 by the merger of the National Clearing Corporation, owned by the NASD, and the clearing facilities of the New York Stock Exchange and the American Stock Exchange. It is a medium through which trades in the respective participants' markets are cleared and settled.

open order An order to buy or sell a security that remains in effect until it is either executed or canceled by the customer.

OTC Bulletin Board service An electronic bulletin board for displaying firm and nonfirm quotes and unpriced indications of interest in over-the-counter securities. The NASD introduced this service in June 1990.

PORTAL Market, The A market for qualified investors to privately trade unregistered, world-class international securities. The NASD has operated this market since June 1990.

position The number of shares of a security held by an investor or a broker-dealer.

right A privilege granted to shareholders in a company to buy shares of a new issue of common stock before they are offered to the public.

risk See systematic risk or unsystematic risk.

secondary market Trading in a security after the initial distribution of an offering by the underwriter.

short sale The sale of a security that the seller does not own. The seller expects to be able to buy the shares at a lower price later and thus make a profit on the transaction.

Small Order Execution System (SOES) The NASD's automatic trade execution system for customer agency orders of 1,000 shares or less in Nasdaq/NMS securities and, at the market maker's option, for 500 shares or less in other Nasdaq securities.

Stock Exchange Automated Quotations (SEAQ) system The electronic communication facility of the London Stock Exchange, which is modeled after Nasdaq. It collects the quotes of competing United Kingdom market makers and disseminates them via the exchange's TOPIC System.

stock symbol An identifier for a security, consisting of one or more letters, and used in stock market communications systems. Nasdaq symbols consist of at least four letters; additional letters are used to designate special securities or special circumstances affecting securities.

systematic risk The possibility of price increases or decreases across an entire market.

trading halt A suspension of trading in a Nasdaq security to allow its issuer sufficient time to disseminate material news that may affect the price of the stock.

trading unit Normally, 100 shares of a stock. Anything less is known as an "odd lot."

two-sided market A market made by a dealer that stands ready both to buy and sell at its quoted prices.

underwriter An investment banker that, in a firm-commitment underwriting as a member of an underwriting group or syndicate, agrees to purchase a new issue of securities from an issuer and distribute it to investors. The underwriter makes a profit on the difference, called the underwriting spread, between the price paid to the issuer and the public offering price.

unit More than one class of securities, such as a stock and warrant, trading together as one.

unsystematic risk The possibility of an unexpected rise or fall in prices of a particular security (firm-specific) or a whole group of securities (industry-specific) without regard to any historic market trends.

warrant A certificate issued by a company giving the holder the right to purchase its securities at a stipulated price, usually within specific time limits.

NASD List of Publications

NASD List of Publications

The NASD provides a variety of educational and informational materials to its members, Nasdaq issuers, and the public. These materials are free unless otherwise indicated.

General

Introduction to the NASD. Booklet. An overview of the NASD, including its purposes, organizational structure, programs, services, and relationships with government agencies and other organizations. (16 pages, April 1990.)

NASD Annual Report. Booklet. Highlights regulatory, automation, research, and market-development activities in the U.S. and overseas. Contains lists of Board of Governors members, national and regional officers, and financial results. (Published in April.)

NASD Manual. Book. Soft-cover edition. Includes list of members, the NASD By-Laws, Rules of Fair Practice, Code of Procedure, Uniform Practice Code, and pertinent SEC and Federal Reserve Board rules. (Updated once a year, usually in the Fall; about 1,200 pages.) **$19.95**

NASD Member Brochures, Books

Compliance Check List. Book. Provides basic guidelines for securities firms to follow in evaluating their operational and compliance needs. Divided into two parts: Main Office Compliance and Branch Office Compliance. (24 pages, January 1991.) **$25**

NASD Guide to Rule Interpretations (Net Capital/Customer Protection Rules). This guide contains interpretations to the SEC's Net Capital Rule (15c3-1) and Customer Protection Rule (15c3-3). Each interpretation has been distilled from one or more of the following sources: letters from the SEC Division of Market Regulation to the NASD; letters from the SEC to other self-regulatory organizations; letters from the SEC to attorneys, accountants, members, and others; SEC releases; and discussions between self-regulatory organizations and the SEC. (85 pages, August 1989.) **$35**

NASD Member Kit. Kit of materials for prospective members of the NASD containing such items as *Introduction to the NASD, How to Become a Member of the NASD, NASD Manual,* forms for registering a member firm and its associated persons, information on qualifications testing, fingerprint information, and fingerprint cards. **$60**

Understanding Your Role as an RR. Brochure. Explains to new registered representatives their obligations to their firms and their customers. (12 pages, 1991.) **1-50 copies, $.50 each; 51-500 copies, $.40 each; 501+ copies, $.35 each.**

Nasdaq Market

Nasdaq/CQS Symbol Directory. Book. Lists Nasdaq securities; market makers with their symbols; names and symbols of exchange-listed securities included in the Consolidated Quotation Service and available on Nasdaq Level 2/3 terminals; information on the Nasdaq/London link; and rules and procedures governing the Nasdaq market. (Updated semiannually; about 90 pages.) **$10**

Nasdaq Fact Book & Company Directory. Book. Extensive data on the performance of Nasdaq securities and the Nasdaq market in the preceding year and historically. Also lists Nasdaq companies, their securities' symbols, industry codes, addresses, media and investor relations contacts, and telephone numbers. (Available each year in April; about 230 pages.) **$20**

Academic/Research Studies

The Economic Impact of Initial Public Offerings. A 1989 study by Glenn Yago and Jeff Tanenbaum, Economic Research Bureau, W. Averell Harriman School for Management and Policy, State University of New York at Stony Brook, on how initial public offerings affect employment, capital spending, sales, and other measures of company performance. (28 pages, with charts, December 1989.) **$10**

Final Report of the Regulatory Review Task Force. Recommendations of the NASD's Regulatory Review Task Force in March 1988 for improving the effectiveness of the NASD's regulatory programs. (42 pages, March 1988.) **$15**

Final Report of the Special Committee on NASD Structure and Governance. Contains committee recommendations in five broad categories: the Board of Governors, the districts, committees of the Board, the National Business Conduct Committee, and The Nasdaq Stock Market. (40 pages, March 1990.) **$15**

Inducements for Order Flow. Booklet. A report from a six-month study conducted by a special committee of the NASD to examine cash payments and other practices in the securities industry that directly affect the routing of aggregated small orders to dealers for execution. It concludes that cash payments for order flow are not sufficiently different from other inducements for order flow to justify greater regulation than applies to comparable noncash payments. (48 pages, 1991.) **$15**

Organized Exchanges and the Regulation of Dual-Class Common Stock. This 1986 study of shareholder voting rights by Daniel R. Fischel, Professor of Law and Director of the Law and Economics Program, University of Chicago, finds that while one share, one vote appears to be the preferred standard for the vast majority of companies, there is no pattern of abuse to warrant a legally mandated standard of one share, one vote for all companies. (36 pages, March 1986.) **$15**

Quality of Markets. A report of the Special Committee of the Regulatory Review Task Force that makes recommendations on major quality-of-markets issues raised by the October 1987 market break. Issues discussed include Nasdaq National Market standards and segmentations of the Nasdaq market, financial integrity aspects of market quality, issuer concerns, international linkages, trading arrangements, and other market-quality issues. (60 pages, 1988.) **$15**

Short-Sale Regulation of Nasdaq Securities. The NASD commissioned Irving M. Pollack, a former SEC Commissioner, to produce this 1986 study of short-sale regulation. The study calls for added regulation of short selling in the Nasdaq market. (87 pages, July 1986.) **$15**

Subscriptions

The NASD offers subscriptions to members, investors, and others interested in the NASD and the Nasdaq market. The following subscriptions are available:

NASD Notices to Members—$225 a year, $25 per single copy. Monthly newsletter to inform members about regulatory issues. Requests for member votes and comments are disseminated through *Notices to Members*, as are summaries of actions taken at the bimonthly NASD Board meetings.

Subscriber Bulletin—$80 a year, $15 per single copy. Bimonthly newsletter with information on developments in The Nasdaq Stock Market, The PORTAL Market, and the OTC Bulletin Board.

NASD Regulatory & Compliance Alert—$80 a year, $25 per single copy. Quarterly newsletter dealing with NASD, federal, and state compliance developments and updates on NASD regulatory policy. Also lists NASD disciplinary actions by district.

NASD Full-Service Subscription—$350 annually. The NASD also offers a subscription service for members and others interested in receiving NASD publications. The following items are included in the subscription: *NASD Annual Report, NASD Notices to Members, Nasdaq Fact Book & Company Directory, Nasdaq/CQS Symbol Directory, Subscriber Bulletin, Regulatory & Compliance Alert, NASD Guide to Information and Services,* and special studies/reports.

Ordering Information

To obtain single copies of the free publications, send requests with a gummed, self-addressed mailing label to:

NASD
Information Services
9513 Key West Avenue
Rockville, MD 20850

To order publications or material for which there is a charge, send a check or money order to:

NASD
Book Order Department
P.O. Box 9403
Gaithersburg, MD 20898-9403

Checks or money orders should be made payable to the **National Association of Securities Dealers, Inc.** Allow three to four weeks from receipt of order for delivery. There are no refunds, and all prices are subject to change.

Index

Index